Hands-On
SCIENCE
ACTIVITIES

For Grades 5-6
Science Curriculum Activities Library
Book 3

Marvin N. Tolman

PARKER PUBLISHING COMPANY
West Nyack, New York 10994

Library of Congress Cataloging-in-Publication Data

Tolman, Marvin. N.
   Hands-on science activities for grades 5-6 / Marvin N. Tolman.
      p.   cm. — (Science curriculum activities library ; Book III)
   Includes bibliographic references.
   ISBN 0-13-011330-1
   1. Science teachers—Training of.   2. Science—Study and teaching
(Elementary)—Methodology.   3. Science—Study and teaching—Activity
programs. I. Title. II. Series: Science curriculum activities
library ; bk 3.
   Q181.T592   1998
   372.3'5044—dc21   98-29440
                                        CIP

© 1999 by
PARKER PUBLISHING COMPANY
West Nyack, New York

Printed in the United States of America

10 9 8 7 6 5 4 3 2 1

ISBN 0-13-011330-1

Computer illustrations by
Michelle Sullivan and
David Bentley

The activities in this resource were adapted from three specialized books in the "Science Problem-Solving Curriculum Library," including Hands-On Earth Science Activities for Grades K-8, Hands-On Life Science Activities for Grades K-8, *Hands-On Physical Science Activities for Grades K-8, all published in 1995 by Parker Publishing Company.*

ATTENTION: CORPORATIONS AND SCHOOLS
Parker books are available at quantity discounts with bulk purchase for educational, business, or sales promotional use. For information, please write to: Prentice Hall Career & Personal Development Special Sales, 240 Frisch Court, Paramus, NJ 07652. Please supply: title of book, ISBN, quantity, how the book will be used, date needed.

PARKER PUBLISHING COMPANY
West Nyack, NY 10994

A Simon & Schuster Company

On the World Wide Web at http://www.phdirect.com

Prentice Hall International (UK) Limited, *London*
Prentice Hall of Australia Pty. Limited, *Sydney*
Prentice Hall Canada, Inc., *Toronto*
Prentice Hall Hispanoamericana, S.A., *Mexico*
Prentice Hall of India Private Limited, *New Delhi*
Prentice Hall of Japan, Inc., *Tokyo*
Simon & Schuster Asia Pte. Ltd., *Singapore*
Editora Prentice Hall do Brasil, Ltda., *Rio de Janerio*

ABOUT THE
SCIENCE CURRICULUM ACTIVITIES LIBRARY

The *Science Curriculum Activities Library* provides teachers with nearly 500 activities that give students hands-on experience related to earth, life, and physical science topics covered in the K-6 curriculum. The activities follow the discovery/inquiry approach and encourage students to analyze, synthesize, and infer based on their own hands-on exploration.

For easy use, the activities are organized into three separately printed grade-level books, each containing a selection of age-appropriate investigations in the different fields of science. The books are individually titled:

- *Hands-on Science Activities for Grades K-2*
- *Hands-on Science Activities for Grades 3-4*
- *Hands-on Science Activities for Grades 5-6*

All of the activities in each grade-level volume are tested, complete, and ready for use with virtually any science program or text and with students of varying ability levels.

More than ever before, children of today grow up in a world impacted by science and technology. A basic understanding of nature and an appreciation for the world around them are gifts too valuable to deny these precious young people who will be the problem solvers of tomorrow. In addition, a strong science program with a discovery/inquiry approach can enrich the development of mathematics, reading, social studies, and other areas of the curriculum. The activities in the *Library* develop these skills. Most activities call for thoughtful responses, with questions that encourage analyzing, synthesizing, and inferring instead of simply answering yes or no.

Development of thinking and reasoning skills, in addition to learning basic content information, are the main goals of these hands-on activities. Learning how to learn and how to apply the various tools of learning are more useful in a person's life than is the acquisition of large numbers of scientific facts. Students are encouraged to explore, invent, and create as they develop skills with the processes of science. The learning of scientific facts is a byproduct of this effort, and increased insight and retention associated with facts learned are virtually assured.

ABOUT THE AUTHOR

Dr. Marvin N. Tolman

Trained as an educator at Utah State University and the University of Utah, Marv Tolman began his career as a teaching principal in rural southeastern Utah. The next eleven years were spent teaching grades one through six in schools of San Juan and Utah Counties, and earning graduate degrees.

Currently professor of elementary education, Dr. Tolman has been teaching graduate and undergraduate courses at Brigham Young University since 1975. Subject areas of his courses include math methods, science methods, and formerly computer literacy for teachers. He has served as a consultant to school districts, taught workshops in many parts of the United States, and published numerous articles in professional journals. Dr. Tolman is one of two authors of *What Research Says to the Teacher: The Computer and Education* (co-author Dr. Ruel Allred), published in 1984 by the National Education Association, and a co-author of *Computers in Education*, published by Allyn & Bacon, 1996 (3rd edition). Dr. Tolman also wrote *Discovering Elementary Science: Method, Content, and Problem-Solving Activities,* 2nd ed., (co-author Dr. Garry R. Hardy), 1999, Allyn & Bacon. With Dr. James O. Morton, Dr. Tolman wrote the three-book series of elementary science activities called the *Science Curriculum Activities Library*, 1986, Parker Publishing Co.

Dr. Tolman now lives with his wife, Judy, in Spanish Fork, Utah, where they have raised five children.

ACKNOWLEDGMENTS

Mentioning the names of all individuals who contributed to the *Science Curriculum Activities Library* would require an additional volume. The author is greatly indebted to the following:

- Teachers and students of all levels.

- School districts throughout the United States who cooperated by supporting and evaluating ideas and methods used in this book.

- Dr. James O. Morton, my mentor and my dear friend.

- Dr. Garry R. Hardy, my teaching partner for the past many years, for his constant encouragement and creative ideas.

- Finally, my angel Judy, for without her love, support, encouragement, patience, and acceptance, these books could never have been completed.

HOW TO USE THIS BOOK

This book consists of 187 easy-to-use, hands-on activities in the following 19 areas of earth, life, and physical sciences:

Earth Science	Life Science	Physical Science
• Air	• Plants and Seeds	• Nature of Matter
• Water	• Animal Adaptations	• Energy
• Weather	• Body Systems	• Light
• The Earth	• The Five Senses	• Simple Machines
• Ecology	• Health and Nutrition	• Magnetism
• Above the Earth		• Static Electricity
• Beyond the Earth		• Current Electricity

Teacher Qualifications

Two important qualities of the elementary teacher as a scientist are (1) commitment to helping students acquire learning skills and (2) recognition of the value of science and its implications in the life and learning of the child.

You do not need to be a scientist to conduct an effective and exciting science program at the elementary level. Interest, creativity, enthusiasm, and willingness to get involved and try something new are the qualifications the teacher of elementary science needs most. If you haven't really tried teaching hands-on science, you will find it to be a lot like eating peanuts—you can't eat just one. Try it. The excitement and enthusiasm you see in your students will bring you back to it again and again.

Capitalize on Interest

These materials are both nongraded and nonsequential. Areas of greatest interest and need can be emphasized. As you gain experience with using the activities, your skill in guiding students toward appropriate discoveries and insights will increase.

Organizing for an Activity-centered Approach

Current trends encourage teachers to use an activity-based program, supplemented by the use of textbooks and many other reference materials. The activities herein encourage hands-on discovery, which enhances the development of valuable learning skills through direct experience.

One of the advantages of this approach is the elimination of the need for all students to have the same book at the same time, freeing a substantial portion of the textbook money for purchasing a variety of materials and references, including other textbooks, trade books, audio and video tapes, videodiscs, models, and other visuals. References should be acquired that lend themselves developmentally to a variety of approaches, subject matter emphases, and levels of reading difficulty.

Grabbers

The sequence of activities within the sections of this book is flexible, and may be adjusted according to interest, availability of materials, time of year, or other factors. Most of the activities in each section can be used independently as *grabbers*, to capture student interest. Used this way, they can help to achieve several specific objectives:

- To assist in identifying student interests and selecting topics for study.
- To provide a wide variety of interesting and exciting hands-on activities from many areas of science. As students investigate activities that are of particular interest, they will likely be motivated to try additional related activities in the same section of the book.
- To introduce teachers and students to the discovery/inquiry approach.
- To be used for those occasions when only a short period of time is available and a high-interest independent activity is needed.

Unique Features

The following points should be kept in mind while using this book:

1. Most of these activities can be used with several grade levels, with little adaptation.
2. The student is the central figure when using the discovery/inquiry approach to hands-on learning.
3. The main goals are problem solving and the development of critical-thinking skills. The learning of content is a spin-off, but it is possibly learned with greater insight and meaning than if it were the main objective.
4. It attempts to prepare teachers for inquiry-based instruction and to sharpen their guidance and questioning techniques.
5. Most materials needed for the activities are readily available in the school or at home.
6. Activities are intended to be open and flexible and to encourage the extension of skills through the use of as many outside resources as possible: (a) The use of parents, aides, and resource people of all kinds is recommended throughout; (b) the library, media center, and other school resources, as well as classroom reading centers related to the areas of study, are essential in the effective teaching and learning of science; and (c) educational television and videos can greatly enrich the science program.

7. With the exception of the activities labeled "teacher demonstration" or "whole-class activity," students are encouraged to work individually, in pairs, or in small groups. In most cases the teacher gathers and organizes the materials, arranges the learning setting, and serves as a resource person. In many instances, the materials listed and the procedural steps are all students will need in order to perform the activities.

8. Information is given in "To the Teacher" at the beginning of each section and in "Teacher Information" at the end of each activity to help you develop your content background and your questioning and guidance skills, in cases where such help is needed. For teachers who desire additional background information on elementary science topics, the following book written by the same author is recommended: *Discovering Elementary Science: Method, Content, and Problem-Solving Activities,* 2nd ed. (co-author Dr. Garry R. Hardy), 1999, Allyn & Bacon.

9. Full-page activity sheets are offered when needed throughout the book. These sheets can easily be reproduced and kept on hand for student use.

At the end of the book are a bibliography, sources of free and inexpensive materials, and a list of science supply houses, as well as sources for videotapes, videodiscs, and computer software. This information can save you time in locating additional resources and materials.

Final Note

Discovering the excitement of science and developing new techniques for critical thinking and problem solving should be the major goals of elementary science. The discovery/inquiry approach also must emphasize verbal responses and discussion. *It is important that students experience many hands-on activities* in their learning of science *and that they talk about what they do.* Each child should have many opportunities to describe observations and to explain what they do and why. With the exception of recording observations, these activities usually do not require extensive writing, but that, too, is a skill that can be enriched through interest and involvement in science.

There is an ancient Chinese saying: "A journey of a thousand miles begins with a single step." May the ideas and activities in this book help to provide that first step.

Marvin N. Tolman

CONTENTS

Section One
EARTH SCIENCE ACTIVITIES   1

Topic 1   Air • 3

Topic 5   Ecology • 93

Topic 6   Above the Earth • 99

Section Two
LIFE SCIENCE ACTIVITIES   135

Topic 11   The Five Senses • 163

Topic 12   Health and Nutrition • 177

Section Three
PHYSICAL SCIENCE ACTIVITIES   193

Topic 13   Nature of Matter • 195

Topic 14   Energy • 219

Topic 15   Light • 249

Topic 16   Simple Machines · 267

Topic 17   Magnetism · 305

LISTING OF ACTIVITIES BY TOPIC AND SUBTOPIC

AIR

Subtopic	Activities				
Air Expands and Contracts	1.1	1.2	1.4	1.5	
Air Pressure	1.3	1.4	1.5	1.6	1.11
Bernoulli's Principle	1.7	1.8	1.9	1.10	

WATER

Subtopic	Activities		
Buoyancy	2.5		
Effect of Heat on Water	2.1		
Surface Tension	2.2	2.3	2.4

WEATHER

Subtopic	Activities		
Air Currents	3.8	3.10	
Clouds	3.1		
Precipitation	3.9		
Measuring the Atmosphere			
Moisture	3.4	3.5	3.6
Pressure	3.3		
Temperature	3.2		

THE EARTH

Subtopic	Activities				
Forces That Shape the Earth	4.16	4.19	4.20		
Fossils	4.15				
Land Forms	4.6	4.7	4.17	4.18	
Maps	4.1	4.2	4.3	4.4	4.5
Rocks	4.8	4.9	4.10	4.11	4.12	4.14

ECOLOGY

Subtopic	Activities
Energy Transfer	5.1
Decomposition	5.2

ABOVE THE EARTH

Subtopic	Activities				
Action/Reaction	6.1	6.2	6.3	6.4	6.5
Gravity	6.8	6.11	6.12	6.13	
Inertia	6.9	6.10	6.11	6.12	
Rockets	6.5	6.6	6.7		

BEYOND THE EARTH

Subtopic	Activities	
Eclipses	7.3	7.4
Moon	7.1	7.2

PLANTS AND SEEDS

Subtopic	Activities
Basic Needs	8.2
Growing Plants	8.1
Plant Parts	8.3

ANIMAL ADAPTATIONS

Subtopic	Activities	
Eating	9.1	9.2
Teeth	9.3	

BODY SYSTEMS

Subtopic	Activities				
Bones	10.2	10.3	10.4	10.5	10.6
Fingerprints	10.1				
Muscles	10.7				
Reactions	10.8				

THE FIVE SENSES

Subtopic	Activities						
Sight	11.1	11.2	11.3	11.4	11.5	11.6	11.7
Smell	11.8	11.9					
Taste	11.8	11.9					

HEALTH AND NUTRITION

Subtopic	Activities			
Calories	12.5	12.6		
Fat	12.4			
Protein	12.1			
Starch	12.3			
Sugar	12.2			
Teeth	12.7	12.8	12.9	12.10

NATURE OF MATTER

Subtopic	Activities			
Acids and Bases	13.13			
Atoms and Molecules	13.3	13.4	13.5	13.6
Buoyancy	13.1			
Elasticity	13.11			
Mixtures and Solutions	13.3	13.4		
Physical and Chemical Changes	13.2	13.10		
Polyethylene	13.12			
Solids, Liquids, and Gases	13.1	13.8	13.9	13.10
Viscosity	13.7			

ENERGY

LIGHT

SIMPLE MACHINES

Subtopic	Activities			
Mechanical Advantage	16.1	16.2		
Simple Machines				
Second-Class Lever	16.3	16.4		
Third-Class Lever	16.5	16.6		
Pulley	16.9	16.10	16.11	16.12
Wheel-and-Axle	16.7	16.8		

MAGNETISM

Subtopic	Activities			
Attraction and Repulsion	17.2	17.3	17.6	
Compasses	17.3	17.4	17.5	17.6
Magnetic Fields	17.6	17.8	17.9	17.10
Making Magnets	17.7			
What Magnets Are Like	17.1	17.6		

STATIC ELECTRICITY

Subtopic	Activities	
Attraction and Repulsion	18.1	18.2
Electrostatic Charge	18.2	
Induction	18.3	

CURRENT ELECTRICITY

Subtopic	Activities				
Batteries	19.7	19.8	19.19		
Circuit—What It Is	19.2				
Complete and Incomplete Circuits	19.3	19.5			
Conductors and Insulators	19.1				
Electromagnets	19.11	19.12	19.13	19.14	19.15
Relationship Between Magnetism and Electricity	19.9	19.10			
Electricity Can Produce Magnetism	19.9	19.10	19.16		
Magnetism Can Produce Electricity	19.20				
Resistance	19.8				
Series and Parallel Circuits	19.6	19.7			
Short Circuits	19.4				
Sunlight to Electricity	19.21				

EARTH SCIENCE ACTIVITIES

Topics

- Air
- Water
- Weather
- The Earth
- Ecology
- Above the Earth
- Beyond the Earth

Topic 1:   Air

TO THE TEACHER

A fundamental understanding of air is important to further studies in such areas as weather, air flight, plants and animals, and pollution. Although children live in an ocean of air, they often have difficulty realizing it really exists.

Air is a vital natural resource. Until recent decades, many people thought Earth's supply of air was so vast that it could not be significantly affected by the actions of living creatures. We now know that this precious resource is vulnerable to the pollutants that are put into the atmosphere every day by humans. And we know that the quality of life for all inhabitants of this planet depends on the way humans care for the huge, yet fragile supply of air that surrounds it.

Air is colorless, odorless, and tasteless. Although it is invisible, it is real, it takes up space, it has weight, and it is held to the earth by gravity. *Air pressure*, or *atmospheric pressure*, presses on all surfaces and in all directions. It presses upward and sideways just as hard as it presses downward; this is a characteristic of fluids.

The weight of the air at sea level exerts a pressure of about 1 kilogram per square centimeter (14.7 pounds per square inch). At higher altitudes the pressure decreases because the weight of the layer of air above is less.

Air pressure in a sealed container can increase or decrease as certain conditions change. The pressure is caused by the air molecules inside the container striking against the walls of the container. If the pressure on the inside of the container is equal to the pressure on the outside of the container, the container is said to have zero pressure. Pressure inside the container will increase if more air is added (there are more air molecules striking the same amount of inside wall space), if the air inside the container is heated (the air molecules have increased energy and strike the wall with greater force), or if the size of the container is decreased while the amount of air inside the container stays the same (there are more air molecules per unit of wall space). Pressure inside the container will decrease if some air is removed (there are fewer air molecules striking the same amount of inside wall space), if the air inside the container is cooled (the air molecules have less energy and strike the wall with less force), or if the size of the container is increased but the amount of air inside remains the same (there is more wall space for the same number of air molecules).

Bernoulli's Principle states that the pressure in a fluid decreases as the speed of the fluid increases. The principle applies to air, water, or any other fluid. If air, for example, is blown across a strip of paper that is in the form of an air foil (See Activity 1.7) the paper will rise. With air rushing across the top of the paper, air pressure is reduced at that point and the paper is lifted by atmospheric pressure from underneath. Airplane wings are designed with a curved top and a nearly flat bottom to force air to travel faster over the top than across the bottom, reducing the pressure on the top surface, thus providing lift from atmospheric pressure beneath the wing.

3

Activity 1.1
HOW CAN YOU CRUSH A GALLON CAN WITHOUT TOUCHING IT?

(Teacher demonstration)

Materials Needed

- Gallon can with tight-fitting lid
- Hot plate
- Water
- Hot pad

Procedure

1. Put a small amount of water (1/2 cup or so) in the can.
2. Put the can on the hot plate *with the lid off* and turn the hot plate on high.
3. When there is a good stream of steam coming out the spout, use the hot pad to remove the can from the hot plate.
4. Put the lid on tight, immediately after you remove the can from the hot plate. (See Figure below.)
5. Have students predict what will happen to the can.
6. As students observe for a few minutes, discuss what is happening and why.

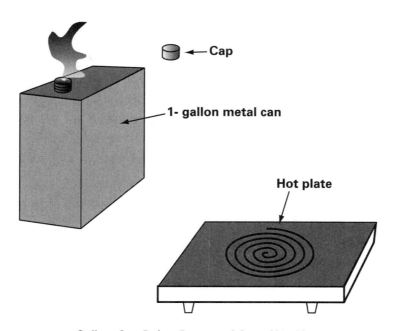

← Cap

— 1- gallon metal can

Hot plate

**Gallon Can Being Removed from Hot Plate
and Cap Ready to Put On**

Teacher Information

Caution: There are two possible hazards with this activity. First, students could get burned. Second, the can should never be left on the hot plate with the lid on, as the can will likely explode. This activity really should be done by the teacher as a demonstration.

This is one of the more popular demonstrations of the great force of air pressure. For older students it's an excellent time to apply math skills. Have them measure the dimensions of the can and compute the air pressure (about 14.7 pounds per square inch at sea level). Their figures will probably show that there are approximately 3,000 pounds of force on the can, and they will see the effect of that pressure as the can is crushed in the activity. This assumes that you were successful in driving out all of the air by water vapor, and that won't happen, but it will come close enough to provide students with a lasting memory about the force of air pressure.

The overabundant supply of gallon cans at school went out with the ditto machine. Even the little bit of ditto fluid that is still used generally comes in plastic jugs. Gallon cans are available, however, at paint-supply stores. Businesses that mix paint usually even have new cans that they will sell at a reasonable price. Another possible source is your local auto-body shop. These shops get some of their reducers (thinners) in gallon cans, and they throw away empties every day. **CAUTION: If you use cans that have had flammable material in them, be sure to *rinse them well* before putting them on a hot plate!**

INTEGRATING: Math, language arts

SKILLS: Observing, inferring, measuring, predicting, communicating

Activity 1.2
HOW CAN YOU CRUSH A SODA CAN WITH AIR PRESSURE?

(Teacher demonstration)

Materials Needed

- Empty soda can
- Hot plate
- Pan of water
- Hot pad

Procedure

1. Put a small amount of water (1/8 cup or so) in the can.

2. Put the can on the hot plate and turn the hot plate on high.

3. When there is a good stream of steam coming out the spout, use the hot pad to remove the can from the hot plate.

4. Immediately turn the can upside down in the pan of water. Only the top of the can needs to enter the water. (See Figure below.)

5. Have students hypothesize as to what they think happened to cause what they saw.

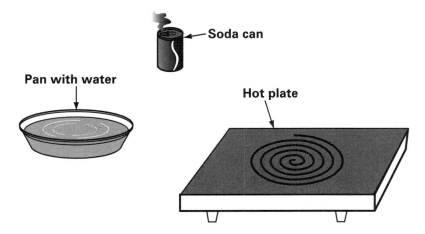

**Soda Pop Can Being Removed from Hot Plate.
Pan of Water Ready**

Teacher Information

Caution: This activity should be done by the teacher as a demonstration, to avoid the possibility of students getting burned.

This is an excellent substitute (or addition) for the gallon-can crusher to demonstrate the force of air pressure. For older students the math skills can still be applied by computing the amount of air pressure on the surface of the can. Many people collect aluminum cans, and they usually stomp on the cans to minimize storage space. Here's a more exciting way to crush the cans!

INTEGRATING: Math, language arts

SKILLS: Observing, inferring, measuring, predicting, communicating

Activity 1.3
HOW HARD CAN AIR PUSH?

 Take home and do with family and friends.

Materials Needed

- Clear glass soda bottle
- Balloon

Procedure

1. Put the balloon into the soda bottle. Hold onto the balloon's open end.
2. Stretch the lip of the balloon over the mouth of the bottle.
3. Inflate the balloon inside the bottle.
4. What happened? Can you explain why?

Soda Bottle with Balloon Hanging Inside

For Problem Solvers: Try this activity with bottles of different sizes. Be sure all of them have small openings, so you can stretch the balloon over them. Can you blow the balloon up any farther with some of the bottles than with others? What seems to make the difference? Try it with your friends and discuss your ideas about it.

Teacher Information

When the child blows into the balloon, the increased air pressure inside the balloon will push against the air trapped in the bottle. The pressure of the air in the bottle will increase and push harder on the balloon. The child will discover the balloon cannot be inflated inside the bottle. Remember, the lip of the balloon must cover the mouth of the bottle and completely seal it.

Just for fun, make a small hole in the bottom of a plastic bottle (rigid plastic works best), then use this bottle for the above activity. Seal the hole with your finger as the student tries to blow up the balloon. Then remove your finger from the hole and let the student try again. The student will now be able to blow up the balloon. Seal the hole again with your finger, just as the student stops blowing, and the balloon will remain inflated just from atmospheric pressure. Of course, the students don't know about the hole in the bottom of the bottle. Let them puzzle over it and discover the hole.

SKILLS: Observing, inferring, measuring, communicating, identifying and controlling variables, experimenting

Activity 1.4
WHAT CAN AIR PRESSURE DO TO AN EGG?

(Teacher demonstration or supervised activity)

Materials Needed

- Hard-boiled egg, peeled
- Glass milk bottle or juice bottle, 1 liter (1 qt.) or larger
- Kitchen matches

Procedure

1. Insert two kitchen matches into the pointed end of the egg.

2. Holding the bottle upside down, light the matches and put the egg into the mouth of the bottle, pointed end first. Hold the egg lightly against the mouth of the bottle—don't push! Keep the bottle upside down.

3. What happened? What can you say about this?

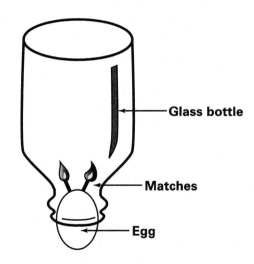

Bottle with Egg and Matches

11

Teacher Information

The mouth of the bottle should be somewhat smaller (5 mm or 1/4 in.) in diameter than the egg. If the old-style milk bottle is not available, you might find a juice bottle that will be about right if you use large eggs. Pullet eggs could be used with bottles having a smaller opening. (A pullet is a young hen, and it lays small eggs.)

The lit matches in the pointed end of the egg will heat the air inside the bottle, causing the air to expand. When this happens, warm air is forced out of the bottle (don't push the egg into the top of the bottle or the air can't get out). Soon the matches will go out and the air inside the bottle will cool and contract, leaving less pressure inside the bottle than outside the bottle. When this happens the outside air pressure will force the egg into the bottle.

If the egg is not broken, you can get it out of the bottle by reversing the process. Hold the bottle above your head with the pointed end of the egg in the mouth of the bottle. Blow very hard into the bottle. The blowing will increase the air pressure inside the bottle and push the egg out. If the egg comes only part way out, try pouring warm water on the bottle. The air inside will expand and force the egg out.

SKILLS: Observing, inferring

Activity 1.5
HOW CAN YOU PUT A WATER BALLOON INTO A BOTTLE?

(Teacher demonstration)

Materials Needed

- Large bottle (with an opening of at least 4 cm [1 1/2 in.])
- Balloon
- Bowl of water
- Paper towel
- Match
- Aluminum foil (or other fireproof surface)

Procedure

1. Place a sheet of aluminum foil or other fireproof surface on the table and place the bottle and the bowl of water on the foil.
2. Put water in the balloon, making a water balloon that is a bit larger than the opening of the bottle.
3. Place the water balloon in the bowl of water, just to get it wet and provide lubrication.
4. Take half a sheet of paper towel (or other paper) and twist it lengthwise, so it fits easily into the opening of the bottle, but don't drop it into the bottle yet.
5. Hold the twisted paper above the spout of the bottle, light it with the match, and drop the burning paper into the bottle. (See Figure below.)
6. Immediately place the water balloon on the bottle, while the paper is still burning, holding the balloon lightly by the neck.
7. Discuss what happened and why you think it did that.

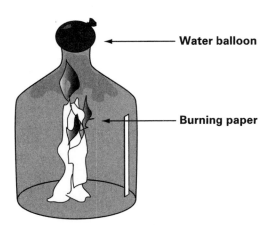

Large Bottle with Water Balloon on Top and Paper Burning Inside

Teacher Information

Caution: This activity should be done by the teacher as a demonstration, to avoid the possibility of students getting burned.

This is an excellent substitute (or addition) for the egg-in-the-bottle demonstration of air pressure, except that it doesn't provide breakfast. The water balloon has the advantage of flexible size, so most any bottle can be used.

Without disclosing conceptual information, you might want to describe the steps of the activity before lighting the paper afire and get students to predict what will happen when you put fire in the bottle and place the water balloon on the top of the bottle.

After the balloon is in the bottle, have students hypothesize about what made the water balloon go into the bottle. Be sure they don't leave with the notion that vacuum in the bottle "sucked" the balloon into the bottle. Vacuum is only a lack of pressure. Lack of force can't do work. The air expanded as it heated, and you probably noticed that the water balloon danced on the top of the bottle as the heating air escaped. As soon as the fire went out, the air began to cool and contract. With the water balloon sealing the spout and preventing air from reentering the bottle, air pressure inside the bottle went down, resulting in less air pressure inside the bottle than outside the bottle. The balloon was pushed into the bottle by atmospheric pressure.

Have students hypothesize also about how you might get the water balloon out of the bottle. If you will turn the bottle upside down, position the balloon over the opening to seal air from coming out of the bottle, then blow air into the bottle, the increased air pressure will force the balloon out of the bottle just as air pressure pushed the balloon into the bottle.

INTEGRATING: Math, language arts

SKILLS: Observing, inferring, measuring, predicting, communicating

Activity 1.6
HOW MUCH CAN YOU LIFT BY BLOWING?

(Teacher-supervised activity)

 Take home and do with family and friends.

Materials Needed

- Small garbage bags, newspaper bags, or other plastic bags (at least 6)
- Two tables (alike and medium size)
- Chair

Procedure

1. Place a book on a bag and blow into the bag to see if you can lift the book.
2. Do you think you can lift three books by blowing into the bag? Try it.
3. If you could lift three books, find something heavier and try lifting it the same way.
4. Turn one table upside down on top of the other.
5. Have several students circle the table, each one inserting his or her bag between the two tables. (See Figure below)
6. Have everyone blow together, on signal and in unison. Did the table rise?
7. If you were successful in raising the table by blowing into the bags, place a chair on the upside-down table and repeat steps 5 and 6.
8. Finally, put a person on the chair and do it again.
9. Discuss everyone's ideas about why they were able to lift such a lot of weight by blowing.

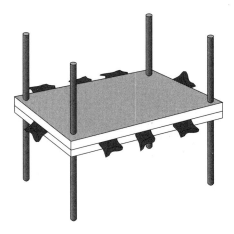

Two Tables with Plastic Bags Ready to Use

15

For Problem Solvers: Talk to someone who works in a mechanic shop and find out how much air pressure is used to lift a car on a hydraulic hoist. How can that much air pressure lift a car?

Find out how much air pressure is in the tires of your family car, or ask someone about theirs. Find out how much the car weighs. Discuss your information with your teacher and other class members. How can that much air pressure hold a car up?

Teacher Information

Students will be amazed at how much weight they can lift by blowing. Talk about the fact that automobiles ride on a cushion of air. A two-thousand-pound car (or more) is held up by tires that have approximately 30 pounds of air in them. How can that happen? Discuss the meaning of "pounds per square inch" and how that applies to the above activity. Older students will be able to devise a way to compute how much air pressure they can blow and the total amount of weight that could be lifted by a bag if they blow that much pressure into it. If they blow into an opening that has an area of 1 square inch, the pressure can be multiplied by the number of square inches of surface area of the bag.

The total force that can be applied by a small amount of air pressure is astounding.

INTEGRATING: Math, language arts

SKILLS: Observing, inferring, measuring, predicting, communicating, formulating hypotheses, researching

Activity 1.7
HOW CAN AIR PRESSURE HELP AIRPLANES FLY?

Materials Needed

- One sheet of standard-sized notebook paper

Procedure

1. Hold the sheet of paper by the corners just below your lower lip.
2. Permit the paper to hang down in front of you.
3. Blow across the top of the paper.
4. What happened? What can you say about this?

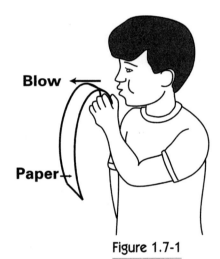

Figure 1.7-1

Student Blowing Air Over Paper

For Problem Solvers: Place two textbooks flat on the table, leaving about 10 cm (4 in.) of space between them. Put a sheet of notebook paper on top of the books. Blow in the space between the books. What happened to the paper? Air pressure above forces it down between the books.

Teacher Information

When the student blows across the top of the paper, it will rise. As air moves faster, its pressure is reduced and the greater air pressure below pushes the paper up. This is called *Bernoulli's Principle*, and airplane wings are shaped to take advantage of it. The same principle is applied to move gasoline out of the carburetor of an automobile or to move chemicals out of the bottle of a garden-hose sprayer.

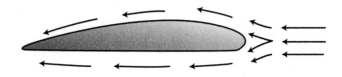

Figure 1.7-2

Air Moving Over and Under an Airplane Wing

SKILLS: Observing, inferring

Activity 1.8
HOW FAR CAN YOU BLOW A PING-PONG BALL FROM A FUNNEL?

 Take home and do with family and friends.

Materials Needed

- Standard kitchen funnel
- Ping-Pong ball

Procedure

1. Place a Ping-Pong ball in your funnel.

2. Hold your funnel at enough of an angle that the ball will stay in the funnel (see Figure below).

3. Blow into the small end of the funnel, and see how far you can blow the ball across the room.

4. How far did the ball go?

5. What happened? Can you explain it?

6. Discuss your ideas with others.

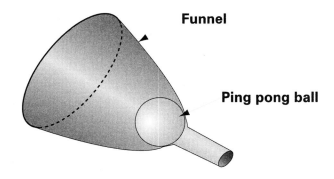

Funnel at an Angle So Ball Will Stay in Place

Teacher Information

If you get three (or several) funnels and Ping-Pong balls, you can have a contest with a group of students. Of course, it's important that they haven't already tried the activity, so they will earnestly compete as you give them the signal to blow. Ask the other students in the class to predict which of the "blowers" will be able to blow the ball the farthest across the room, and notice the surprised looks on the faces of all when the balls go nowhere.

This is an application of Bernoulli's Principle. As air rushes past the ball, pressure is reduced where the air is moving fastest. Atmospheric pressure pressing in on the center of the ball is then greater than the pressure around the perimeter of the ball. The harder you blow, the tighter the ball is held in the funnel by atmospheric pressure.

Try it with the funnel upside down. Hold the ball in place, then release it after you begin to blow hard. The ball will fall *after* you stop blowing.

Note: Be sure to wash the funnels with soap and water before using them with another group.

SKILLS: Observing, inferring, predicting, communicating, formulating hypotheses

Activity 1.9
WHY CAN'T THE BALL ESCAPE THE AIR STREAM?

 Take home and do with family and friends.

Materials Needed

- Hair dryer (with "no heat" setting)
- Ping-Pong ball

Procedure

1. Set the hair dryer on "no heat" and turn it on high speed.
2. With the air blowing upward, hold the ball in the air stream.
3. Carefully let go of the ball and move your hand away.
4. What happened?
5. Can you explain this?
6. With the ball still in the air stream, tilt the hair dryer back and forth slightly.
7. How can this happen? Discuss your ideas with your teacher and with your group.

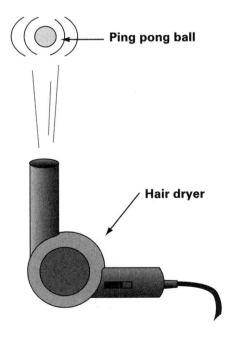

Ping-Pong Ball Suspended in a Stream of Air

21

Teacher Information

This is another application of Bernoulli's Principle. As the ball moves to the side of the air stream due to the force of gravity, the air moving past the ball on the air stream side is moving faster than the air on the other side of the ball, reducing the pressure on the air stream side, and the ball is pushed back into the air stream by atmospheric pressure. As you direct the air stream vertically you will see the ball waver back and forth, and as you tip it at a slight angle atmospheric pressure will support the ball.

This activity also works fine with a tank-type vacuum as the blower. Plug the hose into the rear of the tank, so air blows out through the hose.

SKILLS: Observing, inferring, communicating, formulating hypotheses

Activity 1.10
HOW CAN YOU MAKE AN ATOMIZER WITH A DRINKING STRAW?

 Take home and do with family and friends.

Materials Needed

- Drinking straw
- Small cup of water
- Scissors

Procedure

1. Cut the drinking straw almost through, with about 1/3 of the straw on one end of the cut and 2/3 of the straw on the other end. (See Figure below)
2. Bend the straw at a right angle.
3. Insert the short end of the straw into the water.
4. Predict what will happen if you blow on the other end of the straw.
5. Blow hard on the other end of the straw.
6. What happened? Was your prediction correct?
7. From what you have learned about *Bernoulli's Principle*, can you explain this?
8. Discuss your ideas with your group.

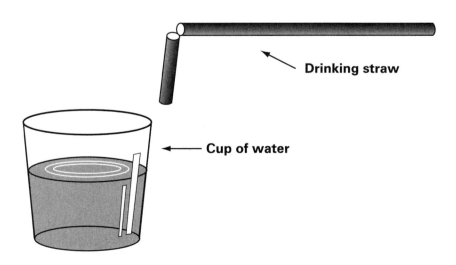

Straw Cut and Bent, Ready to Use in Cup of Water

23

For Problem Solvers: Does the angle of the vertical straw change the way the atomizer works? I wonder if the length of the vertical straw makes any difference in how easy it is to use. I wonder if the size of either straw matters, or the size of the cup. These are all variables that you could test. Think of ways to test these variables and answer the "I wonders." What other variables do you wonder about? Test them, too, and share your information with your teacher and with other students.

Teacher Information

This is another application of Bernoulli's Principle. Air pressure is reduced in the vertical straw as air rushes over its opening. Atmospheric pressure is now greater than the pressure inside the straw, and the liquid is forced up the vertical tube by atmospheric pressure pushing down on the surface of the liquid in the cup.

Squeeze-bulb atomizers use this principle, as do paint sprayers and the type of weed sprayer that attaches to a garden hose. This principle has many other applications in life, including in the operation of a carburetor of a gasoline engine. Airplanes are supported in the air largely by atmospheric pressure, in another application of Bernoulli's Principle.

Incidentally, you might want to do this activity at the end of the day, or at least just before recess, because students will spray water everywhere. Isn't that terrific!

INTEGRATING: Language arts, social studies

SKILLS: Observing, inferring, predicting, communicating, formulating hypotheses, experimenting

Activity 1.11
HOW CAN A BALLOON REMAIN INFLATED WITH ITS MOUTH OPEN?

 Take home and do with family and friends.

Materials Needed

- Balloon
- Rigid plastic bottle with small hole in bottom

Procedure

1. Tuck the balloon into the bottle, but hold onto the mouth of the balloon.
2. Stretch the mouth of the balloon over the mouth of the bottle as shown in the Figure on page 26.
3. Put your finger over the hole in the bottom of the bottle, to seal the hole.
4. Try to blow up the balloon.
5. What happened? Explain why.
6. Now remove your finger from the hole in the bottom of the bottle and try again to blow up the balloon.
7. When the balloon is blown up and fills the bottle, remove your finger from the hole in the bottle, then remove the bottle from your mouth.
8. What happened to the balloon? Explain why it does this.

For Problem Solvers: You can have fun at home with this activity by holding the bottle for the person who is blowing up the balloon. You can hold your finger over the hole in the bottle the first time the other person tries, and he or she won't be able to blow up the balloon. The second time the person tries, secretly move your finger off the hole. Then after the balloon is blown up, quickly put your finger over the hole again and take the bottle away from the mouth. Let him or her wonder why the balloon is still blown up. Explain it to the person if he or she can't figure it out on his or her own.

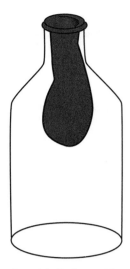

Plastic Bottle with Balloon Hanging Inside

Teacher Information

For this activity you need a rigid plastic bottle. A small hole can be easily drilled in the bottom of the bottle with a knife or other sharp instrument. Some juices are sold in rigid bottles, as are other materials. Two-liter soda bottles are flexible and will be crushed by atmospheric pressure, instead of the balloon remaining inflated. This still demonstrates the force of atmospheric pressure, but in a different way. With a rigid bottle, the balloon will remain inflated with the mouth of the balloon open to the atmosphere. This is a very impressive demonstration of the force of air pressure.

This activity is related to Activity 1.3, but with a little humor added.

SKILLS: Observing, inferring, predicting, communicating, formulating hypotheses, identifying and controlling variables

Topic 2: Water

TO THE TEACHER

Water is essential to all forms of life. People can live for weeks without food but only for a short period of time without water. Because it is usually available we often take it for granted, yet it plays an important role in almost every area of science. Even the study of nonliving materials includes the study of how water acts upon and interacts with them.

Water is the most abundant substance on the planet, yet much of the earth suffers from water shortages. Huge amounts of water are required for agriculture, for the manufacture of goods, for personal needs, and for many other purposes. Although there is a global abundance of water, getting the right amounts in the right places and in the right form is a constant challenge in many parts of the world.

Water evaporates into the air, then condenses and returns to the surface of the earth in various forms of precipitation. Called the *water cycle*, this process is vital to all forms of life as it recycles and redistributes this precious resource.

Activity 2.1
HOW CAN YOU BOIL WATER IN A PAPER CUP?

(Teacher demonstration)

Materials Needed

- Nonwaxed paper cup (not plastic or foam)
- Candle or alcohol lamp
- Water

Procedure

1. Put about 5 cm (2 in.) of water in a paper cup.
2. Put a candle or alcohol lamp under the cup.
3. What happened? Can you think of a reason why?

For Problem Solvers: Different class members probably have cousins and friends in many parts of the country—north, south, east, and west. Write letters to people in various locations. Ask them to boil some water on the stove and tell you what temperature the water boiled at for them. Ask them to use distilled water if they can and to let you know if they used distilled water or tap water. Ask them to include their altitude in the information they send.

Plot on a map the boiling points and altitudes for each location. Be sure to include the same information for your own location. Analyze your data. Is boiling point the same for all locations? What seems to have made a difference? Longitude? Latitude? Altitude? What effect, if any, does each of these variables seem to have on boiling point?

Teacher Information

Soon the water will become hot enough to boil, but the paper cup will not burn. Water boils at 100 degrees Celsius at sea level. Paper must be much hotter to reach its kindling point. As long as water remains in the cup, it will keep the paper cool enough to prevent it from burning. Remember, once water reaches its boiling point, it does not get hotter if the pressure on the surface remains the same.

If the pressure on the surface of the water is increased, the boiling point will be increased and the water can become hotter (as in a pressure cooker). If the pressure on the surface is decreased, water will boil at a lower temperature, which is why high-altitude cooking requires more time.

29

Your problem solvers will have a valuable experience in writing to people in various parts of the country and in analyzing the data they obtain. They will learn that boiling point decreases with increasing altitude. Impurities in water will be somewhat of a confounding variable, because boiling point increases with the addition of impurities, but it shouldn't be a big problem. The only way to control for impurities would be to ask everyone to use distilled water, which would likely decrease the number who respond. There will also be minor differences in thermometer accuracy, but these differences also should not be significant.

INTEGRATING: Math, language arts, social studies

SKILLS: Observing, inferring, measuring, communicating, identifying and controlling variables, experimenting, researching

Activity 2.2
HOW MANY NAILS CAN YOU PUT INTO A FULL GLASS OF WATER?

 Take home and do with family and friends.

Materials Needed

- 8-ounce glass
- Water
- Paper and pencil
- 200 finishing nails 5 cm (2 in.) long

Procedure

1. Fill an 8-ounce glass with water. Make sure the water is level with the top of the glass. (If you lay a pencil across the top of the glass, the water should barely touch the pencil.)

2. Get some finishing nails about 5 cm (2 in.) long.

3. On a piece of paper, write down the number of nails you think will go into the glass before water spills over the top.

4. Carefully put the nails in one at a time, head first to avoid splashing. What happened?

5. What can you say about this?

For Problem Solvers: Try the same activity with paper clips, with pennies. Be sure you write your estimate before you begin putting items in the water. Are you improving your estimates?

Fill a small cup level full of water. Estimate how many drops of water you can put on it without running it over. Write your estimate, then try it. Do the same thing with another cup with a smaller opening, and another with a larger opening. Be sure you write your estimate each time, then test your estimate by counting the drops.

Try the same thing with coins. How many drops of water can you put on a dime? A penny? A quarter? Be sure you estimate first, and see if you can improve your estimating skills.

Teacher Information

Students will probably be able to put many nails into the glass. Smaller nails, pennies, or paper clips will also work well. Water molecules have an attraction for each other (called cohesion). This attraction forms a bond at the surface (called surface tension). Water on the surface of the glass will bulge above the rim as the molecules cling together. Gravity soon overcomes this force, however, and the water spills over.

Water forms in drops because of surface tension.

INTEGRATING: Math

SKILLS: Observing, estimating, identifying and controlling variables

Activity 2.3
HOW CAN SURFACE TENSION BE DISTURBED?

Materials Needed

- Saucer
- Pepper
- Liquid detergent
- Water
- Toothpicks

Procedure

1. Cover the bottom of the saucer with water.
2. Sprinkle pepper lightly on the surface of the water.
3. Dip the tip of a toothpick into the center of the water. What happened?
4. Now dip the tip of another toothpick into the liquid detergent.
5. Dip the toothpick with detergent on it into the middle of the saucer. What happened?
6. Try to explain what you saw, and why it happened.

For Problem Solvers: Place a staple very carefully on its side on the surface of the water. Add a drop of detergent and see what happens. Use hot water. Try cold water. Try soft water. Try distilled water. Predict what will happen each time you try a new idea, then try it and test your prediction. What do you think will happen if you put detergent on the bulging surface of the water created in Activity 2.2? Try it.

Teacher Information

Pepper will float on the surface of the untreated water. Because of adhesion (attraction of unlike molecules for each other), water molecules cling to the side of each pepper particle. The attraction of water molecules to each other at the surface (surface tension) results in a tugging effect on the pepper particle all the way around. Adding detergent breaks the surface tension on the near side, and the pepper is pulled to the edge of the dish by the tugging of water molecules on the other side of the pepper particle.

SKILLS: Observing, inferring, predicting, communicating, formulating hypotheses

Activity 2.4
HOW CAN YOU MAKE A SOAP MOTORBOAT?

 Take home and do with family and friends.

Materials Needed

- One popsicle stick cut in half crosswise
- Eye dropper filled with liquid detergent
- Large bowl or pan of clean, fresh water
- Knife (older students only)

Procedure

1. Carve one end of the popsicle stick to a point so it looks like a boat. Make a small notch in the opposite end.

2. Float your boat near the center of the pan of water.

3. Use the eye dropper to put a small amount of detergent in the notch. What happened?

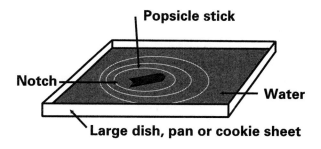

Popsicle Stick Floating in Pan

For Problem Solvers: Do some more research with surface tension, and explain the actions of the boat in terms of surface tension. Did the soap push the boat?

Lay a paper clip very carefully on a pan of water. Put a drop of liquid soap or detergent in the water near the paper clip and observe. Can you make other objects float that normally do not float on water? With each item, predict whether it will float or not before you try it. Can you explain what's happening?

33

Teacher Information

The drop of detergent will gradually dissolve, breaking the surface tension of the water behind the boat. Water molecules tug on the boat at the front, pulling it through the water.

Note: If liquid detergent is not available, scrape a bit of soap from a bar of hand soap into the notched area of the boat. It will work just the same. Before attempting to repeat any activities involving soap or detergent, rinse everything thoroughly in clean water, being certain that no soap film is left from the previous activity.

SKILLS: Observing, inferring, classifying, predicting, communicating, identifying and controlling variables, experimenting, researching

Activity 2.5
HOW DOES A HYDROMETER WORK?

Materials Needed

- Lipstick tube cap (or other small, narrow container)
- Several small nails (or screws)
- Tape (or gummed label)
- Marker
- Plastic tumbler
- Water
- Salt
- A variety of liquids
- Paper and pencil

Procedure

1. Fill the tumbler about two thirds full of water.
2. Put the gummed label or a piece of tape lengthwise on the lipstick cap.
3. Place several weights (small nails or screws) in the lipstick cap.
4. Place the lipstick cap, open end up, in the glass of water. Add or remove weights until the cap floats vertically with the water level about halfway up the cap.

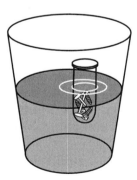

Lipstick Cap Floating Vertically with Weights Showing

5. Mark the water level on the cap.
6. Your cap is now a hydrometer. Hydrometers are used for measuring density of liquids, comparing them with the density of water. If the density is greater than that of water, the cap will float higher. If the density is less than that of water, the cap will sink deeper.

7. Dissolve about 1/4 cup of salt in your jar of water. Without changing the number of weights in the cap, put it in the salt water. Does your hydrometer float deeper than it did in plain water, or does it float higher? What does this tell you about the density of salt water?

8. Test other liquids, such as milk, vinegar, and rubbing alcohol.

9. As you test various liquids, make a list of those you think have a greater density than water has, and those that have a lesser density.

For Problem Solvers: Get several plastic tumblers and fill them about one half full, each with a different liquid, such as water, salt water, cooking oil, and rubbing alcohol. Line up the containers in order of least dense to most dense, according to your prediction. Use your hydrometer to compare the liquids, then arrange the liquids in order, with the liquid of least density on the left and the liquid of greatest density on the right. Did you predict them correctly?

Gather a variety of small objects that are made of plastic, wood, metal, etc. Place these items in the liquids, one at a time. Try to find at least one item that will float on each liquid but not on the next liquid to the left.

Pour a small amount of the most dense liquid into an empty jar. Very carefully pour about the same amount of a second liquid into the first and see if one liquid will float on the other. Try a third liquid. After you have the liquids layered in the same container, carefully drop the items into it that you worked with in the above paragraph. Explain to your teacher what happened.

Teacher Information

Any object that floats displaces an amount of liquid equal to its own weight (Archimedes principle). If the specific gravity (density) of the liquid is greater, the object floats higher, since it has to displace less liquid to equal its own weight. If the hydrometer floats deeper, it is in a liquid of lower density.

Hydrometers are used to test such liquids as antifreeze and battery acid, using the Archimedes principle.

It is easier for swimmers to float in ocean water than in fresh water. Salt increases the density of water. Swimmers bob like a cork in the Great Salt Lake because of extremely high salt content. If salt water gets in the eyes, it will burn. A shower following the swim is necessary, as a film of salt is left on the skin after the water evaporates.

SKILLS: Observing, inferring, predicting, communicating, identifying and controlling variables

Topic 3:   Weather

TO THE TEACHER

Weather is crucial in our lives. It influences where we live, what (and if) we eat, what we wear, what we do, and, sometimes, how we feel. Weather appears as a part of the first recorded history of man. Early civilizations grew and developed in favorable climates. The history of man is interwoven with myths, legends, stories, customs, religious beliefs, poems, art, music, dancing, and many other expressions that tell the story of man's continuing concern with the mysteries, beauties, and dangers of the often unpredictable nature of weather.

Today, sophisticated weather instruments circle the earth to report weather conditions on a global scale. Countless weather stations, with both professional and amateur meteorologists, study and report on a daily basis, yet frequently the news carries a report of some unpredicted or unusual occurrence. This section should help students understand some of the many variables that must be taken into account in a study of weather and to appreciate its importance in our lives.

This study draws heavily on information from the "Air" section and should follow it as closely as possible. You may even see a need to repeat some of the activities from the "Air" section.

Several activities require simple construction. Please take time to read all the activities before you begin. Parents and other resource people can be a great help in gathering and assisting as you build a convection box. Be sure to plan to construct several of each of them.

We hope you will use poetry, stories, music, and art liberally throughout the study.

Finally, please don't blame the weather on the weather forecaster.

Activity 3.1
HOW CAN YOU MAKE A CLOUD?

(Teacher demonstration)

Materials Needed

- One 2-liter bottle with cap
- Kitchen matches
- Water

Procedure

1. Put a small amount (about 1/4 cup) of water into the bottle.
2. Light a match. Hold it down in the bottle to make smoke.
3. Put the lid on the bottle.
4. Shake the bottle to add moisture to the air inside the bottle.
5. Squeeze the bottle, then release it quickly and observe what is inside the bottle.
6. Squeeze and release several times. What's happening inside the bottle?
7. Share your observations and ideas with others who are interested in this activity.

**Two-liter Bottle with Small Amount of Water
and Small Amount of Smoke**

For Problem Solvers: Experiment with different temperatures of water and different amounts of smoke in the bottle for this activity. Also, do some research and learn all you can about how clouds form in the atmosphere. What causes changes in pressure in the atmosphere, and how does this affect temperature? And what do pressure and temperature have to do with cloud formation?

Teacher Information

Air pressure increases the temperature of the air. As air temperature increases, the air is able to contain more moisture. Squeezing the bottle increases the temperature of the air inside the bottle. Releasing the pressure on the bottle reduces the temperature of the air and decreases the ability of the air to hold moisture. The smoke particles that are suspended in the air act as condensation nuclei, and moisture condenses, or collects, around them. Each time you release the pressure a cloud forms, and when you squeeze the bottle the cloud disappears.

Smoke and dust particles in the atmosphere act as condensation nuclei when moisture content is high and temperature drops. Changes in atmospheric pressure create changes in atmospheric temperature, similar to the way these changes occur in the mini-atmosphere in the bottle.

INTEGRATING: Reading, social studies

SKILLS: Observing, inferring, communicating, researching

Activity 3.2
HOW CAN YOU MAKE A THERMOMETER?

Materials Needed

- Commercial thermometer
- Clear, thin, stiff plastic tubing at least 30 cm (12 in.) long (balloon sticks are just right)
- 1-hole rubber stopper to fit bottle
- Warm water
- Red food coloring
- Flask or small-mouthed glass bottle (cough medicine, juice bottle, etc.)
- 3″ × 5″ index card (or larger card)

Procedure

1. The first thing most people notice about weather is the temperature. Thermometers, which measure temperature, are easy to make. You might have learned from earlier science activities that liquids expand when they are heated and contract when they are cooled.

2. Fill the bottle with warm water. Add several drops of red food coloring.

3. Insert the plastic tube through the stopper and fit the stopper tightly in the bottle. Water should be forced into the tube as you press the stopper into place.

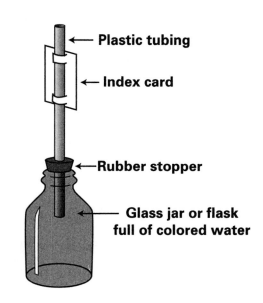

◄— Plastic tubing

◄— Index card

◄— Rubber stopper

◄— Glass jar or flask full of colored water

Homemade Thermometer

4. Adjust the water level so the water will rise nearly halfway up the tube.

5. Make a slit near the bottom of the index card and another near the top and slide it behind the tube.

6. Wait about an hour for the water to reach room temperature.

7. Consult the commercial thermometer and mark the present temperature with a line on the index card.

8. Each morning and afternoon, compare the commercial thermometer with the one you have made. Make new lines to show changes.

For Problem Solvers: Check the temperature on your thermometer each morning, noon, and night for at least one month. Try to do it at about the same time each day. For the first few days, compare the temperatures shown on your thermometer with those of a commercial thermometer to be sure you have calibrated your thermometer accurately. You will gain confidence in your thermometer as you use it.

Make a graph of day-by-day temperatures, using your homemade thermometer. Be sure to check the temperature at the same time each day. Estimate the temperature each time before you read the thermometer.

What are the temperature limits of your thermometer? At what temperature does the liquid rise to the top of the tube, if at all, and at what temperature does it drop out of sight at the bottom? Design a way to find out, and compare with others who are doing this activity.

Your thermometer works on the principle of expansion and contraction of liquids with temperature change. Do some research and find out what other ways are used to measure temperature. Learn what you can about instruments people have used for this purpose through the years.

Teacher Information

Ordinary methyl alcohol (or rubbing alcohol) may be substituted for water if the thermometer is to be left outside in below-freezing temperatures. CAUTION: Methyl alcohol is poisonous if taken internally.

The water expands because the molecules move more rapidly and push against one another as they are heated. As water cools, the molecules move more slowly and require less space, so the water contracts. This same principle is demonstrated with air several times in Section 1.

Balloon sticks are perfect as thermometer tubes. They are stiff, they fit the one-hole rubber stopper, and they are readily available at party supply outlets.

INTEGRATING: Math, reading, social studies

SKILLS: Observing, inferring, measuring, estimating, communicating, comparing and contrasting, using space-time relationships, identifying and controlling variables, experimenting, researching

Activity 3.3
HOW CAN WE MEASURE ATMOSPHERIC PRESSURE?

(Teacher-supervised activity)

Materials Needed

- Wide-mouthed 1-quart glass jar
- Round balloon
- Heavy-duty rubber band
- Commercial barometer
- Soda straw
- Index card
- Milk carton cut into a stand
- Glue
- Scissors
- Pencil

Procedure

1. Cut the narrow neck off a balloon and stretch the balloon very tightly over the mouth of the glass jar.
2. Hold the balloon in place by placing the rubber band below the threads of the jar.
3. Glue one end of the drinking straw to the center of the balloon in a horizontal position. Cut the other end of the straw to a point.
4. Attach the index card to the horizontal stand and bring it near the balloon.
5. Make a mark on the index card in the place where the straw points.
6. Consult your commercial barometer or call the local weather station to determine today's barometric pressure. Write the number beside the mark on your index card.
7. Repeat steps 5 and 6 every day for a week. What is happening? Discuss this with your teacher and class.

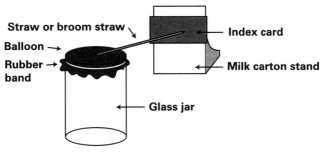

Homemade Barometer

For Problem Solvers: With this activity you made a barometer. Each time you read this barometer the temperature of the air in the room must be the same. Think about that statement and see if you can explain why it is true. Discuss your hypothesis with your friends, then with your teacher. Then keep a thermometer near your barometer so you can be sure of the temperature before you read the barometer.

Do some research and find out what other types of instruments are used to measure atmospheric pressure. Find out how they work.

Keep track of the barometer movement each day—is it moving up or moving down? Whenever there is a change in atmospheric pressure, write a description of current weather conditions, then write a description of weather conditions the next day. See if you can identify a pattern of weather change following pressure changes.

Teacher Information

Close supervision for safety reasons is recommended because of the use of the glass jar, which could cause injury if broken.

Before discussing the barometer, you may want to remind the students of the air pressure activities in the section on air. Atmospheric pressure varies and is one indicator of weather conditions. Generally, decreasing barometric pressures accompany storm fronts, while rising pressures indicate fair weather.

When the balloon is stretched tightly over the bottle, the pressure inside the bottle will be the same as that of the atmosphere in the room. As the atmospheric pressure increases or decreases, it will change the amount of pressure on the balloon and cause the straw to move up or down. Because some air will pass through the balloon diaphragm, the air should be balanced by reattaching the balloon every few days.

Changes in air temperature will cause the air inside the barometer to expand and contract, making the diaphragm move up and down and invalidating the accuracy of this device as a barometer. This effect can be controlled by keeping a thermometer nearby and always reading the barometer at the same room temperature. Following this procedure, you know that any change in the reading is due to change in atmospheric pressure, not change in temperature.

INTEGRATING: Reading, language arts

SKILLS: Observing, inferring, communicating, comparing and contrasting, formulating hypotheses, identifying and controlling variables, researching

Activity 3.4
HOW CAN WE MEASURE MOISTURE IN THE AIR?

Materials Needed

- Empty half-gallon milk carton with the top cut off
- Drinking straw
- Small metal washer
- 5″ × 7″ index card
- Freshly washed human hair at least 20 cm (8 in.) long
- Paper fasteners (4)
- Glass bead with hole
- Glue (latex cement works well)
- Ruler
- Toothpick
- Pencil

Procedure

1. Push a paper fastener through the end of the drinking straw and then through the bead. Near one edge of the carton, measure up from the bottom 10 cm (4 in.) and push the paper fastener into the carton.

2. Slide the small metal washer over the straw just beyond the opposite edge of the carton.

3. Use a paper fastener and glue to attach the hair to the top of the carton near the same edge as the washer. Tie and glue the hair to the straw at a point directly below.

4. Use two paper fasteners to attach the index card to the carton so it extends beyond the length of the straw.

5. Glue a toothpick in the end of the straw as a pointer.

6. When you finish, your model should look like the figure shown below.

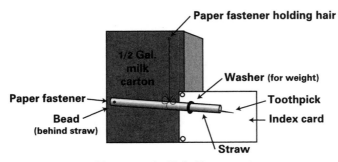

Homemade Hair Hygrometer

45

7. This is a hair hygrometer. Make a pencil mark on the index card where the end of the toothpick is pointing.

8. In the next activity, you will learn how to use this and another kind of hygrometer to measure the moisture or humidity in the air.

For Problem Solvers: I wonder if there is a difference in how well different types of human hair work in this activity. Does light-colored hair stretch when it gets wet more than darker hair does? Does coarse hair respond differently from finer hair? Design an experiment to find the answers to these questions. Discuss your design with other interested students, then discuss it with your teacher and carry out your experiment.

Calibrate your hair hygrometer by comparing it each day to a commercial instrument. Then record the humidity reading for one month and graph the data.

Do meteorologists use human hair to measure moisture in the air? Do some research and find out.

Teacher Information

Hair absorbs moisture and becomes longer in humid air. In dry air, the hair contracts. The straw moves up and down, with the changes in length of the hair attached to it and the top of the milk carton. The washer attached to the straw provides extra weight to help the straw move down freely as the hair stretches in moist conditions. The toothpick and index card will make small movements easier to measure.

Be sure to make several hygrometers, using different colors and textures of clean hair. If there are differences in the hair, your encyclopedia can tell you why.

INTEGRATING: Reading, language arts

SKILLS: Observing, inferring, measuring, communicating, comparing and contrasting, using space-time relationships, researching

Activity 3.5
WHAT CAN EVAPORATION TELL US ABOUT HUMIDITY?

Materials Needed

- Two identical commercial thermometers (preferably Celsius)
- Shoelace (with tips cut off) 20 cm (8 in.) long
- Two rubber bands
- Plastic bottle

Procedure

1. Cut a small hole in the side of the bottle (see Figure below).
2. Use the rubber bands to fasten the two thermometers to the outside of the bottle.
3. Put some water inside the bottle.
4. Moisten the shoelace. Wrap one end around the bulb of one thermometer, and put the other end of the shoelace in the water.
5. After several minutes, compare the temperature of the thermometers.
6. What happened? Can you think of a way to explain this? Discuss this with your teacher and the class.

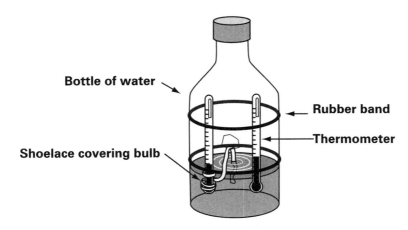

Bottle of water

Rubber band

Thermometer

Shoelace covering bulb

Wet-dry Bulb Hygrometer

For Problem Solvers: Why is there a difference in the temperature readings of these two thermometers? Moisten the back of your hand, then blow on it. Explain why this instrument can be used to measure moisture in the air. Discuss your hypothesis with someone else who is doing this activity.

Meteorologists use an instrument that is a lot like this one. They call it a wet-dry bulb hygrometer. How do they use it? With your research skills you should be able to easily find out.

Locate a relative humidity table (see your encyclopedia) and use it with your home-made wet-dry bulb hygrometer. Record both morning and afternoon readings for one month (same times of day each day) and graph your data. At the same time graph the readings from the commercial instrument, if you have one available. Compare the data from the two instruments.

Teacher Information

After a few minutes, the wet bulb will have a lower temperature, because evaporation is a cooling process. This instrument is called a wet-dry bulb hygrometer. Meteorologists often whirl wet and dry thermometers together in the air. The handle and instrument containing the thermometers are together called a sling psychrometer. Your hygrometer works the same way, but not as rapidly. Students will often assume that the water is colder than the air and is making the wet bulb cooler. Actually, it is being cooled by the evaporation of moisture into the air.

Relative humidity is usually reported in percent. One hundred percent is the total amount of moisture air can contain.

The dryer the air, the faster is the evaporation from the wet-bulb thermometer, cooling the thermometer and resulting in a lower temperature reading. The dry bulb thermometer remains unaffected by moisture content in the air. Therefore, the greater the *difference* in temperature between the wet and dry bulbs, the lower the humidity (amount of moisture in the air).

The next activity compares the hair hygrometer and the wet-dry bulb.

INTEGRATING: Reading

SKILLS: Observing, inferring, communicating, comparing and contrasting, formulating hypotheses, researching

Activity 3.6
HOW CAN YOU COMPARE THE WET-DRY BULB AND HAIR HYGROMETERS?

Materials Needed

- Hygrometers from Activities 3.4 and 3.5
- Empty aquarium or large cardboard box lined with plastic garbage bags
- Pan of hot water
- Warm, moist bath towel
- Paper
- Pencil

Procedure

1. Mark the position of the pointer on the index card of the hair hygrometer.
2. Compare and record the temperatures and difference in the wet-dry bulb hygrometer.
3. Put an open pan of hot water in the aquarium or box.
4. Carefully lower the hair hygrometer into the box and cover the box top with the warm, moist towel. What do you think is happening inside the container? Can you predict what will happen to the hygrometers?
5. After waiting five minutes, gently remove the hygrometer from the box and on the index card mark the position of the pointer.
6. Repeat steps 3, 4, and 5 exactly, using the wet-dry bulb hygrometer, except at the end record the temperatures and the difference between them.
7. What kind of environment (conditions) did you create inside the container?
8. What can you say about the reactions of your hygrometers?

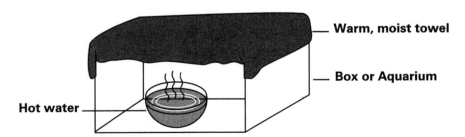

Aquarium with Pan of Water and Warm, Moist Towel

For Problem Solvers: This activity will help you to decide which of the hygrometers you prefer. Do the activity several more times, but vary the amount of moisture you put in the box by varying the amount of moisture you put in the towel. Also, include a commercial hygrometer with the two homemade devices. Estimate the humidity each time before you read the instruments and record your estimate. Record the readings from all three and graph your data. Include your estimates in your graph. Which of the two homemade instruments is more consistent with the commercial instrument? Are your estimates getting more accurate?

Teacher Information

If possible, do this on a "normal" day for your climate. The pan of hot water and moist towel will create a very humid environment. The hair should lengthen and show a measurable difference on the card. The temperature of the wet bulb thermometer should increase more than that of the dry bulb, but with little difference (both will go up some). The normal readings at the beginning of the activity, plus the moist reading at the end, should give students the beginning of a scale upon which they can record daily "readings" of the humidity.

SKILLS: Observing, inferring, measuring, estimating, communicating, comparing and contrasting, using space-time relationships, formulating hypotheses, identifying and controlling variables, experimenting, researching

Activity 3.7
HOW DO HEATING AND COOLING AFFECT AIR CURRENTS?

(Teacher-supervised activity)

Materials Needed

- 10-gallon aquarium and sheet of cardboard to cover the top or a cardboard box approximately the same size
- Two glass lamp chimneys
- Large cup or small pan
- Incense or hemp rope to produce smoke
- Roll of 5-cm (2-in.)-wide plastic tape
- Drawing compass
- Transparent plastic wrap if a cardboard box is used instead of an aquarium
- Match
- Small bowls
- Hot water
- Warm water
- Very cold water
- Knife or scissors

Procedure

1. If the aquarium is used, fit the cardboard covering snugly on top. (See Figure on page 52.)
2. Measure the diameter of the bottom of a lamp chimney and use the compass to make a circle near each end of the cardboard top.
3. Cut out the circles and fit a lamp chimney in each.
4. If you use a cardboard box, cut off the top flaps and use the plastic wrap to make a window. Seal the wrap and all other openings in the box with plastic tape. Lay the box on its side and make holes in the top for lamp chimneys as explained in steps 2 and 3. In one end of the box, cut a door that can be opened and closed.
5. Whether you use an aquarium or a cardboard box, seal any space around the lamp chimneys with plastic tape.
6. Light the incense or rope and put it in a large cup or small pan in the center of the box. Observe what happens.
7. Place a cup of warm water in the box under one lamp chimney. What happened?
8. Repeat steps 6 and 7 using very hot and very cold water.
9. Look in your window to observe what happens.
10. This is called a convection box. Using information you have learned about air, explain what happened.

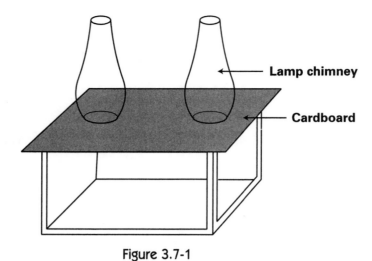

Figure 3.7-1

Aquarium with Lamp Chimneys in Cardboard Top

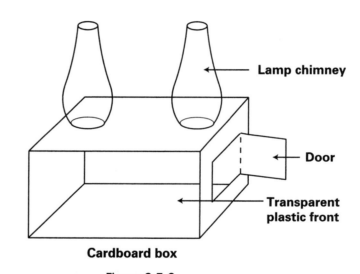

Figure 3.7-2

Box with Lamp Chimneys and Transparent Side

For Problem Solvers: Draw a circle to represent the earth. Label the north and south poles. Draw and label the equator. Think about regions of the earth that are warm and regions that are cold, and consider the effect these temperature differences might have on air movement. Draw arrows showing the movements of air masses that you would expect to occur in the atmosphere, based on the warm and cold regions that you have identified.

Do some research on winds and learn about major wind patterns around the globe. Do air masses move the way you showed them? What other factors seem to influence wind patterns? Add arrows to your drawing, showing major global wind patterns.

Teacher Information

Before you begin this activity, you may want to review concepts from the section on air. When warm water is placed under one of the lamp chimneys in the box, the air around it will be heated and rise. Cooler air will be drawn into the box through the other chimney. Smoke will clearly show the currents.

If you think of the bottom of the convection box as a large area of the earth's surface that heats and cools irregularly due to the shape and material (land, water) of its surface, perhaps you can visualize how large warm and cold air masses develop and cause constant movement of the air.

Each time the water is changed, the smoke should be exhausted from the box. When fresh smoke and a different temperature of water are used, allow several minutes for the atmosphere to change in the box.

INTEGRATING: Reading, social studies

SKILLS: Inferring, predicting, communicating, using space-time relationships, formulating hypotheses, identifying, researching

Activity 3.8
WHAT CAN WE LEARN FROM A CONVECTION BOX?

(Upper-grade activity)

Materials Needed

- Lamp chimney convection box from Activity 3.7
- Two sheets of 9″ × 12″ newsprint
- Pencil
- Large cups
- Smoke source
- Hot water
- Cold water

Procedure

1. Study the convection box and draw a picture of it.
2. Use hot water and smoke to start air movement in the convection box.
3. Since we know that faster-moving air has lower pressure, where might a difference in air pressure be inside your box? Write "high" and "low" in the places where you think the pressures might be different.
4. Since we know warm air can hold more moisture than cold air, where might the differences in humidity be inside your box? Write "moist" and "dry" where you think the air contains more and less humidity.
5. Draw another picture of the convection box.
6. Replace the hot water with ice water in the actual box.
7. Observe the behavior of the smoke. Repeat steps 3 and 4, marking the places in the box where you think air pressure and humidity might differ.
8. Under what conditions does the air (wind) move faster?

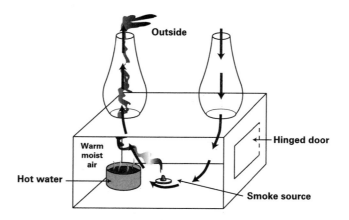

Figure 3.8-1

Convection Box with Hot Water

54

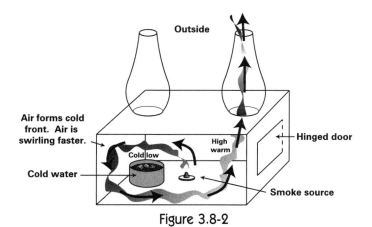

Figure 3.8-2

Convection Box with Cold Water

For Problem Solvers: Go back to the drawing of air mass movements that you made for the "Problem Solvers" section of Activity 3.7. Consider the effect of rising and falling air on atmospheric pressure. Label each of the areas that you think will have high pressure as a "high" and each low pressure area as a "low."

In what areas of the globe will air masses most likely pick up large amounts of moisture from the earth's surface? Label these as "moist." Label as "dry" those areas where air masses will be least likely to pick up moisture. Consult a globe of the earth, or a map, if you need help in locating water and land surfaces.

Teacher Information

The students should not see Figures 3.8-1 and 3.8-2 until they have completed the activity. Although it would require very sensitive instruments to measure the differences, they do occur.

Some students may have difficulty with the abstract thinking this activity requires. A class discussion and review at the end of the activity should help.

This activity may also help you determine how well children understand the basic principles of weather and air that have been developed up to this point.

The next activities will use these basic concepts to make generalizations about the causes of weather regionally and worldwide.

INTEGRATING: Reading, social studies

SKILLS: Inferring, predicting, communicating, comparing and contrasting, using space-time relationships, formulating hypotheses, identifying variables, researching

Activity 3.9
WHAT MAKES RAIN?

Materials Needed

- One profile weather picture for each student (Figure on page 57)
- Paper
- Pencil

Procedure

1. Study Figure on the following page. Can you see the relationships?
2. Write a story that describes what is happening from left to right in the picture. Can you explain why?

For Problem Solvers: Design and build a model that demonstrates the water cycle. You will need a closed box with a clear lid. This could be a plastic-lined cardboard box with clear plastic stretched over the top, or a plastic box with a clear lid. Make a land form in your box. Include a mountain at one end of the box, sloped into a lake or sea at the other end. Plaster of Paris or paper maché work well for making your land form, and all of this needs to be waterproofed. You can waterproof it by painting it with a sealer.

Now put some water in the lake and find a way to put a few ice cubes at the other end, up high. A plastic baggy could be mounted at the top of the box, over the mountain, for the ice cubes. This can be your cloud; it represents the cold air in the upper atmosphere.

You need to include a warm sun. The sun could be a lamp, with the bulb positioned near the lake end, either protruding through the box or near the plastic cover.

Now be patient for a few minutes and watch the rain come down on the mountain and flow down into the lake. Share your model with others, and describe for them what's happening, step-by-step, through the water cycle. This is a model of the world's largest recycling operation.

Teacher Information

This is a simplified diagram of one way weather can change. Reading from left to right: Sun shines on water, causing it to warm and evaporate. The air above is warm and moist and rises until it reaches the upper atmosphere and begins to cool. As it cools, moisture condenses and clouds begin to form. Prevailing winds that move from water to land carry the clouds inland, where they continue to pick up moisture.

When the clouds reach the mountain, they are forced upward into cooler air. As the air in the clouds cools rapidly, it must reduce its moisture content, which it does at lower elevations in the form of rain and at higher elevations in the form of snow (depending on temperature).

Profile of Water, Land, and Mountains

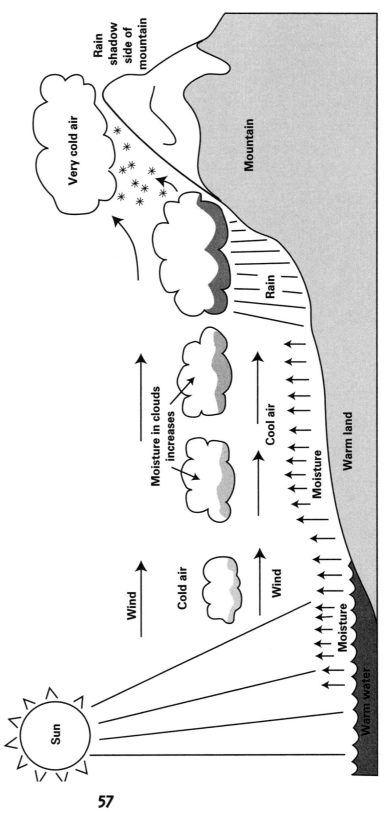

As clouds are forced up by a high mountain range, they may give up much of the moisture they contain, so less precipitation falls on the far side of the mountain. This area is called a rain shadow.

Your problem solvers will create a water cycle model that will show the process of evaporation, condensation, and precipitation, somewhat as it occurs in nature.

INTEGRATING: Language arts, social studies

SKILLS: Observing, inferring, communicating, using space-time relationships, identifying and controlling variables

Activity 3.10
WHAT IS A COLD FRONT?

Materials Needed

- One copy of Figure for each student
- Crayons

Student Information

If all weather patterns were as simple as the one shown in Activity 3.9, the weather forecaster's job would be easy. Actually, different air masses form over water, ice, and dry land. Many different kinds of air masses are moving over the earth at different altitudes at the same time. When they collide, they often do not mix. At the point of impact, weather disturbances, sometimes of unpredictable extent, occur.

Procedure

1. Study the picture of colliding air masses. In this case, the cold air mass is somewhat like a moving mountain. Use your red crayon to write "warm" where you think warm temperatures would be found.

2. Use a blue crayon to write "cold" and "very cold" where you think cold temperatures might occur.

3. Use a green crayon to write "moist" where the most humidity will be found.

4. Use a yellow crayon to write "dry" where you think there is less moisture.

5. Use a black crayon to write "high" or "low" where you think air pressure differences might occur.

6. Compare and discuss your picture with your teacher and with other members of the class.

For Problem Solvers: You can see by now that the earth's atmosphere is a very complex system. This activity considers movements of very large masses of air. On a smaller scale, can you see how winds are generated at a lake? Does water cool and heat faster or slower than the land surface? What effect would this have on air temperature after sundown? What about after sunup?

With this in mind, examine the water cycle model you made for Activity 3.9. Which direction would you expect winds to blow in the morning? What about in the evening? Think about temperature changes that occur over land regions and over sea regions during the night and during the day. Share your ideas with others who are interested in this activity.

Teacher Information

The temperature will be warmer near the ground in the area before the approaching front. Temperatures behind and above the front will be colder.

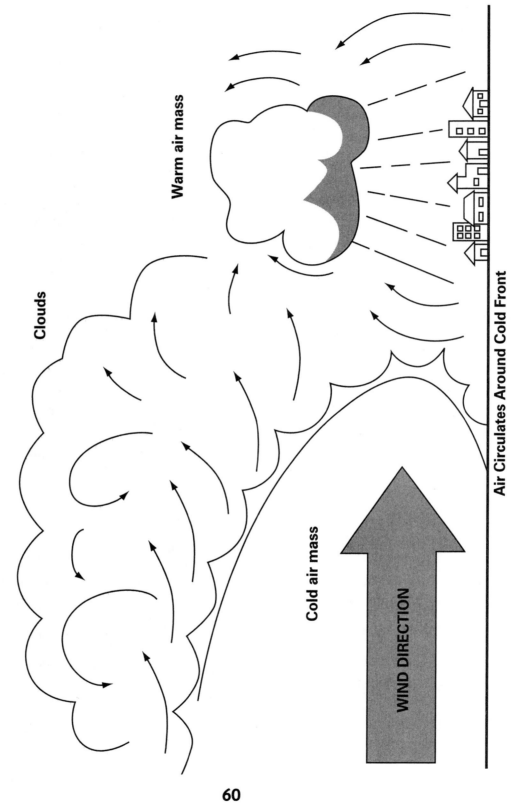

Colliding air masses

Clouds

Warm air mass

Cold air mass

WIND DIRECTION

Air Circulates Around Cold Front

60

As the cold front pushes the warm air upward, precipitation may occur. The type of precipitation will depend on the temperature of the air. The common weather prediction of "rain turning to snow" tells the progress of the cold front.

Because cold fronts move faster, the air pressure will be lower behind the front.

The humidity will be greater in areas before and following the front line.

If the cold front should stop over the town, it would be called stationary. Stationary lows and highs often determine weather for long periods of time over large regions of the country.

Occasionally, especially in mountainous areas, a cold front may become stationary with a warm air mass above it. The warm air forms a blanket and retards circulation of the cold air. This is called a temperature inversion. If a temperature inversion occurs over a city, air does not circulate and smog will develop.

If you live in an area near a large body of water, such as an ocean or gulf, your weather is controlled to a great extent by the water mass. Since the air temperature over water does not change as much as it does over land, your temperatures could vary less. Latitude and ocean currents will be of greater importance. Severe storms will most often develop over the body of water and move onto land, especially in the southern latitudes. Weather is also greatly influenced by large lakes, rivers, mountains, and valleys.

A final evaluation for this study could be to have the students draw, label, and explain a picture of the last storm that occurred in their area.

SKILLS: Observing, inferring, predicting, communicating, using space-time relationships, formulating hypotheses, identifying, experimenting, researching

Topic 4:   The Earth

TO THE TEACHER

We live on a combination of rock, soil, and water known as the earth's crust. We depend on this relatively thin layer (along with air and sunlight) to provide our food, medicine, and clothing—and the materials to build our homes, cars, and other things. Geologists continually search the earth's surface for clues to the location of mineral resources and answers to questions about the origin, early history, and current changes of the surface of this planet. A study of its structure and evolutionary history helps to increase our appreciation for the earth and its resources.

Scientists are interested in the composition of the earth, the forces that shape and change it, and how it came to be as it is. From a career point of view, exposure to some of these ideas can help students begin to develop a perception of geology-related occupations and even stimulate possible early interests. From the standpoint of general interest, horizons are broadened within the mind as students acquire a glimpse of the significance and majesty of this great planet.

The first several activities of this unit are map oriented. The objective of these activities is not to present a thorough treatment of map reading, but to develop the concept of representing the earth, or small portions of it, on paper or other surface that can be used for observation and study. The map-related questions in this section deal with the problems arising from efforts to represent size and shape in miniature form. Even in the very early grades, students can begin forming concepts about the earth's magnitude and structure.

Children are natural collectors. This interest can be stimulated and broadened by encouraging them to watch for new kinds of rocks; then provide simple ideas for recognizing likenesses and differences in rocks they find and categorizing them according to those recognized attributes.

Along with involvement in the activities of this section, emphasis should be placed on appropriate geologic concepts. The earth's crust, for instance, consists largely of rock layers that have been formed and layered by such factors as heat, pressure, and the effects of water and cementing material. Under the earth's crust is molten rock, called magma. Great pressures sometimes force magma to the surface, forming volcanoes. Other forces shift the outer layers of the earth's surface, causing earthquakes and forming mountains and valleys, sometimes causing much destruction in life and property.

Many locations are rich with nearby sites where geologic changes are evident—exposed rock layers on a mountainside or at an excavation site, a glacier-formed canyon, or a terrace that was once the beach of an ancient lake. These examples and many more stand as evidence of the ever-changing nature of the earth's surface. A geologist, forest ranger, or rock collector could provide fascinating information about local geologic interests.

Those living in the city are limited in availability of rocks for collection from natural settings, but a little creative effort can compensate rather well. Samples can be obtained from science supply catalogs or from local rock collectors. Possibly one or more students have collected rocks while on vacation that they would be pleased to bring to class and share with the group. As a group, the class might acquire an impressive rock collection by writing to friends and relatives. Trips to a local museum can provide meaningful geologic field trips.

Activity 4.1
HOW CAN A FLAT MAP SHOW THREE DIMENSIONS?

(Individual or small-group activity)

Materials Needed

- Clay
- Pencil
- Paper or cardboard

Procedure

1. Form your clay into the shape of a mountain.
2. Now draw your mountain on paper. Think of a way to show the high and low places on your "map." If others are doing the same activity, talk about ways this could be done.
3. Use whatever idea you think is best to show the high and low places of your mountain on your map.

Teacher Information

The purpose of this activity is to help students discover ways to show a third dimension on a flat surface. This is commonly achieved with relief maps. Depending on maturity of students and prior experience with maps, they may or may not think to use shading or color coding. These methods could be suggested, but students should first be encouraged to devise their own ways to show the highs and lows of their mountain on paper. Original ideas that communicate the information, as well as the tried-and-true techniques, should be accepted and praised.

As a test of accuracy in their use of techniques for showing three dimensions, students might enjoy trading maps with a classmate. Each should leave his or her original mountain intact, get additional clay, and construct a second mountain from the borrowed map. Then each child should compare the second mountain with the classmate's original, to see how well the intended communication was given and interpreted.

INTEGRATING: Math, language arts, social studies, art

SKILLS: Observing, inferring, measuring, communicating, using space-time relationships

Activity 4.2
WHAT ARE CONTOUR LINES?

Materials Needed

- Clay
- Pencil
- Paper
- Thick book
- Thin book

Procedure

1. Form your clay into the shape of a mountain. Include hills and valleys, steep slopes, and gradual slopes.

2. Lay a thick book on the table beside your "mountain."

3. Sight across the book to your mountain and put marks all the way around your mountain at the same level as the top of the book.

4. Draw a line around the mountain, connecting the marks you made for step 3.

5. Now stand above your mountain and look down at the line you drew. Does the line form a circle? What shape does it form? This is called a *contour line*.

6. Use a thinner book and draw a contour line further down the mountainside. Then stack two books and draw a contour line further up the mountainside. Draw still more contour lines if you wish, but keep them apart from each other.

7. Stand over your mountain and look down at the contour lines. Are they the same distance apart all the way around the mountain?

8. Draw your mountain on paper, including all contour lines as they appear from above. When you finish you will have a *contour map*.

9. Trade contour maps with a classmate. Look at your classmate's map and try to visualize what the mountain looks like. Then look at the actual mountain and see if you were right.

Teacher Information

The contour map is a very popular and practical way of illustrating elevation on a flat surface. This activity should add meaning to the next, as students try to interpret an actual contour map to determine the highs and lows and the gradual and steep slopes.

INTEGRATING: Math, language arts, social studies, art

SKILLS: Observing, inferring, measuring, communicating, comparing and contrasting, using space-time relationships

Activity 4.3
WHAT IS A CONTOUR MAP?

Materials Needed

- Commercial contour maps
- Clay

Procedure

1. Examine your contour map. Your experience from Activity 4.2 should help you understand the lines on this map.

2. How much elevation (height) is represented from one contour line to the next?

3. Select one section of the map. Study it carefully and try to visualize the area it represents.

4. Make a clay model of this section of the map.

5. Trade maps with a classmate. Examine and evaluate each other's work.

Teacher Information

This activity can be done individually or in small groups. Before you begin, the previous activity should be reviewed. Any contour maps can be used, but if maps can be obtained that represent a local area familiar to students, the experience will be more meaningful. Students might need help in determining the *contour interval* (amount of elevation change represented from one contour line to the next).

If the maps used represent a local area, consider taking a field trip to that area. Students could then compare the maps with the actual terrain and evaluate their own interpretation of the map. If a class field trip is not possible, perhaps some students could take a field trip of their own, with the family or a group of friends.

If the class or group of students visits a local area with contour maps in hand, consider having them try to walk the contour lines for a distance. After determining the contour interval, each of several students could stand at the point best determined to be a contour line on the map. Then all in the group walk in unison around the terrain, being careful not to walk up or down the slope, each remaining as nearly as possible at the same elevation as the starting point. The vertical distance between participants should remain constant, but the horizontal distance will vary as they walk along the terrain, as it varies on the contour map.

INTEGRATING: Math, language arts, social studies, art

SKILLS: Observing, inferring, measuring, communicating, using space-time relationships

Activity 4.4
HOW HIGH AND LOW ARE THE EARTH'S MOUNTAINS AND VALLEYS?

Materials Needed

- World relief map or globe
- Pencil
- Paper

Procedure

1. Study your relief map until you know how to determine the elevations of the different areas.

2. Write down several of the highest elevations you can find. Include the name of the mountain each one represents and the country it is in.

3. Write down several of the lowest elevations you can find and the name of the area each represents.

4. How much higher are the highest points than the lowest points?

5. The distance through the earth is approximately 8,000 miles. Draw a circle to represent the earth and make a mark to show how high above the line the highest mountain would be. Show the lowest ocean floor also.

6. If others are doing this activity, compare notes and discuss your findings.

For Problem Solvers: Look at a ream of paper. Each sheet of paper is very thin, but the ream of 500 sheets is about two inches thick. If you think of one sheet of paper as representing one mile, how many sheets would it take to represent the diameter of the earth? How many reams? If you let the top of the ream of paper represent the earth's surface at sea level, how many sheets of paper do you need to add to show how high the highest mountain is? How many sheets would you remove to show the deepest part of the ocean?

Using reams of paper or your own creative ideas, make a model of the earth that shows the highest and lowest parts of the earth's surface.

Teacher Information

Locating some of the highs and lows on the earth will help students visualize the earth. When they do step 5, some might be surprised to find that, although the elevation differences between mountain peaks and ocean floors seem great, they actually represent very slight distortions on the earth's skin.

INTEGRATING: Math, language arts, social studies, art

SKILLS: Observing, inferring, measuring, communicating, using space-time relationships

Activity 4.5
HOW CAN A FLAT MAP REPRESENT THE EARTH?

(Teacher-supervised activity)

Materials Needed

- World relief globe
- World relief map
- Fresh orange
- Dull knife
- Pencil
- Paper

Procedure

1. Carefully remove the peel from your orange, keeping it all in one piece or in as large pieces as possible.
2. Try to lay the orange peel out flat on the paper. What happened?
3. Cut off a piece of orange peel about 2–3 cm (1 in.) square and lay it out flat on your paper. Did that work any better?
4. On the globe, compare the size of the United States with the size of Greenland.
5. Now compare the same two countries on the flat map. What do you find?
6. Think about what you did with the orange peel in step 2. What problems do there seem to be with representing a ball-shaped object on a flat surface?
7. If you were a map maker, what could you do to show the earth on a flat map?

For Problem Solvers: Put yourself in the place of the map maker. Brainstorm with others who are interested in this activity and try several different ways to represent the earth accurately on a flat surface. Share your ideas with your teacher and with the rest of the class.

Teacher Information

In doing this activity, students should begin to understand the problems involved with representing the spherically-shaped earth on a flat map. After students have struggled with the question in step 7, discuss the ideas that were suggested. This would be an excellent time to discuss different types of projections used in map making. Bring samples to class if possible. Consider having students try to make one or more of these with their orange peel (or a new one), by cutting along the "meridians," then flattening it out on paper. Discuss the advantages and disadvantages of the different types of projections.

INTEGRATING: Math, language arts, social studies, art

SKILLS: Observing, inferring, measuring, communicating, using space-time relationships

Activity 4.6
HOW DOES THE NATURE OF THE EARTH'S SURFACE AFFECT ATMOSPHERIC TEMPERATURE?

Materials Needed

- Relief maps
- Temperature maps
- Paper
- Pencil

Procedure

1. Study your temperature maps and identify at least 10 areas that have high average temperatures.
2. Find these same areas on the relief map. Do they seem to be areas of high altitude, low altitude, medium altitude, or a mixture of all three?
3. Are these areas commonly near mountain ranges, near oceans, or far away from both? Or does it seem to be a mixture?
4. Are these areas near the equator or nearer to the North Pole or South Pole?
5. Next, identify at least 10 areas that have low average temperatures. Do steps 2, 3, and 4 with them.
6. What can you say about the effect altitude seems to have on temperature?
7. What effect do mountain ranges and oceans seem to have on temperature?
8. What effect does latitude (distance from the equator) have on temperature?

For Problem Solvers: Do some research and find out how atmospheric temperature is affected by land masses and by oceans and other large bodies of water. What other surface features affect air temperature?

Teacher Information

Temperatures are affected by altitude. In general, the higher the altitude, the cooler the climate will be. Even near the equator, areas of higher altitude have cooler temperatures than do those near sea level. Oceans tend to have a moderating effect on nearby land masses, as water heats up and cools down more slowly than does land. Air masses coming from the oceans can have a great cooling or warming effect on temperature over land areas, depending upon whether they are coming from the cold Arctic waters or from warmer ocean currents.

Latitude affects temperature more than any other single factor. Regions near the equator are said to have a low latitude. High latitudes are near the poles. The higher the latitude of a region, the colder the climate will be. Low latitudes get the direct rays of the sun. Higher latitudes get slanted, less concentrated rays.

INTEGRATING: Math, language arts, social studies

SKILLS: Inferring, communicating, comparing and contrasting, using space-time relationships, formulating hypotheses, identifying and controlling variables, experimenting, researching

Activity 4.7
HOW DO MOUNTAINS AFFECT YEARLY RAINFALL?

Materials Needed

- Relief maps
- Rainfall maps
- Paper
- Pencil

Procedure

1. Study your rainfall maps and identify at least 10 areas that have high average rainfall.

2. Find these same areas on the relief map. Do they seem to be areas of high altitude, low altitude, medium altitude, or a mixture of all three?

3. Are these areas usually near mountain ranges, near oceans, or far away from both? Or does it seem to be a mixture?

4. Are these areas near the equator or nearer to the North Pole or South Pole?

5. Next, identify at least 10 areas that have low average rainfall. Do steps 2, 3, and 4 with them.

6. What can you say about the effect altitude has on rainfall?

7. What effect do mountain ranges and oceans seem to have on rainfall?

8. What effect does latitude (distance from the equator) have on rainfall?

For Problem Solvers: Do some research and find out how annual precipitation is affected by altitude. Does latitude affect annual precipitation? What about longitude? What else do you think causes one region of the earth to have more or less precipitation than another? How does precipitation amount seem to coincide with population centers? Continue your research and see what you can learn. Share your information with others.

Teacher Information

Latitude determines which *wind belt* a region is located in and, to a large degree, whether the region will have warm, moist air creating rainy weather, or cool, dry air bringing dry weather. Rainfall is also affected by mountains, usually favoring the windward side of the mountain. As the air moves up the mountainside it is cooled and condensed, and rainfall results. The leeward side of the mountain gets the air mass after much of the moisture has been condensed from the air. As winds blow inland from the ocean, the regions nearest the ocean get the most rainfall. See Activity 3.9.

INTEGRATING: Math, reading, language arts, social studies, art

SKILLS: Observing, inferring, communicating, comparing and contrasting, using space-time relationships, formulating hypotheses, researching

Activity 4.8
HOW DO ROCKS COMPARE IN HARDNESS?

(Teacher-supervised activity)

 Take home and do with family and friends.

Materials Needed

- Variety of rocks
- Dull knife, piece of glass, and other "scratchers"

Procedure

1. Select two rocks from the collection.

2. Try to scratch one with the other.

3. Which would you say is harder—the one that will scratch or the one that can be scratched?

4. Keep the harder of the two rocks and set the other aside.

5. Select another rock and use the same scratch test to compare it with the first one you kept.

6. Again keep the harder of the two rocks and set the other one aside.

7. Repeat the procedure until you have identified the hardest rock in the collection.

8. Now compare the other rocks and find the second hardest one. Put it next to the hardest.

9. Continue this process until you have all the rocks lined up in order of hardness.

10. Use the scratch test to compare other objects with rocks. Some things you might try are your fingernail, a penny, a knife blade, and a piece of glass. Be extremely careful with the sharp objects.

11. Try to find other rocks that are harder or softer than any you have in this collection.

For Problem Solvers: Learn about the Mohs hardness scale. What does it do? Why is it used? Make a hardness scale of your own that will provide the same kind of information. What materials will you use? How does each one compare with the items used by the Mohs scale?

Compare your list of materials with that of some of your classmates. If you used some of the same items for your hardness scale, do you agree as to the hardness of these items on the Mohs scale?

Teacher Information

The label "rock" is often used rather loosely to mean either rock or mineral. Actually, rocks are made of minerals. Minerals have physical properties and chemical composition that either are fixed or vary within a limited range. A rock is often an aggregate of minerals.

Minerals are scaled in hardness in a range of 1 to 10, with 1 being very soft and 10 very hard. A common method of determining hardness is the "scratch test." Fingernails have a hardness of about 2.5, so if a rock will scratch the fingernail, the rock has a hardness greater than 2.5. If it will not scratch the fingernail, or if it can be scratched by the fingernail, the rock has a hardness less than 2.5. A penny has a hardness of three, so if a rock scratches the penny, it has a hardness greater than three. Other common materials that can be used in the scratch test are steel knife blades (hardness about 5.5), glass (hardness about 5.5 to 6.0), and other rocks.

The Mohs' hardness scale is helpful in comparing hardness of rocks. It uses the following minerals, representing hardnesses of 1 to 10:

1. talc
2. gypsum
3. calcite
4. fluorite
5. apatite

6. orthoclase feldspar
7. quartz
8. topaz
9. corundum
10. diamond

CAUTION: In step 10 on page 72, you will need to judge whether students are to use knife blades and glass in their comparisons. Other objects can be tested to see where they lie in the range of hardness.

INTEGRATING: Reading, language arts

SKILLS: Observing, inferring, classifying, predicting, communicating, comparing and contrasting, researching

Activity 4.9
WHAT COLOR STREAK DOES A ROCK MAKE?

Materials Needed

- Collection of rocks
- Porcelain (non-glazed)
- Sheets of paper in various colors
- Colored pencils

Procedure

1. Select one of the rocks from the collection.
2. Try to make a streak on the porcelain with the rock.
3. Does it make a streak? If so, what color streak does it make?
4. Try to make a streak with each of the other rocks in the collection.
5. Does the color of the streak usually match the color of the rock that made it?
6. Put the rocks in groups according to the color of the streak.
7. Will any of your rocks write on paper? Try it. If you have one that will, draw a picture with it. Try different colors of paper as well as different types of rocks.

Teacher Information

One of the common tests made in classifying rocks is the streak test. A porcelain plate, called a streak plate, is used. The rock is rubbed on the streak plate to see what color dust it makes. A piece of white porcelain tile will suffice as the streak plate. Use the back of the tile—not the glazed side.

    (CAUTION: If you use a broken piece of porcelain as the streak plate, close supervision is needed to assure safety.) The color of the streak is frequently different from the color of the rock that made it.

    If the rock collection includes talc, anthracite (coal), or gypsum, students should be able to write on paper with them.

INTEGRATING: Language arts

SKILLS: Observing, inferring, classifying, predicting, communicating, comparing and contrasting

Activity 4.10
HOW DO ROCKS REACT TO VINEGAR?

Materials Needed

- Collection of rocks
- One plastic cup for each rock
- Vinegar
- Chalk

Procedure

1. Put a small sample of each rock in a separate cup. Put a small piece of chalk in a cup as one of the rock samples.
2. Pour a small amount of vinegar on each sample.
3. What happened?
4. Group the rocks according to the way they responded to the vinegar.

Teacher Information

This test is called the acid test and is normally performed with dilute hydrochloric acid (HCl). Vinegar is a weak acid and works satisfactorily.

The acid test is used to identify rocks that contain calcium carbonate. Any such rock will fizz when vinegar (or dilute HCl) is applied. Limestone, marble, calcite, and chalk are made of calcium carbonate and will fizz in the presence of vinegar. Before applying the vinegar, scratch the surface of the rock to expose fresh material.

INTEGRATING: Language arts

SKILLS: Observing, inferring, classifying, predicting, communicating, comparing and contrasting

Activity 4.11
WHICH ROCKS ARE ATTRACTED BY A MAGNET?

Materials Needed

- Collection of rocks
- Magnet

Procedure

1. Select one of the rocks and touch it with the magnet.
2. Is this rock attracted by the magnet?
3. Test each rock in the collection to see if any seem to be attracted by the magnet.
4. Make two groups of rocks—those that are attracted by the magnet, and those that are not.

Teacher Information

Try to include at least one rock that contains iron, such as galena, in the collection of rocks used for this activity. If no rocks that are attracted by a magnet are available, this activity should be omitted.

If you have, or can acquire, a piece of lodestone, it would make an excellent addition to the collection for this exercise. Lodestone is nature's magnet. After the activity is completed as written, have students suspend the lodestone from a string and see how it responds to the magnet. It will be attracted or repelled, depending on the position of its poles, the same as any magnet behaves in the presence of another magnet.

INTEGRATING: Language arts

SKILLS: Observing, inferring, classifying, predicting, communicating, comparing and contrasting

Activity 4.12
WHICH ROCKS CONDUCT ELECTRICITY?

Materials Needed

- Collection of rocks
- Dry cell battery
- Small light socket with flashlight bulb
- Two pieces of insulated wire about 20 cm (8 in.) long
- One piece of insulated wire about 5 cm (2 in.) long
- Small bolt or nail

Procedure

1. Connect the bulb to the battery with the pieces of wire, as illustrated in Figure 4.12-1, to be sure the battery and bulb are working properly. Be sure you can light the bulb before going on to the next step.

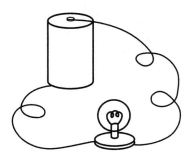

Figure 4.12-1

Flashlight Cell, Bulb, and Wires

2. Use both wires and connect the system again, this time with the bolt held between the two wires (Figure 4.12-2). Be sure you can light the bulb this way before you continue. The bolt is a good conductor of electricity.

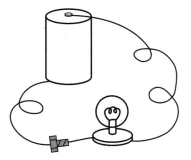

Figure 4.12-2

Same as Figure 4.12-1, but with a Bolt in the Circuit.

3. Remove the bolt and put one of the rocks in its place. Does the bulb light? If so, the rock is a conductor of electricity.

4. Put the rocks in two groups—those that are conductors of electricity and those that are nonconductors. (If the bulb lights, the rock is a conductor.)

Teacher Information

Some rocks conduct electricity (such as those containing significant amounts of copper, zinc, or iron). This is one of the characteristics scientists use in classifying and identifying rocks.

SKILLS: Observing, inferring, classifying, predicting, communicating, comparing and contrasting

Activity 4.13
WHAT TYPE OF CRYSTALS DO ROCKS HAVE?

 Take home and do with family and friends.

Materials Needed

- Collection of rocks
- Hand lens

Procedure

1. Examine each rock with the hand lens.
2. Can you see any crystal structure?
3. Are the crystals lined up or are they arranged randomly?
4. Do the crystals seem to be somewhat interlocking (melted together) or do they appear to be glued together by a cementing material?
5. Put the rocks in groups according to your findings.

For Problem Solvers: Do some research in encyclopedias, field manuals, and whatever sources you have. Find out about common types of rock crystals. How many of these do you have in your collection? Try to find more. Share your information with others who are interested in rock crystals.

Teacher Information

Igneous and metamorphic rocks have undergone intense heat in their formation and the crystals are interlocking, or melted together by nature, with materials that settled to the bottom of a body of water where the rock was formed. Beautiful arrangements of quartz crystals are found in the centers of hollow rocks called geodes. Try to include at least one geode in the collection used.

INTEGRATING: Language arts

SKILLS: Observing, classifying, communicating, comparing and contrasting, researching

Activity 4.14
HOW CAN YOU MEASURE THE DENSITY OF A ROCK?

(Enrichment activity or for older students)

Materials Needed

- Variety of small rocks
- Gram balance
- Jar or soup can
- Small tray or pan
- Water
- Paper
- Pencil

Procedure

1. Select a rock. It must fit inside your jar.

2. Weigh your rock on the gram balance and record the weight.

3. Determine the weight of a volume of water equal to the volume of your rock by following these steps:

   a. Place the tray on the balance. Weigh the tray and record its weight. Then place the jar on the tray.

   b. Pour as much water into the jar as you can get in it without overflowing water into the tray. If any water spills into the tray, it must be cleaned up.

   c. Carefully put your rock into the jar of water. The water that is displaced by the rock will spill into the tray. It will have exactly the same volume as the rock.

   d. Carefully remove the jar without spilling any more water.

   e. Weigh the tray containing the water and subtract the weight of the empty tray to obtain the weight of the water that was displaced by the rock.

4. Divide the weight of the rock by the weight of the water it displaced.

5. What is the result? This number represents the *specific gravity* of the rock.

6. Follow the same procedure with rocks of other types and compare the specific gravity of the rocks.

For Problem Solvers: The specific gravity of water is 1.0. Is the specific gravity of your rock greater or less than the specific gravity of water? Specific gravity is a measure of *density*.

Find other small objects—some that seem to be heavy for their size and some that seem to be light for their size. For each one, predict whether it is lighter than water or heavier than water. Test your prediction by measuring the density of each object using the technique you learned by doing the above activity. Were your predictions right?

Teacher Information

Specific gravity is a number expressing the ratio between the weight of an object and the weight of an equal volume of water at 4 degrees Celsius. If a rock weighs twice as much as an equal volume of water, its specific gravity is 2. If it weighs three times as much as an equal volume of water, its specific gravity is 3, and so on. Most common minerals have a specific gravity of about 2.5–3.0. Those outside these limits feel noticeably light or noticeably heavy.

If a gram balance is not available, try a postage scale or other sensitive scale.

INTEGRATING: Math

SKILLS: Observing, inferring, comparing and contrasting, classifying, measuring, predicting

Activity 4.15
HOW CAN YOU MAKE A PERMANENT SHELL IMPRINT?

Materials Needed

- Seashell
- Pie tin
- Petroleum jelly
- Plaster of Paris
- Water
- Paper towels
- Newspapers

Procedure

1. Coat the bottom and sides of the pie tin with a thin layer of petroleum jelly so the plaster will release easily.

2. Coat your shell with a thin layer of petroleum jelly.

3. Lay your shell in the bottom of the pie tin. Place it with the rounded side up (Figure 4.15-1).

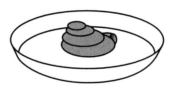

Figure 4.15-1

Shell, Rounded Side Up, in Pan

4. Mix plaster with water according to the instructions on the package. Prepare sufficient plaster to make a layer in the pan about 15 mm (at least 1/2 in.).

5. Pour the plaster carefully over the shell and let it harden (leave it at least one hour).

6. Turn the pie tin upside down on a table covered with newspaper and tap it lightly. The plaster cast with shell should fall out onto the table.

7. Remove the shell but handle the plaster cast very carefully. The plaster will be quite soft until it has had at least a day to cure (harden).

8. After at least one day of curing time, carefully wipe the excess petroleum jelly off the plaster cast with a paper towel. Then wash the rest off lightly with warm water.

9. You now have an imprint of the shell in plaster much like those often found in limestone and other sedimentary rock (Figure 4.15-2). When found in rock, this imprint is called a fossil because it is evidence of an ancient animal.

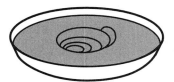

Figure 4.15-2

Shell Imprint in Plaster

For Problem Solvers: Begin a collection of fossils, especially any that might be found in your area. Watch for opportunities to expand your collection. If you know a geologist or a rock hound, they will be able to help you get started. Find out what kind of fossils you have and what period of time they represent. What conditions do you think they lived in? Study about the fossils and find out if scientists agree with you. Encyclopedias will be very helpful. Share what you learn with others who are interested in fossils.

Teacher Information

Plaster of Paris can be obtained at a local builders supply store or hobby shop. It is easy to work with, and if students follow the directions, the project should be successful. As the plaster cures, it will become quite warm, then will cool. It should be allowed to cool completely before being removed from the mold (pie tin).

If you have an area nearby where fossils can be found, that would be an excellent field trip. Otherwise, perhaps a few fossil samples could be borrowed from a friend or purchased from a science supply house. The experience of making a "fossil" will make a more lasting impression on the minds of students if they can see just how similar their "fossil" is to the real fossil formed by nature.

The imprint resulting from the above activity is a negative imprint. If a positive image is desired, spread a thin layer of petroleum jelly on the entire surface of the plaster, wrap and tie a piece of cardboard around it to provide sideboards to hold plaster, and pour another layer of plaster on top of the first. After it has cured, remove the cardboard, separate the two pieces of plaster with a knife blade, and presto—you have both a positive and negative of the shell. Clean up the petroleum jelly after the plaster has cured thoroughly, as indicated above.

An imprint of a leaf can be made following the same steps.

INTEGRATING: Reading, language arts, social studies

SKILLS: Observing, classifying, communicating, using space-time relationships, formulating hypotheses, researching

Activity 4.16
HOW IS SNOW COMPACTED INTO ICE TO FORM GLACIERS?

Materials Needed

- Tall, narrow jar with lid
- Rocks or other weights that can fit into jar
- Scissors
- Cardboard
- Masking tape
- Fresh marshmallows (miniatures preferred)
- Pencil

Procedure

1. Fill the jar with fresh marshmallows, loosely packed.
2. Cut a cardboard circle to fit inside the jar without rubbing the sides.
3. Place the rocks, or other weights, on top of the cardboard circle.
4. Stick a strip of masking tape to the side of the jar from top to bottom.
5. Make a pencil mark on the masking tape at the level of the cardboard.
6. Put the lid on the jar and set the jar in a safe place.
7. Twice each day for four days, check the jar and make a pencil mark on the jar at the level of the cardboard.
8. At the end of four days, discuss your observations with others. Tell how you think this is like the forming of a glacier.

For Problem Solvers: Do some research about glaciers. What makes a glacier a glacier? Where is the nearest one to where you live? What do glaciers do to alter the surface of the land?

Where do icebergs come from? Are they the same as glaciers? What is the difference between a glacier and an iceberg? Why do ship captains have to be careful when they are around icebergs? Draw a picture of an iceberg, showing how much of it is above the water and how much of it is below the surface of the water.

Teacher Information

As snow accumulates and remains for long periods of time, the weight of the snow compacts the lower layers into ice. If conditions are such that the accumulation continues season after season, a snowfield is formed. If it moves, it's a glacier. In this activity, the compacting action is demonstrated with marshmallows. The weights substitute for upper layers of heavy snow. The lid is used to keep the marshmallows from drying out so the compacting action can continue for a longer period of time.

INTEGRATING: Reading, language arts, social studies, art

SKILLS: Inferring, communicating, researching

Activity 4.17
HOW IS THE EARTH LIKE YOUR BODY?

(Total-group activity)

Materials Needed

- Pencil
- Lined paper
- Picture of the earth
- Picture of the moon

Procedure

1. Scientists often refer to our earth as a living planet. Unlike the moon, which is considered dead, the earth is constantly changing its surface, using energy from the sun to grow new life, repairing damage to itself and adjusting its surface in response to many stresses. Compare the pictures of the earth and the moon. Can you see how one might be called living and the other dead?

2. Your body works in much the same way. Its surface changes, it has mountains and valleys, it is covered by a thin crust (skin), and it uses energy from the sun to grow. It also has the ability to repair itself when it is injured.

3. With your teacher and others, discuss what it means to be alive and why our living earth is so important to us.

Teacher Information

This activity and Activity 4.18 are intended to provide the foundation for the more specific activities that follow. First are activities concerned with general major phenomena, such as mountain building through earthquakes, folding, faulting, volcanic activity, and water and glacial erosion. Other activities focus on collecting and testing rocks in the student's immediate environment.

INTEGRATING: Health, language arts, social studies

SKILLS: Observing, inferring, predicting, communicating, comparing and contrasting, using space-time relationships, formulating hypotheses

Activity 4.18
HOW IS THE EARTH LIKE A JIGSAW PUZZLE?

(Total or small-group activity)

Materials Needed

- Globe of the earth
- Soccer ball
- Tennis ball cut in half

Procedure

1. Look at the three objects on the table. They represent different models of the earth.

2. The thin outer cover of the tennis ball represents the earth's crust, the part on which we live. The model would be more accurate if we filled the rest of the ball with very hot metal, but we won't do that.

3. Examine the soccer ball. Notice it is not just a smooth, round ball, but appears to be made of many pieces. In some ways, the crust of our earth is like the soccer ball; scientists believe it is not a single, solid piece or cover, but many pieces that fit together in different ways. This idea is called *plate tectonics.*

4. Now look at the globe of the earth. Pretend it is a big jigsaw puzzle. If you could move the continents around, could you find a way to make them fit together?

5. Most scientists believe that millions of years ago the continents were joined together in some way and have gradually drifted apart. They call this idea (theory) *continental drift.*

For Problem Solvers: Look up Pangaea in the encyclopedia. Make a puzzle that shows how the super continent seems to have split up into the continents as they are today. Learn what you can about Pangaea. What is the "ring of fire"? What does *plate tectonics* have to do with all of this? Share your information with others in your class. Discuss your ideas. Do you think the continents were once one?

Teacher Information

Some students may be unable to visualize the shapes of the continents in such a way that they can put them together. It may be helpful to make outline maps (cutouts) of the major continents to assist them.

CAUTION: Carefully puncture the tennis ball before cutting it.

Plate tectonics is the study of the formation and deformation of the Earth's crust. It is considered by many to be the most significant scientific breakthrough in the history of geology. Although some scientists have suggested related theories for over 100 years, clarification of it into a unifying theory of Earth's dynamics is credited to research and writing of the 1960s. It explains the origin of mountains, the history of ocean basins, and the forces and changes within the earth's crust that bring about volcanoes and earthquakes. Students who do "For Problem Solvers" can continue learning about these effects as far as their interests take them. It will be a truly fascinating journey of study for those who are motivated to pursue it.

INTEGRATING: Reading, language arts, social studies, art

SKILLS: Observing, inferring, measuring, communicating, using space-time relationships, formulating hypotheses, researching

Activity 4.19
WHAT CAUSES EARTHQUAKES?

Materials Needed

- Several colors of clay (or fabric)

Procedure

1. Select one color of clay and make a flat sheet of it about 25 cm long × 10 cm wide × 5 mm thick (10 in. × 4 in. × 1/4 in.).
2. Make similar sheets of other colors of clay, varying the thickness somewhat.
3. Stack several strips of clay on top of each other.

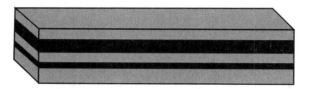

Stacked Clay Strips

4. Put one hand on each end of the stack of clay and push toward the middle.
5. What happened?
6. If the layers of clay were layers of rock on the earth's surface, and they were forced together as you forced the clay in step 4, what would happen?

For Problem Solvers: In this activity you demonstrated what happens as rock layers push together due to pressures in the earth's crust. Such pushing together is called *convergent* movement. The earth's crust shifts in other ways, too. Find out about *divergent* movement and *lateral* movement, and make a model that you can use to demonstrate these movements. What else causes earthquakes? Can you think of any other ways to make models that show earthquake action?

What was the most recent earthquake that you have heard about? What damage was done? Could some of the damage have been avoided if buildings, roads, and bridges had been built the way earthquake experts recommend?

What should you do if you are where an earthquake strikes? Share your ideas and your research with your class.

Teacher Information

Any soft plastic clay will work as clay for this activity. If sufficient clay is not available, carpet samples will do. You might think of other material that could be substituted, such as colored bath towels. Anything that can be layered and pushed together to show folding is adequate.

Although the layers of rock in the earth's surface are very hard and very heavy, heat and pressure under them are sometimes strong enough to cause them to shift, slide, and buckle. This results in earthquakes, and if it occurs in populated areas, much damage can occur.

You might want to let the layers of clay dry somewhat in order to better resemble the brittle rock layers as folding occurs, or wet the surface of each layer, so the layers are more likely to slide on each other as rock layers sometimes do.

If cracks are noted in the layers of clay, point out that these represent joints. Sometimes rock layers shift at joints. Cracks along which movement has occurred are called *faults*. If there is an earth fault reasonably nearby, a visit to it would make an excellent field trip. Students could construct a model of the earth layers from clay as they think the area of the fault might appear.

You might want to consider doing "Cakequakes" with your students (see Hardy and Tolman's "Cakequakes! An Earth-Shaking Experience," *Science and Children,* September 1991.)

INTEGRATING: Reading, language arts, social studies

SKILLS: Inferring, classifying, predicting, communicating, using space-time relationships, formulating hypotheses, researching

Activity 4.20
HOW CAN YOU MAKE A VOLCANO REPLICA?

Materials Needed

- Large pan
- Rubber tubing 50 cm (20 in.) long
- Flour
- Salt
- Water
- Puffed rice
- Brown tempera paint
- Paintbrush
- Pencil

Procedure

1. Make at least two quarts of salt-flour paste in the pan.
2. In the same pan, form the salt-flour paste into a volcanolike cone, leaving a cone-shaped hole in the center (Figure 4.20-1).

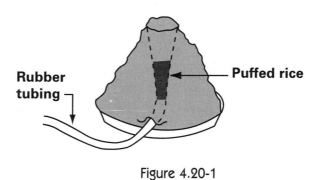

Figure 4.20-1

Volcano Replica

3. Use a pencil to form a small tunnel under one side of the volcano. Then insert the tube into the tunnel and bring it up in the center of the volcano so that the end of the tube comes up in the bottom of the cone. Seal the channel by pressing the paste around the tube.

4. When the model dries and hardens, paint it with brown tempera paint and with other colors if you have them and want to use them.

5. Pour some puffed rice into the cone.

6. Blow on the end of the tube, gently at first, then harder.

7. What happened? From the way your model works, tell what you can about real volcanoes.

For Problem Solvers: Make another design of a volcano model that will show how material from within the earth is thrust out by forces that are there. Use your creativity. Check your encyclopedia and other reference books that are available to you. Discuss your ideas with others who are working on the same activity. Together you will probably be able to think of several different ways to design a volcano model. Construct at least one of these and try it out.

Do you know where there is an active volcano, or one that has been active during your lifetime? If not, find out about one. Do some research, talk to people who know about it, and learn what you can about it. In what ways did it change the shape of the earth's surface? What damage did it do? What did people do to avoid getting hurt by it? Is it expected to be active in the future? How soon? Share your information with others.

Draw a cross-section of this volcano, showing what you think is within the volcano and beneath it, deep in the earth's crust. Share your drawing with others who did the same activity.

Did you study about the "ring of fire"? If not, this would be an excellent time to learn about it. The encyclopedia would be an excellent place to begin.

Teacher Information

In this model, air pressure forces the cereal out of the vent, simulating an eruption. In real volcanoes, the pressure is created by heat, steam, and movements beneath the earth's surface. This experience should be followed by a discussion of the similarities and differences between the model and a real volcano. Volcanic eruptions form mountains. Some islands, such as the Hawaiian islands, are the tops of such mountains formed in the ocean.

A more realistic model can be made by using ammonium dichromate (crystal form) for the erupting material (Figure 4.20-2). If you use this, certain changes should be made in the construction of the volcano. Instead of forming the inside cone, place a small tin can in the top and mold the clay around it. Omit the rubber tube and the puffed rice. You might want to make the volcano out of plaster of Paris instead of salt-flour clay. The ammonium dichromate is placed in the can and is to be lit with a match. You might need to add a bit of alcohol or lighter fluid to get it to light. **CAUTION: The operation of this volcano must be closely supervised and the volcano must be used outdoors. Fumes from the ammonium dichromate are poisonous. Have students stand back before the volcano is lit.** With proper supervision, this volcano is safe and provides a rather realistic impression of the volcanic eruption. Be sure to wash your hands thoroughly after this activity, as the ash produced during the eruption is poisonous, and the ammonium dichromate is more so. The volcano should be placed on newspapers, then, when finished, gathered up and thrown away.

Figure 4.20-2

Volcano Replica Made for Use with Ammonium Dichromate

If you have access to a compressed air source, even a portable air tank, you should consider another style of volcano model that is safe, realistic, and easy to construct. Insert a rubber tube through the bottom of a cardboard box at the center and attach it with tape (the opening of the tube should be very near the bottom of the box). The box should be at least 30 cm (12 in.) square. Put a layer of sand in the box, at least 10 cm (4 in.) deep. Turn on the air slowly at first, then increase the pressure. Too much air pressure will blow sand farther than you probably want it. A "volcanic" cone will form in a natural way, as the sand is blown up and falls back to the surface (Figure 4.20-3).

Figure 4.20-3

Volcano Replica Made for Use with Compressed Air

INTEGRATING: Math, reading, language arts, social studies, art

SKILLS: Observing, inferring, measuring, predicting, communicating, using space-time relationships, formulating hypotheses, researching

Topic 5:   Ecology

TO THE TEACHER

Ecology is both interdisciplinary and intradisciplinary. It is interdisciplinary because it involves content from the biological, physical, and earth sciences, plus all areas of the social sciences. It is intradisciplinary because the ecologist attempts to use information from many sources to produce a unique field.

Many of the ecological problems we read about, see on TV, or hear on the radio are global in nature. Some are highly sensitive and fall in the political realm. National and international relations often deteriorate over ecologically-based issues. This section does not attempt to deal with moral, economic, or political issues. It deals with some basics of the science of ecology and attempts to help students realize their place, as individuals, in the ecological system.

The first portion of the area deals in very simple ways with nature's balance, food cycles, and food webs. The cycles of soil, water, and air are alluded to but not introduced formally. If you care to pursue these in greater depth, your library can provide ample resources.

People are introduced into an ecological system in this section. Liberties are taken with the term ecosystem to generalize it to apply to the student and his or her interaction with the immediate environment. Human interaction with the immediate environment becomes the focal point. Conservation, cooperation, and individual responsibility are emphasized. You may be tempted, as many are, to become preachy at this point; however, the effectiveness will be greatly increased if students are helped to discover these ideas on their own.

Many of these activities could be enhanced by the use of movies on nature and wildlife. Teachers of young children should be aware that some movies show predators killing prey and portray life and death as they occur in a true ecosystem. Be sure to preview the movies and use only those you consider to be appropriate for your students.

Try to include as much art, music, poetry, and aesthetic experience as you can. Opportunities for enrichment are almost limitless.

Activity 5.1
HOW IS ENERGY TRANSFERRED IN AN ECOSYSTEM?

Materials Needed

- Simple food chain chart (Figure 5.1-1)
- Simple food web (Figure 5.1-2)

Procedure

1. Figure 5.1-1 is a diagram of a simple *food chain* showing how energy from the sun is used and stored in food molecules manufactured by the producers from nonliving materials. In turn, they are consumed by primary and secondary consumers. The waste products and remains of dead animals and plants are returned to the soil, where the scavengers and decomposers complete the cycle so that it can begin again.

2. There are many different ways food chains can work. Some consumers eat only certain producers. Other consumers eat both primary and secondary consumers. Ecologists call these many variables the *food web*. Just as a spider spins a web one strand at a time, food webs are made up of many food chains. Compare the food web (Figure 5.1-2) with the food chain (Figure 5.1-1).

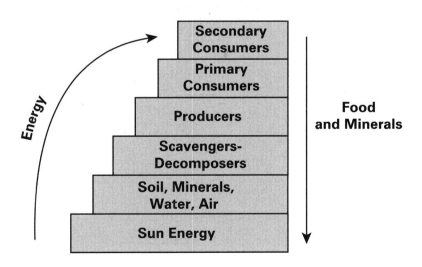

Figure 5.1-1

Food Chain

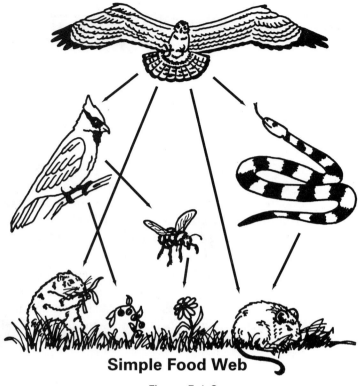

Simple Food Web

Figure 5.1-2

Food Web

4. Weather and chemicals produced from the nonliving portions of the ecosystem (air, water, soil) influence the conditions within the system. Can you think of other factors that might change the food web? What would happen if there were no mice?

5. Ecosystems are very complex. Can you see why ecology is an interesting and exciting science?

Teacher Information

Figures 5.1-1 and 5.1-2 are simple, but should still give students a feeling for the highly complex interrelationships that occur in nature. Also, chance is always part of the interplay.

Using charts may convey a feeling of a static process. Ecosystems are actually highly dynamic, with countless variables. Students may need additional experience in constructing ecosystems and applying them to life situations.

The next activity introduces the most complex variable in ecology—people.

SKILLS: Observing, inferring, classifying, communicating, comparing and contrasting, using space-time relationships

Activity 5.2
WHICH SOLIDS DECOMPOSE EASILY?

Materials Needed

- Large, deep tray, such as a suit box
- Plastic liner or plastic garbage bag
- Water
- Soil
- Samples of small items (solid waste) out of garbage cans
- Paper
- Pencil

Procedure

1. Line the box with the plastic.
2. Put a layer of soil about 3-5 cm (1-2 in.) deep in the bottom of the box. Spread it out so it is uniform.
3. Place your samples of solid waste around on top of the layer of soil.
4. Make a "map" on paper, showing which items you used and where they were placed on the tray.
5. Cover the items with another layer of soil about the same thickness as the first.
6. Sprinkle some water on it, enough to wet the soil.
7. Let the box sit for a period of four to six weeks. Sprinkle a little bit of water on it each day or so to keep the soil moist.
8. When the time period is up, remove the top layer of soil and check the samples.
9. Refer to your map so each item can be located easily. Record the amount of decomposition of each item.
10. Which items decomposed the most? What were they made of?
11. Which items decomposed the least? What were they made of?

For Problem Solvers: What type of material is most of our solid dry waste made of? What can we reuse, or even avoid using in the first place? To answer the first question, for both home and school, try this:

(1) Make a list of common materials that are frequently put in the garbage, such as paper, plastic, glass, and so on.

(2) Ask your school custodian which of these materials make up most of the garbage at school. List the materials in order of quantity, with the material that comprises most of the garbage at the top of the list. Estimate the number of pounds of each type of garbage

discarded daily by the school. Maybe your custodian would allow you or a member of your group to help empty the waste baskets of the school for a day or two, so you can record types and amounts of garbage.

(3) Ask each of your classmates to examine their garbage at home and make a similar list. Then compile all the lists into one, showing categories and estimated amounts of the most common garbage discarded at home.

(4) Make a line graph or a bar graph that shows types and amounts of garbage discarded, both at school and at home.

Discuss your findings with your class. Use your information to estimate the amount of garbage discarded at school and at home in a week, a month, and a year. What type of material do we discard the most of? Is there something we should do to use less of it? Do we need to recycle more of our garbage? Could we use some of it for art creations, for useful containers, or can you think of other uses for it? Share your ideas and try to come up with a plan to reduce the amount of waste.

Teacher Information

The average solid waste in the United States has been estimated at about 5.3 pounds per person per day. Have some students use that rate to figure out the amount for your school, city, state, or nation. Much of this waste material is hauled to sanitary landfills and covered with dirt. Sometimes it is crushed first. After it is covered with soil, bacteria and moisture begin their work of decomposing the material. However, some of the solids don't cooperate very well. Such materials are very difficult to completely dispose of. To keep our environment clean, materials that become garbage must either be recycled or decomposed.

This activity is to give students a way to find out which materials will decompose readily and which will not. Samples used should be small and thin. Students could use a tin can lid, a piece of aluminum foil, a toothpick, a piece of a plastic bottle, various types of paper and fabric, a rubber band, and so on. They also need to be very patient. Decomposing matter by natural means requires a lot of time. At least four to six weeks should be allowed in order for changes to be observed. For some materials, observable changes might require many years.

INTEGRATING: Math, language arts, social studies, art

SKILLS: Observing, inferring, classifying, measuring, communicating, comparing and contrasting, using space-time relationships, formulating hypotheses

Topic 6:   Above the Earth

TO THE TEACHER

Suppose a small child at play on the beach at Kitty Hawk, North Carolina, had paused to watch the first flight of Orville and Wilbur Wright, in December 1903. Less than seventy years later, that same individual could have watched on television as the first man walked on the moon. The incredible and fascinating story of flight above the earth is introduced in this section.

Learning to simulate controlled flight can be exciting and enjoyable. You may even find yourself helping to build a large cardboard mock-up of a pilot's cockpit with simulated controls. (If, as a result of these activities, you decide to fly a real airplane or space ship, we strongly recommend that you take additional lessons first.)

The following activities are offered to help you and your students learn about our remarkable progress in the quest to move into the unknown, and perhaps to challenge some of you to dream of what lies beyond.

Activity 6.1
HOW CAN A BALL HELP YOU MOVE?

Materials Needed

- Heavy ball, such as a medicine ball or an old basketball stuffed with cloth

- Skateboard (or roller skates or roller blades)

- Water-soluble felt pen (or chalk)

Procedure

1. Stand on the skateboard. Be sure you are on a smooth, flat surface.

2. Have a friend mark the spot where the back rollers of your skateboard touch the floor and then have the friend stand in front of you, no closer than two meters (2 yards).

3. Hold the ball in both hands close to your chest. Throw it to your friend with a pushing motion.

4. Mark the position of the back rollers of your skateboard.

5. Repeat steps 3 and 4 several times.

6. What happened? What can you say about this?

For Problem Solvers: Find some objects to throw that are different weights. Be sure they are objects that you can throw and catch without hurting anyone and that the objects won't be damaged if they are dropped on the ground. Do the activity again, but this time recording the weight of the object each time, as well as the distance the skateboard moves. Compare the distance with the weight of the object thrown. Does it seem to make a difference? Graph your information.

Find an object you can throw that is a different weight from all your other objects. From the information you now have, predict how far the skateboard will move as you throw this object. Try it several times and find the average distance. Was your prediction accurate, or nearly accurate?

Teacher Information

Each time the person on the skateboard throws the ball in one direction (action) he or she will move in the opposite direction (*reaction*). Newton stated this principle as his third law of motion: "For every action there is an equal and opposite reaction."

The student throwing the ball will not move the same distance as the ball travels due to such factors as friction and the fact that the person is bigger and heavier than the ball. However, each time the ball is thrown in one direction, the person on the skateboard will move an observable and measurable distance in the opposite direction.

Your problem solvers will do some scientific research comparing the effect of the weight of the thrown object. If no one in the group is sensitive about his or her weight, it would be interesting to use the weight of the person on the skateboard as another variable in the experiment.

INTEGRATING: Math, language arts

SKILLS: Observing, inferring, measuring, predicting, communicating, comparing and contrasting, formulating hypotheses, identifying and controlling variables, experimenting

Activity 6.2
WHAT TYPE OF ENERGY IS THIS?

(Teacher-supervised activity)

Materials Needed

- Metal can
- Large nail
- Hammer
- Heavy string 1 m (1 yd.) long
- One fishing swivel
- Scissors
- Sink
- Water

Procedure

1. Use the hammer and nail to punch four holes at equal distances around the can near the bottom edge. Drive the nail in at a steep angle so the holes appear semicircular. Be sure all holes point in the same direction.

2. Make three small holes around the top of the can (large enough for string).

3. Cut the string into four 25-cm (10-in.) lengths.

4. Tie one string to one end of the fishing swivel. Tie the other three strands to the other end.

5. Thread each of the three strings through a hole in the top of the can and tie them securely.

6. Hold your can over the sink at arm's length and have someone else pour water into it.

7. What happened? Can you explain why?

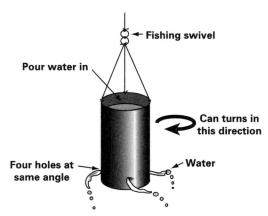

Can with Holes Rotating on Strings

Teacher Information

This principle was discovered by a Greek named Heron of Alexandria nearly 2,000 years ago (see the encyclopedia).

There are other ways of helping children discover the principle of action-reaction (for every action there is an equal and opposite reaction). One is to put an air gun (without the BB) on a roller skate. Each time the air gun is fired in one direction, the skate and gun will move in the opposite direction (*recoil*). A plastic medicine bottle with a snap top (not safety top) may be placed on round pencils as rollers. Put a mixture of bicarbonate of soda and vinegar in the bottle and snap on the top. CO_2 gas will form inside the bottle, pop the top off, and move the bottle along the pencil rollers in the opposite direction of the popped cap. (*Note*: This demonstration can get messy!)

SKILLS: Observing, inferring, measuring, predicting, communicating, comparing and contrasting

Activity 6.3
WHAT CAN A MARBLE GAME TELL US?

Materials Needed

- 1/2-in. garden hose cut in half lengthwise, 2 m (2 yds.) long (or transparent tubing)
- Marbles
- Two chairs

Procedure

1. Bend the half hose, open side up, into a nearly U-shape between two chairs.
2. Put six marbles in the lowest part of the hose. Be sure they move freely.
3. While observing the marbles resting in the bottom of the hose, release one marble in the groove at the top of the hose. What happened?
4. Release two marbles at exactly the same time at the top of the groove. What happened at the bottom?
5. Try releasing different numbers of marbles. What happened? Can you explain why? Can you predict what would happen if you had more marbles?
6. What will happen if you have *two* marbles at the bottom and release three at the top? Try it.

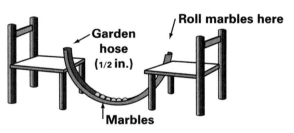

Garden Hose Placed Between Chairs

Teacher Information

If you can obtain small ball bearings (round wheel bearings) and plastic or rubber tubing in half-meter lengths each student can construct this project. This is another investigation of action-reaction. When one marble is released in the groove at the top, it will roll down and strike the end marble in the row at the bottom. The marble at the opposite end of the row will move up the hose on the opposite side. If two marbles strike the row on one side, two will move away on the opposite side. If more marbles strike the row than there are marbles at rest, the nearest moving marble(s) will continue on with the ones set in motion.

INTEGRATING: Math

SKILLS: Observing, inferring, predicting, communicating, comparing and contrasting, identifying and controlling variables

Activity 6.4
HOW CAN WE USE ACTION-REACTION?

Materials Needed

- Long balloons
- Paper bags (large enough to contain blown-up balloon)
- Masking tape
- Monofilament fishline
- Plastic drinking straw
- Paper
- Pencil

Procedure

1. Inflate a long balloon and release it. On your paper write a description of its path of flight.

2. The balloon uses the principle of action-reaction to move. Can you see how it works? Make a picture of an inflated balloon with air coming out. Draw arrows showing the direction of action and reaction.

3. Look at the words you used to describe the path of the balloon's first flight. Try the following to correct the problems.

4. Locate the straw on the fishline stretching across your classroom. Tape the paper bag to the straw, parallel with the fish line.

5. Slide the bag and straw to the center of the line and put a long, inflated balloon in the open bag.

6. Release the air rapidly from the balloon. What happened?

7. Pretend your paper bag is a rocket ship and the balloon is a powerful rocket engine. What could you do to improve its flight? Test your ideas.

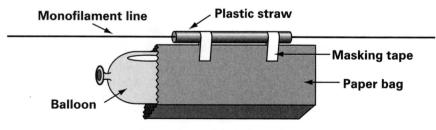

Paper Bag with Balloon in It

Teacher Information

The balloon acts as a simple reaction (rocket) engine. When it is released by itself, its flight will be very erratic or unpredictable.

The monofilament line, straw, and paper bag provide housing, control, and direction for the thrust of the rocket engine. These are three essentials needed for space travel.

While experimenting to obtain greater speed and distance, you might suggest trying different-sized tubes as nozzles for the exhaust end of the rocket. Will a smaller opening (barrel of old ball point pen) make greater distances possible? Should the opening at the end of the balloon be larger (copper pipe)? How can you get both greater speed and greater distance (less mass, larger engine)?

SKILLS: Observing, inferring, predicting, communicating, comparing and contrasting

Activity 6.5
HOW CAN YOU MAKE A SODA STRAW ROCKET?

 Take home and do with family and friends.

Materials Needed

- Two-liter bottle
- Large drinking straw
- Standard-size drinking straw
- Modeling clay

Procedure

1. Insert the large straw into the bottle and seal around it at the mouth of the bottle with clay. (See Figure below.)
2. Seal one end of the regular straw with a small dob of clay.
3. Insert the small straw into the large straw.
4. Squeeze hard on the sides of the soda bottle.
5. What happened?
6. Explain why you think it happened.

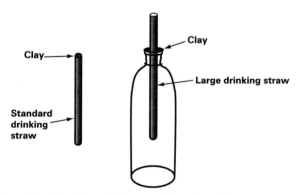

Two-liter Bottle and Straws, Ready to Launch

Teacher Information

This activity will be fun for all ages, and will demonstrate the principle of action-reaction. It also teaches important concepts about air and what happens to air pressure when the size of the container is decreased.

Activity 6.6
HOW DO OTHER FORCES AFFECT OUR ROCKET'S PERFORMANCE?

Materials Needed

- Long balloon
- Plastic drinking straw
- Monofilament line
- Masking tape

Procedure

1. Thread the monofilament line through the straw and attach it, tightly stretched, to opposite sides of your classroom.

2. Inflate a long balloon. Hold its mouth closed while using masking tape to secure it to the straw.

3. Release the balloon. What happened?

4. Compare the performance of this balloon to that of the balloon in the paper bag in Activity 6.4. Can you think of reasons for the differences you observed?

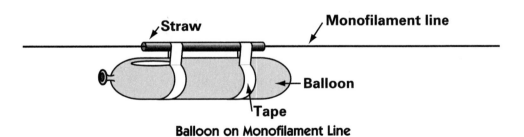

Balloon on Monofilament Line

For Problem Solvers: What can you do to control the distance your balloon rocket moves along the line? Do you think the size or shape of the balloon will make a difference, or the paper bag, or how much air you put in the balloon? What about the way the system is hung on the line? Work with these and other variables that you can think of to help you control how far the rocket travels. Then mark the line with a piece of tape, showing how far you expect the rocket to go, and try it to test your prediction. Do this several times. Are you improving your skill?

Teacher Information

Without the paper bag, the balloon will move down the line at a higher rate of speed for a greater distance. Children may decide that the "weight" of the bag reduced the performance. Others may suggest that the square shape of the bag slowed it down. Some may notice that the balloon without the bag seems to get a faster start. These observations are related to the forces that are acting upon the object: gravity, inertia, and friction (wind resistance). To travel into outer space, all three must be considered.

INTEGRATING: Math

SKILLS: Observing, inferring, measuring, predicting, communicating, comparing and contrasting, formulating hypotheses, identifying and controlling variables, experimenting

Activity 6.7
HOW CAN WE DEVELOP MORE THRUST?

(Teacher-supervised activity)

Materials Needed

- Empty tube from paper towel or toilet tissue
- Heavy cardboard
- Monofilament line (15-lb. test or greater)
- CO_2 capsules
- Screw eyes
- Scissors
- Iron wire
- Hammer
- Sharpened nail
- Strong glue
- Stapler

Procedure

1. Cut three tail fins from the heavy cardboard. Glue them lengthwise around one end of the cardboard tube.

2. Make a circle approximately 10 cm (4 in.) in diameter. Cut from one edge into the center and fold it over to make a cone (glue and hold with staples).

3. Glue the nose cone to the end of the tube opposite the fins.

4. Attach two screw eyes or loops of wire to the top of the tube. Secure them with glue.

5. Use cardboard and crossed pieces of iron wire (tie wire) to make a holder for your CO_2 capsule. Insert it in the rear of the tube.

6. String monofilament line through the cup eyes.

7. Take your rocket outside and locate two uprights (trees or poles) about 50 meters (50 yards) or more apart. Stretch the line with the rocket attached very tightly between the uprights. Be sure there is nothing else near the line.

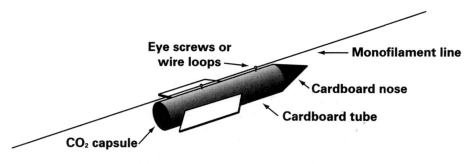

Eye screws or wire loops
Monofilament line
Cardboard nose
Cardboard tube
CO₂ capsule

CO₂ Rocket on Monofilament Line

8. Have a friend hold the rocket while you use a hammer and sharp nail to punch a small hole in the narrow end of the CO_2 capsule. Release the rocket immediately.

9. Try this several times.

For Problem Solvers: Try to find one or more water rockets. Figure out a way to measure how high the rocket goes. Fire the rocket several times, recording the amount of water used, the amount of pressure (number of pumps), and how high the rocket goes. Graph your data, then use it to predict the height with other amounts of water or pressure. Share your results with others who are interested in water rockets.

Teacher Information

The CO_2 capsule rocket is relatively safe, but close supervision is recommended in case of unexpected events. The sharpened nail and hammer, used to puncture the CO_2 capsule, are potential hazards if used carelessly.

When properly punctured and released, the rocket will travel down the line at a high rate of speed. The students may have to practice several times to get a successful launch. CO_2 capsules can be purchased at sporting goods stores and hobby shops.

Be sure all students remain behind the point of the rocket launch and that there are no obstructions along the path of the line. Use heavy-weight monofilament line (at least 15-pound test) and stretch it as tightly as possible (at least 4 feet above the ground).

All students can construct and launch rockets safely if the directions are carefully followed. The purchase of CO_2 capsules will entail some expense. Check local prices before you begin.

Students may notice that the capsules become very cold after they have been "triggered." This is because of a physical principle concerning gas under pressure: When released it takes on heat energy. This same principle is used to cool refrigerating systems (see the encyclopedia).

INTEGRATING: Math

SKILLS: Observing, inferring, measuring, predicting, communicating, comparing and contrasting, using space-time relationships, formulating hypotheses, identifying and controlling variables, experimenting

Activity 6.8
HOW DOES GRAVITY AFFECT OBJECTS?

 Take home and do with family and friends.

Materials Needed

- Objects of different sizes and weights (Ping-Pong ball, tennis ball, golf ball, marble, rock, large plastic foam ball, and so on)
- Meter stick, yardstick, or long board

Procedure

1. Place several of the objects close together on the edge of a flat table.
2. Find several students to be observers.
3. Use the long stick to push all the objects off the table at the same time (a rapid, even push is better than a slow, gradual one).
4. Have your observers report which object hit the floor first.
5. Try several times until you are certain of the results.
6. Find a shelf or ledge to launch the objects from a greater height. What do your observers report?

For Problem Solvers: Find some other objects to test your findings from this activity. Drop a sheet of paper with a marble. Do they fall at the same speed? Wad the paper up into a tight ball and try it again. Did that make any difference? Read about gravity in the encyclopedia. Do scientists know what causes gravity? Share your information with your teacher and with the class.

Teacher Information

If wind resistance (air friction) does not affect them, all objects fall at the same rate. Therefore, if dropped at the same instant and from the same height, they will hit the ground at the same time. The rate of fall does not depend on the size or weight of an object. This is a very difficult concept for children (and many adults) to understand. Our logic seems to say, "Big, heavy rocks will fall faster than tiny pebbles." The story is told of Galileo's dropping large and small objects at the same time from the Leaning Tower of Pisa centuries ago. This was the principle he discovered: Shape and mass do not affect the rate of fall.

SKILLS: Observing, inferring, classifying, measuring, predicting, communicating, comparing and contrasting, formulating hypotheses, identifying and controlling variables, experimenting

Activity 6.9
HOW DOES INERTIA AFFECT OBJECTS?

(Teacher-supervised activity)

Materials Needed

- Plastic tumbler half full of water
- Meter stick or yardstick (sturdy)
- Four or five blocks 10 cm × 10 cm (4 in. × 4 in.) cut from a 2″ × 4″ plank

Procedure

1. Stack the square blocks on a flat, smooth surface (table). Be sure no one is around you.
2. Rest your meter stick on the table behind the stack of blocks.
3. Hold the meter stick at one end and strike the bottom block with a smooth, rapid, sliding movement.
4. Repeat step 4 as many times as you can.
5. Stack the blocks again. Put a plastic tumbler half full of water on the top block.
6. Can you make the glass with the water stand on the table without touching it or spilling any of the water?

For Problem Solvers: Find a dictionary and read the definition of the word *inertia*. Using that definition, try to explain why the activity with the blocks of wood and the glass of water works the way it does. Why didn't the glass go flying with the block it was on? When you ride a bicycle, why does the bike continue to roll when you stop peddling? And why does the wheel skid when you try to stop quickly? What do these events have to do with inertia? What other things do you do that involve inertia? Share your ideas with your group, and together make a list of these.

Teacher Information

Be sure this investigation is done in an area where neither flying blocks nor spilled water will cause damage.

The blocks should be sanded so they are smooth and then polished to reduce friction.

As they strike the blocks, students may need to practice in developing a smooth, gliding motion with follow-through as they would in baseball, golf, or tennis. With practice, the blocks can be removed one at a time. The plastic tumbler should behave as the other blocks do.

Newton's law states that objects in motion remain in motion and objects at rest remain at rest unless acted upon by an outside force. If you try to stop a moving object (catch a ball) or move a stationary object (the block), its resistance to change in motion is called inertia. By using smooth blocks to reduce the friction, we can move a single block with very little disturbance to the others because the inertia of the other blocks will be greater than the friction. If you're tempted to leave the plastic tumbler empty, remember, the greater the mass, the more inertia it has. An empty tumbler is more likely to topple than a full one. Also, a short, squat tumbler will be more stable than a tall, narrow one.

SKILLS: Observing, inferring, predicting, communicating, comparing and contrasting

Activity 6.10
HOW CAN YOU PUT A COIN IN A GLASS WITHOUT TOUCHING THE COIN?

 Take home and do with family and friends.

Materials Needed

- Drinking glass
- Penny
- Index card cut into a square

Procedure

1. Put the card on the top of the glass.
2. Put the coin in the middle of the card.
3. With your middle finger, flip the card sharply so it flies off horizontally. What happened? What can you say about this?

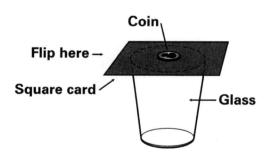

Glass with Index Card and Coin

Teacher Information

If the card is flipped horizontally with the middle finger, the coin will fall into the glass. This demonstrates the principle of inertia. The card slips from under the coin. The inertia of the coin causes it to stay in the same place, and after the card is gone the coin falls in the glass. Remember, one principle of inertia is that force is required to make a body at rest go into motion. When the card slips out, it does not apply enough force to make the coin move.

You can also pull a paper out from under a glass of water if you have the paper about half off the table and pull with a sharp downward motion. Be sure the glass is dry on the bottom.

Activity 6.11
HOW DO GRAVITY AND INERTIA AFFECT SPACE TRAVEL?

Materials Needed

- Blocks used in Activity 6.9
- Paper
- Pencil

Procedure

1. Stack one block on top of another. Pretend the bottom block is an automobile and the top block is the passenger. Touching the automobile part only, move it and the passenger across the table and make it crash head-on into another block. What happened? In most automobiles, there are devices designed to protect passengers in a situation like this. Can you name them? Draw the block and use arrows to show what happened.

2. Put the passenger block on top of the automobile block again. Without touching them, use a third block to crash into the rear of the stationary automobile block. What happened? Can you think of devices in most automobiles designed to protect passengers in this situation? Draw the blocks and use arrows to show what happened to the passenger.

3. Use your understanding of inertia to explain what would happen if these crashes occurred in space without safety devices. Since there is no gravity or friction in space, what would happen to the passenger? Draw the blocks and use arrows to show what happens to them.

For Problem Solvers: Consider what you have learned about gravity and inertia and apply that information to objects in space. Why does the moon continue in orbit around Earth? Why does Earth stay in orbit around the sun? Why can they shut off the engines of a space ship after it gets so far out in space and it continues traveling to the moon? And what effect does the moon have on the movement of the space ship as the ship comes nearer to it? Discuss your ideas together.

Teacher Information

This activity should help students relate inertia to familiar situations. Step 1 illustrates the importance of using seatbelts. The arrows in the first drawing should show the top block continuing forward (inertia) after the "head-on" crash and then falling to the ground (gravity). The arrows in the rear-end collision in step 2 should show the block continuing on with the passenger remaining stationary. Since the passengers cannot remain stationary in a real car, they are thrown back against the seat and unless their heads are protected by a headrest (safety device) they receive a painful and often serious neck injury called whiplash.

In the third step, several possibilities could occur. In a head-on crash the passenger might be thrown forward out of the automobile and, since neither gravity nor friction would stop the forward motion, continue on in a straight line forever. If a rear-end crash occurred and the passengers were not thrown out, they would be pushed against the seats with the same force as they were on earth. If the passengers were thrown out of the automobile, the car would continue on in a straight line and the passengers would be left behind.

INTEGRATING: Social studies

SKILLS: Observing, inferring, measuring, predicting, communicating, comparing and contrasting, using space-time relationships, formulating hypotheses, identifying and controlling variables

Activity 6.12
HOW CAN YOU COMPARE GRAVITY AND INERTIA?

 Take home and do with family and friends.

Materials Needed

- Two rocks of the same size
- Thin cotton thread
- Support

Procedure

1. Tie a thread around each rock and tie the thread to a support so the rocks hang freely.
2. Tie a second thread to each rock. These threads should hang freely from the rocks.
3. Grasp the bottom of one thread and pull down slowly.
4. What happened?
5. Now grasp the thread hanging from the second rock.
6. Pull down very sharply.
7. What happened?

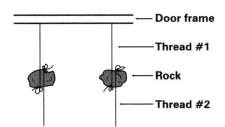

Two Rocks Hanging from Threads

Teacher Information

Note: The rock is suspended by one thread. Use a separate thread to hang down from the rock.

This activity demonstrates the principle of inertia. When the thread attached to the first rock is pulled slowly, the weight (pull of gravity) on the rock will help exert pressure on the upper thread, and the thread will break above the rock. When the thread attached to the second rock is pulled sharply, the inertia of the rock (its resistance to a change in its state of motion) will resist the sudden movement and cause the thread to break below the rock.

To control variables, the rocks and thread should be similar, or a single rock should be used for both parts of the investigation.

Activity 6.13
HOW DOES WEIGHTLESSNESS FEEL?

(Small-group activity)

Materials Needed

- Clear plastic drinking glass
- Lightweight plastic bag
- Hard-boiled egg
- Spring scale
- Salt
- Tablespoon
- String 20 cm (8 in.) long
- Warm water
- Paper
- Pencil

Procedure

1. Put the egg in the plastic bag.

2. Attach a 20-cm (8 in.) piece of string to the spring scale. Attach the other end to the plastic bag, being sure no air is trapped in the bag. Record the weight of the egg.

3. While it is still attached to the string and scale, lower the egg into a glass two thirds full of warm water.

4. While the egg is submerged in the water but not touching the bottom, record its weight again.

5. Lower the egg to the bottom of the glass while it is still attached to the string and scale, but don't support its weight.

6. Add salt, one tablespoon at a time, until the egg begins to move off the bottom of the glass.

7. Predict how much the egg will weigh now. Check and record the egg's weight.

8. Compare your first and last record of the egg's weight.

9. If you have ever gone deep in the water while swimming, you may have felt like the egg. As the density of the medium (substance) in which the egg is placed increases from air, to water, to salt water, the egg will appear to weigh less. In a swimming pool, the water pressure, as you go deeper, creates the same effect, and at a certain depth you feel weightless. You may have felt this same sensation at an amusement park if you took a ride that lifted you off the seat. Astronauts are trained to move around in a weightless

environment by spending time experiencing weightlessness in a deep pool. Discuss this with your teacher and other members of your class.

Teacher Information

Although weightlessness as a result of density and water pressure has different causes, the observed behavior is the same. The egg demonstration will show students that the weight of an object, as measured by a scale, is relative and can be changed in several ways. As you speed over the top to begin the second dip on a roller coaster, or similar ride, the tendency of your body to continue upward (inertia) creates the same weightless feeling for just a moment for a different reason. The pull of gravity decreases rapidly as an object moves away from the earth's surface. Astronauts experience the feeling of weightlessness as they orbit the earth or as they continue out into space.

NASA films of all space flights are available. Check with your local library.

INTEGRATING: Reading, language arts

SKILLS: Observing, inferring, measuring, predicting, communicating, comparing and contrasting, formulating hypotheses, identifying and controlling variables, experimenting

Topic 7:   Beyond the Earth

TO THE TEACHER

The rapid explosion of space technology has provided an overwhelming amount of new information to astronomers. As you read this page, hundreds of satellites and controlled space vehicles are beaming messages, pictures, and other information about our neighbors in space. At the same time, other satellites are studying the earth and communicating new information about the weather, topography, temperature, and other features of our home planet. Astronomy and the resultant technology are on the growing edge of scientific knowledge.

Many of the numbers, distances, temperatures, and figures that we learn today will change tomorrow. If you ask students the number of planets and they say eight or ten instead of the traditional nine, think before marking them wrong. By many criteria, Jupiter can be classified as a sun and many astronomers believe there are planets beyond Pluto in our solar system.

And what of intelligent life in the universe? Many astronomers believe it is just a matter of time until we are in contact. Time is related to speed, distance, and space in ways few of us can even comprehend.

In this rapidly changing field of knowledge, be wary of teaching facts as absolute. Much information is tentative and changing.

As they begin to sense the incredible order and grandeur of the universe, your students will stand in awe and wonder. We invite you to direct the following activities toward that goal.

National Geographic (December 1969) produced exceptionally fine coverage and photographs of the first manned moon landing and exploration. Included was a small phonograph record narrated by astronaut Frank Borman, telling of the Apollo flights that led to the magnificent achievement. Neil Armstrong's first words as he stepped on the moon are recorded. This particular issue of *National Geographic* is strongly recommended, especially for students in grades 4–8. Check with your media center or public library.

Activity 7.1
WHAT ARE PHASES OF THE MOON?

(Teacher-supervised activity)

 Take home and do with family and friends.

Materials Needed

- Lamp with exposed low-watt bulb (15–25 watts)
- Large plastic foam ball
- Meter stick or yardstick
- String 50 cm (20 in.) long
- Masking tape
- Pencil
- Paper
- Chair

Procedure

1. Tape one end of the string to the plastic foam ball and the other end to the meter stick.

2. Have your partner sit on a chair. Stand behind your partner and hold the meter stick horizontally at arm's length so the plastic foam ball is hanging in front of your partner at about his or her eye level.

3. Slowly move the meter stick in a counterclockwise direction. Have your partner turn in the chair and observe the ball (moon) while it makes a complete circle. With room lights on, this is the way the moon would appear to you on the earth if light came from all directions or if the moon produced its own light, as the sun does.

4. Place the lamp on a chair approximately 2 meters (2 yards) behind and to the right of your partner.

5. Turn the lamp on and turn the room lights off.

6. Move the ball around on the meter stick until your partner says it appears brightest. This position should be almost directly opposite the light source.

7. Slowly move the ball one fourth of a revolution, similar to the movement you made in step 3. Stop. Observe the ball carefully. How much is now brightly lighted? Which side(s)?

8. Continue to move the ball slowly in one complete revolution. Stop and carefully observe at intervals of one fourth of a revolution.

9. Trade places with your partner and perform a second revolution. Draw four circles on a sheet of paper and use your pencil to shade the circles so they resemble what you observe.

10. Try stopping between each of the original four stops and draw four additional circles, one between each of the original four. Shade them to show what you see.

11. After everyone has completed the activity, discuss it and compare your diagrams with those of the rest of your group.

Figure 7.1-1

Partners Showing the Phases of the Moon

Teacher Information

Phases of the moon are difficult to portray in a realistic manner. In most schools, it is impossible to find a completely dark room where no light is reflected. The low-watt lamp will provide a soft light with less reflected glare. However, under almost all conditions, the students will be able to see the part of the ball that is in shadow. Students should understand that only the bright part of the ball represents the light the moon reflects.

Eight named phases of the moon are shown in Figure 7.1-2.

If shadows interfere as the ball representing the moon is revolved around the student sitting on the chair, elevate the ball above the shadow.

Note: Each student can experience the phases independently by inserting a popsicle stick into a plastic foam ball and using the stick as a handle. The handle keeps the hand out of the way for viewing.

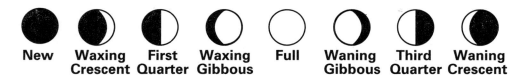

New　Waxing　First　Waxing　Full　Waning　Third　Waning
Crescent　Quarter　Gibbous　　Gibbous　Quarter　Crescent

Figure 7.1-2

Eight Phases of the Moon

SKILLS: Observing, inferring, communicating, comparing and contrasting, using space-time relationships, formulating hypotheses

Activity 7.2
HOW CAN WE MAKE A MOON MODEL WITH A MOVABLE SHADOW?

 Take home and do with family and friends.

Materials Needed

- Hollow plastic baseball
- Plastic foam ball slightly smaller than the baseball
- Hacksaw
- Black permanent marking pen with wide tip
- Lamp

Procedure

1. Using the hacksaw, cut the hollow ball in half.
2. Check the other ball for fit by placing it inside one of the halves of the hollow ball. It should just nest inside.
3. Draw a line around the circumference of the foam ball.
4. On one half of the foam ball, write the words "Seen from Earth." This will be your moon model.
5. With the black marker, color the outside of one of the halves of the hollow ball. This will be your moon's shadow.
6. Nest the moon model inside the shadow.
7. Turn on the lamp. This is your sun.
8. Letting yourself be the earth, hold the moon at arm's length. Turn the moon so that the words "Seen from Earth" face you, the earth. Place the shadow on the moon so that it is opposite the sun.
9. Move the moon around yourself very slowly, to show the moon orbiting the earth. Be sure that the side of the moon that says "Seen from Earth" faces you all the time, and that the shadow remains opposite the sun.
10. As you turn around slowly, watching the moon, say the name of the moon's phase as it appears to progress from new moon, to crescent, first quarter, gibbous, full, gibbous, third quarter, crescent, and back to new moon.
11. Use your moon-and-shadow model to teach someone else about the moon's movements and phases.

For Problem Solvers: Carry this activity farther by showing the earth's movements as the moon orbits the earth. How long does it take for the moon to travel 360 degrees around the earth? How long does it take for the moon to advance from new moon to new moon? Find the answers to these two questions and find out why the two answers are different and teach your friends and family. They will learn new information, and they will probably be excited about it.

Teacher Information

A common practice is to show the moon with one dark side. This is a deceiving and confusing model, and it develops misconceptions. If you think of the light side as the side facing the earth, and the dark side as the shadow, the shadow is shown facing the sun during each new moon. Shadows can't do that. Such a model also perpetuates the misconception that the moon has a dark side. The model used in this activity allows students to keep the correct side of the moon facing the earth *and* the moon's shadow opposite the sun.

It takes a little longer for the moon to progress from new moon to new moon than for it to revolve 360 degrees around the earth. In the four weeks required for the moon to progress 360 degrees around the earth, the earth shifts about 30 degrees in its orbit, so the moon must go a little farther to return to the same *relative* position with the earth and sun.

INTEGRATING: Math, language arts

SKILLS: Observing, inferring, measuring, communicating, comparing and contrasting, using space-time relationships, formulating hypotheses, researching

129

Activity 7.3
WHAT IS AN ECLIPSE?

(Partners in darkened room)

Materials Needed

- Small plastic foam ball
- Large plastic foam ball (about four times the diameter of the small ball)
- Coat-hanger wire 45 cm (18 in.) long
- Two pieces of coat-hanger wire 5 cm (2 in.) long
- Flashlight

Procedure

1. Use the longer wire to attach the two plastic foam balls together. The larger ball represents the earth. The smaller ball represents the moon.

2. Attach the two smaller pieces of wire to the large ball, one at the top and one at the bottom about where the North and South Poles would be located.

3. Darken the room and hold a flashlight about two meters (2 yards) from the larger ball. The light represents the sun.

4. Hold the large plastic foam ball by the wires representing the poles and slowly rotate it in a counterclockwise direction. As the moon passes between the sun and the earth, notice what happens. What can you say about this? How much of the large ball is affected?

5. Continue turning the earth until it comes between the moon and the light. How much of the smaller ball was darkened?

6. Pretend you are standing on the earth at a spot where both steps 4 and 5 happened.

   a. In step 4 you would be observing a solar eclipse. Eclipses of the sun (where the moon is in a position to block the sun's light from reaching the earth) are quite rare. A *total eclipse*, when the moon completely blocks the sun, will occur over a small path across the earth. When this happens, scientists gather from throughout the world to study the corona or bright halo around the sun. **CAUTION: It is extremely dangerous to look at the sun with the naked eye or even with very dark glasses. Eye damage or blindness may occur.**

   b. In step 5 from the earth you would be observing a *lunar eclipse* (when the earth blocks the sun's light from the moon). Since the moon is much smaller than the earth, lunar eclipses (when you see the earth's shadow covering the moon) are much more common.

Teacher Information

Solar eclipses, even partial, occur rarely on any single area of the earth. Media will inform you well in advance when a solar eclipse is to occur. *Never* look directly at the sun. Observing lunar eclipses will not harm the eyes. However, since those you can see only occur at night, they may be damaging to your sleep patterns!

Here are a few lunar and solar eclipse dates, over a ten-year period, that might interest you. All of the eclipses listed are visible from North America. All solar eclipses listed are partial eclipses. The next total solar eclipse to be experienced in North America will be on August 21, 2017. This eclipse will be total for a narrow strip of the United States extending from northwest to southeast. The rest of North America will experience a partial solar eclipse on that day.

Lunar Eclipses

April 4, 1996	Partial eclipse, as seen from North America.
September 27, 1996	Total eclipse in the eastern part of North America and partial eclipse in the west.
March 24, 1997	Near total, as seen from most of North America. Partial on the West Coast.
January 21, 2000	Total eclipse, as seen from North America.
May 16, 2003	Total eclipse, as seen from eastern North America. Partial for the rest, except not seen at all from most of Alaska.
November 9, 2003	Total eclipse, as seen from the east, and partial for the rest of North America.
October 28, 2004	Near total, as seen from most of North America. Partial on the West Coast.

Solar Eclipses

February 26, 1998	Visible from southern and eastern United States. Not visible in the rest of North America.
December 25, 2000	Visible from North America except eastern Canada and Alaska.
December 14, 2001	Visible from North America except Alaska, northern and eastern Canada, and northeastern United States.
April 8, 2005	Visible from south central and southeastern United States. Not visible from the rest of North America.

INTEGRATING: Language arts

SKILLS: Predicting, communicating, using space-time relationships

Activity 7.4
HOW CAN YOU SAFELY VIEW A SOLAR ECLIPSE?

Materials Needed

- Two cards or papers
- Straight pin

Procedure

1. **Never look directly at the sun.**
2. Make a pinhole in one card. Don't make the hole larger—just a pinhole.
3. Stand with your back to the sun.
4. Hold the card that has a pinhole in one hand and the other card in the other hand.
5. Let sunlight pass through the pinhole card and shine onto the other card (see Figure below).
6. The spot of light that you see on the lower card is more than a spot of light—it is an image of the sun. During a solar eclipse you will see part of the spot of light blocked out as the moon passes in front of the sun.
7. Use this method to watch a solar eclipse. **WARNING: Never look directly at the sun, even with dark sunglasses. Sunglasses do not protect your eyes from damage if you look at the sun.**

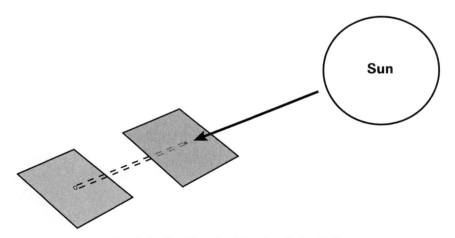

Cards in Position for Viewing Solar Eclipse

For Problem Solvers: People have not always known what causes solar eclipses and lunar eclipses, and at times throughout history these events have created a lot of fear. Do some research and find out what some of the early theories and beliefs were. Are there any superstitions about eclipses today? Share your information with others who are interested in these beliefs.

Teacher Information

Some experts claim that looking at the sun even for a moment will cause some damage to the retina, and a few seconds can cause major and permanent damage. This activity describes a way to view a solar eclipse safely. Invite students to do other things to project small spots of sunlight onto a white paper or sidewalk. If you cross the fingers of one hand with the fingers of the other hand (fingers slightly open), several eclipses can be projected onto the ground. Also, as sunlight filters through the leaves of a deciduous tree, many round spots of light are projected onto the ground. These are not just spots of light; each one is an image of the sun. Place a large sheet of white paper under the tree during a solar eclipse and you will see a mass of solar eclipses on the paper.

There are ways to safely view the solar eclipse directly; unfortunately, using sunglasses isn't one of them—not even dark sunglasses. If you have a planetarium nearby, ask them about inexpensive glasses that are designed especially for viewing solar eclipses. Also, from welding supply outlets you can buy lenses designed for arc welding helmets. **WARNING: To provide adequate protection in looking at the sun, the lens must be #14 or darker.**

INTEGRATING: Reading, language arts, social studies

SKILLS: Observing, inferring, communicating, using space-time relationships, formulating hypotheses, researching

LIFE SCIENCE ACTIVITIES

Topics

- **Plants and Seeds**
- **Animal Adaptations**
- **Body Systems**
- **The Five Senses**
- **Health and Nutrition**

Topic 8:   Plants and Seeds

TO THE TEACHER

A study of plants affords many opportunities for creative imagination. Throughout the study, appreciation of beauty and the wonder of growth should be emphasized. Language arts, music, art, and other subjects should be related as often as possible.

Teachers in urban areas may find some difficulty in conducting a few of the field trip activities; however, window boxes and artificial growing areas may be substituted.

Resource people can be valuable in this area. Most classrooms have mothers or fathers who grow plants as a hobby. Agronomists (soil specialists), horticulturists, florists, botanists, and nutritionists can also be helpful in their areas of specialization. Designing and planting a school garden could be a very worthwhile outgrowth of this study.

Throughout the study, care should be taken to emphasize the danger of eating any unknown substance. Even some parts of plants we eat can be poisonous, such as rhubarb leaves and some varieties of potato plant leaves. Warn children never to eat berries or flowers. On field trips, take into account regional variations to avoid such things as poison ivy and stinging nettle.

Most growing activities suggest the use of potting soil; however, as plants develop they will usually do better in rich, loamy soil. Specialized plants such as cactuses and pine trees will need special alkali or acid soils. Be sure to check reference sources before growing specialized plants.

Older children may be interested in solving a problem as a plant scientist might. Several plants in the same kinds of containers could be presented with the following statement and question:

These are all the same species of plant, planted on the same day from similar seeds. How can you account for the differences?

The plants used will have been grown in different media—gravel, sand, potting soil, or loam. One will have been put in a dark place, one in sunlight. One will have been overwatered, one underwatered. As children observe differences in the conditions of the plants, soil, and moisture, they will form hypotheses they can test through replication: identifying a problem (Some plants don't grow as well as others); stating a hypothesis (This plant is too dry); testing the hypothesis (If I transplant this plant to soil instead of gravel it will grow better); conclusion (What I tried worked or didn't work). This activity is similar to the work of agricultural specialists.

Activity 8.1
WHAT IS A TERRARIUM?

Materials Needed

- Potting soil
- Small plants
- Wild bird seed
- Various containers (one-gallon clear, wide-mouthed bottle; clear plastic shoe box; one-gallon plastic milk bottle cut in half; fish bowl)

Procedure

1. One kind of artificial home for plants is called a terrarium. Terrariums can be made in a variety of ways. The large ones can be covered so air cannot get in or out, and larger ones may contain both plants and animals.

2. Choose a container and make a terrarium of your own. Use the drawings in the Figure below to help you.

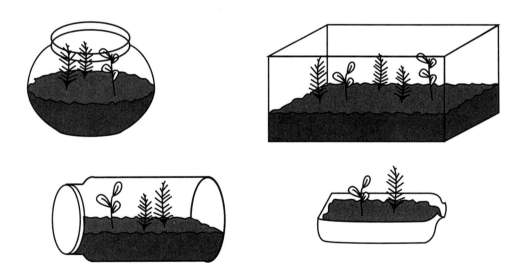

Variety of Terrariums

For Problem Solvers: Experiment with three or four terrariums, each a bit different in types of plant and animal life involved. Try to balance each terrarium with the right amount of plant and animal life so that it is self-sustaining. Observe carefully for needed adjustments, and keep a record of the things you do, including dates, to keep your terrariums thriving.

Study about the efforts people have made to maintain a large, self-contained environment.

Teacher Information

Larger terrariums may be sealed and may continue to grow and develop for many months. The plants will continue to produce oxygen and carbon dioxide, and moisture will be released into the air. Water droplets may form inside the container. The terrarium is then said to be *balanced*. As a class project, you might want to convert a 10-gallon aquarium to a terrarium and include plants and animals such as newts and salamanders. Be sure to check reference sources on terrariums before planning a classroom project.

It is important in balancing a terrarium that you choose plants that require similar amounts of moisture and sunlight. Terrariums in unique containers can make attractive gifts or centerpieces. A plastic two-liter soft-drink bottle with tiny plants and ground cover is an example.

INTEGRATING: Reading, social studies

SKILLS: Observing, inferring, predicting, communicating, using space-time relationships, formulating hypotheses, identifying and controlling variables, experimenting, researching

Activity 8.2
HOW CAN A PLANT A"MAZE" YOU?

(Teacher-supervised activity)

Materials Needed

- Utility knife
- Water
- Large shoe box
- Heavy cardboard
- Masking tape
- Small plant such as wandering Jew (genus *Zebrina*)

Procedure

1. Cut a hole in one end of the shoe box 6 cm high (2 1/2 in.) and 2 cm (3/4 in.) wide.

2. Use the end of the box as a pattern to cut four dividers (pieces of cardboard) as tall as the box but 2 cm (3/4 in. to 1 in.) shorter than its width.

3. Tape the cardboard dividers upright along the inside of the box, alternating from side to side. Be sure the first divider is attached to the same side as the slot you cut in the box.

4. Put your small plant in the end of the box opposite the slot. A box arranged this way is called a *maze*.

5. Put the lid on the box and *turn the opening toward bright sunlight*. Every three or four days, remove the lid enough to water your plant and observe its condition.

6. Observe your plant for several weeks. What is happening? Can you think of reasons why?

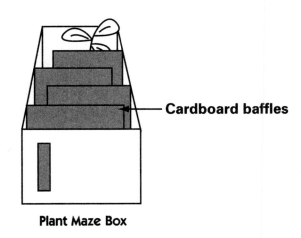

Plant Maze Box

141

For Problem Solvers: Learn as much as you can about *phototropism*. What is it? What does this activity have to do with it? How does phototropism compare with *geotropism*?

Where do you think the light-sensing mechanism on a plant is? Can you design an experiment to find out? Try it. Share your ideas with others who are interested in this experiment.

Teacher Information

This activity is designed to help children discover that green plants need sunlight, and some will travel to find it. The plant will grow around the dividers toward the light source. The attraction of plants to light is called *phototropism*. A sprouting potato may be substituted for the wandering Jew and will not need water.

If you can locate a field of sunflowers near your school, visit it several times on a sunny day. The children should discover that most sunflowers turn their flowers toward the sun and will follow it during the day. (There are usually some that hear Thoreau's "different drummer" and don't conform.)

INTEGRATING: Reading

SKILLS: Observing, inferring, predicting, communicating, using space-time relationships, formulating hypotheses, identifying and controlling variables, experimenting, researching

Activity 8.3
HOW CAN YOU COLLECT BARK WITHOUT DAMAGING THE TREE?

Materials Needed

- Plaster of Paris
- Clay
- Cardboard
- Straight pins
- Newsprint or plastic table cover
- Vaseline

Procedure

1. Form a piece of clay into a rectangular shape, at least 10 cm × 10 cm (4″ × 4″) and about 1 cm thick.
2. Cover one side of the clay with a thin film of Vaseline.
3. Press the clay onto the bark of a tree (lubricated side next to the bark), forming it to the shape of the bark.
4. Carefully remove the clay from the tree, being careful to preserve the shape of the clay the best you can.
5. Cover a table with newsprint or plastic and place the clay on the table.
6. Cut the ends of the clay off straight.
7. Fold the clay to a slight boat-shape and pin a piece of cardboard to each end by pushing straight pins through the card and into the clay (see the figure below). The cardboard pieces will serve as end supports.
8. The clay, along with its end supports, is now a mold for your plaster of Paris.

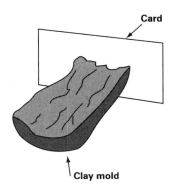

Clay Mold with One End Support in Place

9. Mix a small amount of plaster of Paris with water to the consistency of pancake batter and pour it into the mold.

10. Allow the plaster time to cure, then carefully remove the clay from the plaster.

11. Compare your tree-bark cast with those of others who are doing this activity. Discuss the likenesses and differences in their shapes.

12. Paint your bark the color of the tree.

For Problem Solvers: You might want to expand this activity and make a collection of castings of different types of bark. You should be able to use the same clay multiple times.

You can make castings of leaves by simply pouring a shallow layer of Plaster of Paris into a container, then lay a leaf on the surface. Press the leaf only slightly to smooth it out and to be sure it will leave its shape in the plaster. Avoid letting plaster get on the top of the leaf.

Make matched sets of bark and leaf.

Teacher Information

Students will enjoy making permanent casts of bark. These can be painted if desired. They make fine paperweights and shelf pieces. Those who choose to continue with the problem solvers' challenge will also enjoy collecting pairs of bark-and-leaf casts.

INTEGRATING: Art

SKILLS: Observing, communicating

Topic 9: Animal Adaptations

TO THE TEACHER

The following activities are examples of some specific ways animals adapt to their environment. Feathers and birds are used frequently in these activities because they are common even in large cities and suburban areas, and many types of adaptations are evident. Feathers collected from wild birds should be carefully examined before use. Check on laws pertaining to the possession of feathers before collecting any of them.

The importance of a picture collection is emphasized in the general introduction to this book. This section relies heavily on the use of pictures. Older students might be interested in starting picture collections of their own.

Some household tools used in some of these activities are sharp and potentially dangerous. Careful discretion and close teacher supervision is recommended.

People are the most adaptable animals on earth. Teachers have frequent need to adapt. As you read and prepare to teach this section, feel free to adapt it in any way you choose to meet the needs of your students and the conditions of the environment in which they live. Most important, adapt this study according to your needs, special skills, and knowledge.

Activity 9.1
HOW DO BIRDS ADAPT TO EATING?

(Teacher-supervised total-group activity)

Materials Needed

- Variety of pictures of birds with many kinds of beaks (names of food they eat written on back)
- Household utensils and tools including scissors, two-tined fork, linoleum cutter, sieve, knives (serrated and plain), wooden spoons, nutcracker, salad tongs (hinged at end), tweezers, scissor tongs, tea ball, eye dropper, needle-nosed and standard pliers, hammer, ice pick or punch, chopsticks, grater, ear syringe

Procedure

1. Arrange the pictures of birds on a large table. Carefully study their beaks. What type of food do you think their beaks are best designed for?

2. Look at the household tools. Do any of them remind you of birds' beaks? Be sure you know how each one works.

3. Examine each household implement and put it next to the bird whose beak it most closely resembles. Can you think of other objects around your home or school that work the same as birds' beaks?

4. Test yourself by turning the bird pictures over. On the back is a list of foods they eat.

Teacher Information

Since some implements are sharp, this activity should be carefully supervised. (To avoid the risk of having the sharp instruments, pictures of them could be used instead of the instruments themselves.) Birds do not have teeth, but some of their beaks or bills are highly specialized, depending on the food they usually eat. The terms *beak* and *bill* are generally used interchangeably. Some ornithologists reserve the term *beak* for the sharp, hooked beaks of hawks, eagles, owls, and other birds of prey.

The most common beaks among land birds are varieties of the short, strong seed eaters. If you have a canary or parakeet visiting in your classroom, notice that before it eats some types of seeds, it uses its beak to split and remove the outer covering or husk.

Ducks and many other birds with flat bills often use them in water as strainers or sieves to draw in plants, snails, and small aquatic animals. The varieties, range, and eating habits of ducks make them easily available for study throughout the moderate climates of the world.

Some birds (for example, grebes and cormorants) with long scissorlike bills catch small fish by diving and swimming under the water for short periods of time. Other fishing birds (herons and egrets) stand on long legs and fish near the shore.

147

Marsh and shore birds (for example, sandpipers) have long, often curved bills to catch shrimp and other crustaceans in marshlands and at the seashore.

Some birds (terns, pelicans, kingfishers) circle in the air above the water and dive under to catch fish with their scissorlike bills.

The bills of woodpeckers are mostly long and sharp and have built-in shock absorbers to chisel out tree bark insects and construct nest holes. Some woodpeckers also eat acorns and other nuts, often drilling holes in trees as storage bins for their food.

Some birds (pigeons, jays, gulls) eat a wide variety of foods and may become bothersome intruders at picnics and campsites.

The tiny hummingbird uses its very long bill much like an eye dropper to draw in nectar and pollen. Despite its small size, the hummingbird is an excellent flyer and can hover, dart at high speeds, and even fly backward. Hummingbirds are highly territorial, somewhat aggressive, and usually friendly and curious.

Adaptations of birds are almost unlimited. Probably the most feared and respected are the predatory birds (eagles, hawks, ospreys, falcons, owls) with sharp, hooked beaks and powerful claws. Although of different scientific classifications, these birds are often referred to as *raptors*. They have strong, sharp beaks and claws, superior flying ability, and excellent eyesight.

INTEGRATING: Language arts

SKILLS: Observing, inferring, classifying, predicting, communicating, comparing and contrasting

Activity 9.2
WHAT ARE SOME OTHER EATING ADAPTATIONS?

(Teacher-supervised total-group activity)

Materials Needed

- Household utensils from Activity 9.1, plus picture of hypodermic needle

- Pictures of animals with mouths open showing mouth parts. Write the name of the principal food they eat on the back. Try to include animals that live almost entirely in the water, such as: shark and whale, squid, octopus; other types of animals such as reptiles (crocodile, alligator, rattlesnake, constrictor, lizard with long tongue); common mammals (rodents, dogs, wolves, bears, sheep, cows, horses, cats, bats, shrews, beaver, and deer); and representative dinosaur pictures. Try also to include enlarged insect mouth parts (mosquito, flea, ant, bee, grasshopper, praying mantis) and enlarged spider mouths.

Procedure

1. In Activity 9.1 we found that birds' beaks are often adapted to eating certain kinds of foods. Study the pictures on the table and try to arrange or classify them into different groups whose open mouths look similar.

2. Look at the household utensils. Try to find some that resemble the mouth parts in the animal pictures. Put the utensils near the pictures. You may find some animal mouth parts that have several utensils in them.

3. Look at the pictures of the dinosaurs. The *Brontosaurus* had a long neck and small mouth. Compare it with the picture of *Tyrannosaurus Rex*. Compare the mouths of these giants from the past with the mouth parts of a spider or praying mantis. Can you tell how large the animals are by looking at their mouth parts?

4. One way of classifying animals is by the kind of food they eat. Some animals eat plants, some prefer meat, and some eat both. Arrange your animal pictures into these three groups according to the food they eat. Turn the pictures over and see if you were right. What were the clues that helped you decide?

Teacher Information

As with birds, mouth parts of different species of animals vary greatly. Sharp, curved, tearing teeth (similar to eagles' beaks) usually indicate meat eaters. Cutting and grinding teeth (or the absence of teeth) usually suggest plant eaters. Animals that eat both usually have some combination of tearing, grinding, and cutting teeth.

There appears to be no simple relationship between the size of animals and the food they eat. Quantity and availability of food seems more significant. The largest of the dinosaurs were plant eaters, and so are elephants today.

When the giant lizards ruled the earth, mammals were very small and not plentiful. Today, some mammals are very large. Some species of whales are much larger than any other animal that has ever lived.

The traditional terms *herbivore* (plant eaters), *carnivore* (meat eaters), and *omnivore* (both plants and meat) have not been used in this section. Bears, pigs, people, birds, bats, and many other animals feed in such a variety of ways that the terms may become quite confusing. Your students may also have house pets (cats and dogs) that are basically meat eaters but have become so domesticated that they will eat anything people do, even French fries!

INTEGRATING: Language arts

SKILLS: Observing, inferring, classifying, predicting, communicating, comparing and contrasting

Activity 9.3
WHAT ARE HUMAN TEETH LIKE?

Materials Needed

- Dentures
- Tooth model
- Ear syringe
- Picture of mother dog or pig nursing her young
- Picture of typical six- or seven-year-old child with front teeth missing
- Picture of horse or mule showing its teeth

Procedure

1. What does the saying "Don't look a gift horse in the mouth" mean? Look at the picture of the smiling horse. How does it make you feel? If you were a horse dealer you might react in a different way. Horses eat hay, grass, and some other plants. Over the years their teeth gradually wear down. Looking in a horse's mouth is one way to tell its age. Until recently, looking in a human's mouth might tell the same story. Why is this no longer true?

2. In Activities 9.1 and 9.2 you learned some ways mouth parts are important to animals in getting and eating food. Many of the mouth parts were developed for one kind of food. A few had parts for eating a variety of foods. Examine the dentures (false teeth). They are very similar to the ones you have in your mouth. Find teeth that look like the beaks, bills, and specialized mouth parts of other animals. From looking at their teeth can you tell what humans eat?

3. Baby mammals, including humans, usually don't have teeth when they are born. They get their food in the form of milk by sucking on the soft nipples of their mother. Examine the ear syringe. Put some water in your hand and draw it up. You can draw milk or water into it without damaging the surface it touches. Mammal babies seem to be born with an instinct for sucking.

4. Sometimes at birth but usually after a few months, human babies begin to develop teeth. The first ones are small but allow babies to begin eating soft food other than liquids. These first teeth are temporary and usually fall out. Do you have temporary teeth in your mouth? Find a picture of young children who are losing their temporary teeth.

5. Look at the set of false teeth. By the time you are a young adult (16 to 20 years old) you will have a permanent set of teeth, usually 28 to 32 in number. With care, they will serve you well for the rest of your life.

6. If you haven't figured out what "Don't look a gift horse in the mouth" means, discuss it with your teacher.

Teacher Information

Dentures, real teeth, charts, and models may be obtained from a local dentist. The American Dental Association also provides pamphlets and information about teeth and their care.

"Don't look a gift horse in the mouth" may have originated at the time when horses were as common in everyday life as cars are today. An experienced person can tell a lot about the age and condition of a horse by examining the teeth and mouth. If someone gave you a horse as a gift and you looked in its mouth to see how old it was, it would be as rude as to look for a price tag or brand name on an item received as a gift. Today we often use the expression to describe someone who has had good (unexpected) fortune or received a gift and looks for an underlying or selfish motive behind the gift.

Humans are very adaptable, and their teeth and mouth reflect this pattern. We have fairly good cutting teeth (not as good as those of a beaver) and grinding teeth (but not nearly as good as those of a cow). Our mouths can be shaped for sucking but not nearly as efficiently as that of a hummingbird, mosquito, spider, leech, or lamprey.

Where food is concerned, the size of our mouths and the limited operations of our jaws keep us from being the best at anything, but because they are so generalized we do pretty well at most things, and we are able to handle a wide variety of food.

Human age can sometimes be determined by counting permanent teeth (6- and 12-year molars). For many years the presence of dentures was associated with old age.

INTEGRATING: Language arts, social studies

SKILLS: Observing, inferring, classifying, communicating, comparing and contrasting

Topic 10:   Body Systems

TO THE TEACHER

This section provides opportunities for students to learn about themselves. Activities involve both the muscular and skeletal systems of the body. Students can discover and learn a great deal about their own body structure by studying the bones and muscles of animals. These parts are usually available from the local meat market. Hair, nails, skin, and lung capacity are also dealt with in the activities of this section.

The teacher should invite resource people into the classroom at appropriate times to enrich the experience. Along with the sections "Health and Nutrition" and "The Five Senses," the study of this section provides many excellent opportunities to explore the world of work with respect to the health services occupations and professions.

In a study of the body, the handicapped should be recognized as normal people for whom certain abilities are limited. There is such a broad range of ability among the non-handicapped, and such a broad range among the handicapped, that it is sometimes difficult to distinguish between the two. It is hoped that in the study of this section physical differences will be recognized and treated as normal. We are all different. Being different is normal. It should be noted and stressed, however, that we are more alike than different.

We suggest that the teacher scan all activities in the section before beginning its use in the classroom, taking note of materials required. This will aid in making necessary advance preparations.

Activity 10.1
HOW DO FINGERPRINTS COMPARE?

 Take home and do with family and friends.

Materials Needed

- Ink stamp pad
- Paper

Procedure

1. Have each participant place the tip of the right forefinger on the ink pad with a slight right-to-left rolling motion.
2. Immediately after applying ink to the finger, place it on the paper, using the same rolling motion.
3. Examine the fingerprints.
4. How are they alike?
5. How are they different?
6. Do you notice any patterns that are similar in some of the fingerprints?
7. Do you see any two fingerprints that are exactly alike?

For Problem Solvers: Here's another way of making fingerprints. Rub a pencil on a piece of paper, making a heavy smudge of graphite on the paper. Rub the tip of your finger on the graphite. Next, put a piece of clear plastic tape on the graphite-covered finger, then remove the tape and put it on a piece of white paper. The tape will preserve the fingerprint.

Using this method of fingerprinting, study patterns of fingerprints from one person to another and from finger to finger of the same person. Find patterns and draw them. Are they similar from finger to finger for the same person? How many patterns can you find?

Discuss your findings with your group. Why are fingerprints so valuable in police and detective work?

Teacher Information

Your problem solvers will want to take the prints of all their fingers and study the similarities and differences. They will find that no two fingerprints are exactly alike, not even from two fingers of the same person.

Discuss with the group why fingerprints or footprints are used for identification in some important documents, such as birth records and police records.

INTEGRATING: Math, social studies, art

SKILLS: Observing, inferring, classifying, measuring, predicting, communicating, comparing and contrasting, researching

Activity 10.2
ARE HUMAN BONES LARGE OR SMALL?

Materials Needed

- Encyclopedia or other appropriate reference books
- Ruler
- Pencil and paper

Procedure

1. Make a scale drawing of your femur (upper leg bone). Use a scale of 1 to 4 and check the encyclopedia for help with the shape of the bone.

2. Find the size of the same bone of various animals, such as dog, cat, rabbit, mouse, horse, and maybe one of the large dinosaurs. Use the encyclopedia as a source of information. Perhaps you can actually measure this bone of some animals if you have pets or farm animals.

3. Make a chart showing the comparative sizes of the femur—yours and those of the animals you used.

4. Is your bone large or small?

For Problem Solvers: Compare the length of your femur with your height. If others are doing this activity, make a line graph with length of femur along the bottom and height of the person up the left side of the graph. Plot the height and femur length of several and see if height seems to be related to femur length. Discuss your results.

Do some research on dinosaurs and see if scientists seem to think they can estimate the size of dinosaurs by femur length.

Teacher Information

The student will find that size is relative and that human bones could be considered either large or small, depending on the size of the animals with which they are being compared. Students might prefer to make scale drawings of the bodies of various animals, instead of a single bone, and chart these in a way similar to that suggested above.

The lower grades could do this activity by substituting a general comparison of sizes for scale drawings. When students find information in a book about the size of a bone, have them locate something in the classroom or outside that is about the same size, to help them visualize it.

INTEGRATING: Reading, math, language arts, art

SKILLS: Observing, inferring, classifying, measuring, predicting, communicating, comparing and contrasting, researching

Activity 10.3
HOW MANY BONES CAN YOU COUNT?

Materials Needed

- Paper and pencil
- Encyclopedia or other appropriate reference books

Procedure

1. Feel the bones in the fingers of one hand with the other hand. Count them.

2. How many bones did you count in your hand? Write that number on your paper.

3. See how many bones you can count from your wrist to your shoulder. Write that number.

4. Now begin with your toes and work up as you count all the bones you can find. As you count the bones in your foot, leg, back, and so on, write down the numbers.

5. Using this procedure, count the bones in your entire body. As you write the numbers, remember to include the number of bones in both hands, both feet, and so forth.

6. Draw a picture of the human skeleton, showing the bones you found.

7. If others in your group do this activity, compare your notes and drawing with theirs. If your numbers are different for some part of the body, each of you count again and try to determine where the differences occurred.

8. When you have counted and drawn all the bones in your body that you can find, go to the encyclopedia and see if you can find out how many bones there really are in the human skeleton.

9. How close was your count?

10. Which ones did you miss?

For Problem Solvers: Which of your bones are similar to those of a cat or dog? Bird? Other animals? Decide how you can find out, and study the answer to the question for the animals of your choice. Share your information with your group.

Teacher Information

The human body has at least 206 bones. A textbook that has this information could be substituted for the encyclopedia suggested in the materials list. The process of counting and searching the text or encyclopedia will provide a worthwhile and interesting research experience for students.

Lower grades can count, talk about, compare, and draw the bones they think they feel. The use of reference books can be eliminated for students who are not able to use them.

INTEGRATING: Reading, math, art

SKILLS: Observing, inferring, classifying, measuring, predicting, communicating, researching

Activity 10.4
HOW ARE BONES CONNECTED AT A JOINT?

Materials Needed

- Knee joint of an animal
- Encyclopedia
- Pencils

Procedure

1. Examine the joint.
2. Can you see what holds the two bones together?
3. Use your pencil to probe around on the bone near the joint, in the joint, and away from the joint.
4. Is there any difference in the way the material feels with your probe as you move from one part to another? Where is it harder? Where is it softer?
5. Look up "bone" in the encyclopedia and find names for the parts you see, including what holds the two bones together at the joint.
6. Where do you think you have bones similar to those you are looking at?

For Problem Solvers: Your bones might do things for you that you don't even know about. Do some research about bone marrow. Get a piece of a leg bone of a beef cattle or sheep from a butcher. Examine the marrow. Study about bone marrow in the encyclopedia. What does the marrow do that is very important to the body?

Teacher Information

Bones for this activity are usually available at meat markets. A front knee joint of a calf or sheep would work well, but most any joint will do. In checking the encyclopedia, students should be able to identify the bone, cartilage, and ligaments. Connecting points of tendons might also be visible.

As they probe with their pencils, students should be able to feel the softer cartilage material that cushions the bones at the joint.

Consider asking the butcher for a second joint, sawed lengthwise through the bone and joint, with which students can see where the cartilage is fused to the bone. Marrow will be in the center of the long part of the bones, providing an excellent research topic with the encyclopedia and other available sources.

INTEGRATING: Reading

SKILLS: Observing, communicating, researching

Activity 10.5
WHAT ARE TENDONS AND HOW DO THEY WORK?

Materials Needed

- Chicken leg, complete with foot

Procedure

1. Pick up the chicken leg and locate the tendons. The tendons are like cords and should be visible at the top of the leg.

2. Pull on the tendons one at a time and observe the foot.

3. What happened?

4. Try it again. What do you think the chicken does to curl its toes? What does it do to straighten them out?

5. How does this compare with the way your own fingers and toes work?

6. Locate some of the tendons that operate your fingers. See if you can tell where they connect and what makes them work. Wiggle your fingers quickly and watch the action of the tendons.

7. Grasp the large tendon at the back of one ankle with your fingers. Feel it as you move your foot up and down. This is called the Achilles tendon. Which muscles pull on the Achilles tendon?

For Problem Solvers: Do some research on the mythology of the Achilles tendon and report to the class.

Teacher Information

Chicken legs and turkey legs work equally well for this activity. Be sure the tendons have not been removed. If the tendons are not visible at the top of the leg, cut the skin back to expose enough of the tendon for students to grasp. If some students are squeamish about operating the chicken foot, have others demonstrate for them.

Students should be able to easily identify similar structures on their own hands and feet and observe the tendons that attach muscles to bones. With careful observation they can tell which tendons open each finger and toe and about where they attach to the muscle. Point out that most muscles are attached to bones by tendons.

INTEGRATING: Reading, social studies

SKILLS: Observing, communicating, researching

Activity 10.6
WHAT IS BONE LIKE WITHOUT THE MINERAL MATERIAL?

(Teacher-supervised activity)

Materials Needed

- Chicken leg bones
- Vinegar
- Metal pan
- Gram balance (or other sensitive scales)

Procedure

1. Soak one of the chicken bones in vinegar for four or five days.
2. Remove the bone from the liquid and dry it off.
3. Feel the bone. Bend it. What happened? What does it feel like?
4. What do you think is now missing from the bone?
5. How do you think the materials these bones are made of compare with your own?

For Problem Solvers: Do some research and find out what was removed from the bone by the vinegar. Discuss what problems might occur if our bodies don't get enough of these materials.

Teacher Information

With the minerals removed, this bone will be soft and flexible enough to tie in a knot.

INTEGRATING: Reading

SKILLS: Observing, inferring, communicating, comparing and contrasting, researching

Activity 10.7
HOW MANY MUSCLES CAN YOU IDENTIFY?

Materials Needed

- Paper
- Pencils

Procedure

1. Raise your arm slowly. As it moves, try to identify the muscles that make it move.

2. Write down the movement and describe where you think the muscles causing the movement are located. For instance:

Movement	Muscle Location
Raise the arm	From shoulder to top of upper arm

3. Lower the arm onto a table. Then push against the table top in an effort to lower the arm further. Find the muscles that seem to pull the arm down.

4. Write down the movement and describe where you think the muscles causing the movement are located.

5. Continue this for all the different arm movements you can think of. Do the same with the hand, then the legs and feet, then other body parts.

6. Compare your list of body movements and muscle locations with others. See how many more you can identify together.

For Problem Solvers: Using the references you have available, find a chart that shows the human muscular system. Find out how many muscles there are in the human body. Does the chart show all of the muscles that you found in the above activity? What other muscles can you find on your body with the help of the chart that you didn't find earlier? Add these muscles to your list.

Teacher Information

Essentially every movement of the body is produced by muscular action. Since muscles pull (contract) but do not push, a different set of muscles is used for opening the fingers than for closing them. The same can be said for many other body movements, such as moving the leg forward and backward, raising and lowering the arm, and so on. (Gravity should be taken into account.) Where ball joints are involved, muscular arrangements also allow a twisting motion.

The human body has over 650 different muscles. Students will be able to locate many of these as they examine their own body movements. There is some advantage in putting students in groups of two or three for this activity so they can analyze their movements together, discuss their observations, and learn from one another.

INTEGRATING: Physical education

SKILLS: Observing, inferring, classifying, communicating, researching

Activity 10.8
HOW FAST ARE YOUR REACTIONS?

 Take home and do with family and friends.

Materials Needed

- Meter stick

Procedure

1. In this activity, you will test your reaction time. Reaction time is one indicator of health condition.

2. Have your partner hold the meter stick vertically. Your partner should hold it at the top, and the lower end should be between your thumb and index finger.

3. Ask your partner to drop the meter stick without warning. When the stick drops, grasp it as quickly as you can with your thumb and index finger. Note how far it fell by reading the centimeter scale where you grasped the meter stick.

4. Try it three or four times and see if you can improve your reaction time.

5. Trade places with your partner. This time you drop the meter stick.

6. Practice and see if you can both improve your reaction time.

7. Have you ever had a physical examination by a doctor? If so, did the doctor check the reflexes of your knees?

For Problem Solvers: Place a dime on the back of your hand, then tip it off and try to catch it before it hits the floor. Try left hand, right hand, and both at the same time. Share this activity with others and each of you try to improve your skill.

Find other reaction-challenging activities to try together. Check your resource books. Ask others if they know of one or more of these.

Teacher Information

Students will enjoy comparing reaction times and trying to improve their own with this and other reaction-testing activities you might care to use. A competitive reaction-time activity is the hand slapper. The first person holds a hand palm up and the second places his or her hand on that of the first, palm down. Person 1 tries to slap the back of the hand of person 2 before person 2 can move out of the way. Again, try each hand separately and both together. Caution students not to slap hard enough to hurt the other person.

INTEGRATING: Physical education, math

SKILLS: Measuring, communicating, comparing and contrasting

Topic 11:   The Five Senses

TO THE TEACHER

The human body is a topic of interest, curiosity, and importance to all ages. Formal study of it should begin in the elementary grades. Many things can be done at this early age to increase awareness of the capacities and needs of this marvelous system. As awareness increases, so do appreciation and the ability to care for our bodies properly.

Everything we do involves one or more of the five senses. All that we learn is learned through the senses. Getting acquainted with their bodies is a logical topic for young learners. Scores of activities can be undertaken that involve concrete, firsthand experiences. Many concepts have been encountered before, but new insights and awarenesses should be acquired as those concepts are spotlighted and discussed.

A study of the five senses should include recognition of the handicapped. Those who have lost part, or all, of one or more senses deserve to be recognized and respected as normal human beings. Children should develop an attitude of appreciation for their capabilities without perceiving the handicapped as something less. Indeed, people with full capability of the senses can learn a great deal from those with some degree of loss of hearing, sight, or other capabilities. Frequently, other senses have compensated by becoming sharper and stronger through use, resulting in enhanced awareness.

Activity 11.1
WHICH IS YOUR DOMINANT EYE?

 Take home and do with family and friends.

Materials Needed

- None

Procedure

1. Look at an object that is at least 3 meters (10 ft.) away from you.

2. With both eyes open, point at the object.

3. Without moving your pointing finger, close your left eye. Does your finger still appear to be pointing at the object?

4. Now open your left eye and close your right eye. Does your finger appear to be pointing at the object?

5. Select another object and repeat steps 2 through 4.

6. What happened? Try to explain why.

Teacher Information

The two eyes, being a short distance apart, see objects from a slightly different angle. This has certain advantages, including helping us to perceive depth and distance with much greater accuracy than would otherwise be possible. When we point at an object, the finger is in the line of vision of only one eye. This is called the dominant eye, as it is nearly always the same eye. People with two good eyes usually have one that is dominant.

SKILLS: Observing, inferring

Activity 11.2
HOW WELL DO YOU REMEMBER WHAT YOU SEE?

 Take home and do with family and friends.

Materials Needed

- Tray
- Variety of small objects

Procedure

1. Put a variety of small objects on the tray, such as a pencil, eraser, marble, paper clip, toy car, bracelet, or wad of paper.

2. Ask one or more participants to examine the items on the tray for 30 seconds.

3. Remove the tray from sight. Remove one of the items.

4. Return the tray and ask participant(s) to look over the contents and try to determine which item was removed. Ask them not to say it aloud until all participants have decided what they think it was.

5. Did everyone get it right? Did no one get it right?

6. If time allows, do the same activity again with the same group. See if they can, with practice, improve their visual memory skills.

For Problem Solvers: Repeat this activity many times with different people, changing the number of items. Find out how many items most people can remember well. How many would you predict?

When you know how many items most people can remember with a 30-second examination of the tray, reduce the viewing time to 20 seconds and find out if the number of items most people can remember is the same. What difference do you predict it will make, if any?

Teacher Information

This activity is effective in evaluating visual memory skills. With repeated use, it also provides *practice in developing* visual memory skills. As skills improve, try increasing the number of objects or rearranging them.

SKILLS: Observing, predicting, communicating, comparing and contrasting, using space-time relationships, formulating hypotheses, identifying and controlling variables, experimenting

Activity 11.3
WHAT HAPPENS TO THE IRIS AS LIGHT CHANGES?

Materials Needed

- Mirror

Procedure

1. Hold the mirror close enough to your face so that you can easily see the iris (colored part) of your eyes.

2. Look at the iris of one eye carefully and see if you can detect any movement.

3. Hold one hand up to the side of your eye to shade the light. As you do, watch the iris carefully.

4. Move your hand, allowing more light to reach the eye again, still watching the iris.

5. Close one eye or put your hand over it to shut out the light. When you open it, observe the iris immediately.

6. What happens to the iris as you change the amount of light around it? Why do you think this happens?

Teacher Information

The iris opens and closes to adjust the amount of light entering the eye through the pupil. The diaphragm of a camera operates much the same way (see Activity 11.4).

You might pair students up and have them observe the iris in each other's eyes as light conditions change. Caution them not to shine bright light in their eyes or look directly at bright lights. The movement of the iris is easily observed in room light by closing the eyes or by temporarily shading with the hand.

SKILLS: Observing, communicating, identifying and controlling variables

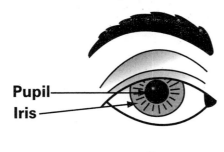

Eye

167

Activity 11.4
HOW IS A CAMERA DIAPHRAGM LIKE THE EYE?

(Teacher-supervised activity)

Materials Needed

- Camera

Procedure

1. The camera must not have film in it and must have an adjustable diaphragm (f-stop).

2. Ask your teacher to be close by for this activity, to assure that no damage will be done to the camera and to help you locate the parts you need to work with.

3. Open the back of the camera.

4. Set the shutter speed on "time" (B) so it will remain open while the shutter release button is depressed.

5. Look through the lens from the back of the camera. Press the shutter release button and hold it down. You should be able to see a dot of light.

6. Move the f-stop setting as you look through the lens.

7. What happened? How does it compare with the movement of the iris of your eye from your observations in Activity 11.3?

For Problem Solvers: The amount of light that reaches the film in a camera is adjusted in two ways; one of these is the f-stop that you experienced in this activity. Find out what the other one is and how it works, and share your information with the class.

Another adjustable setting on the camera is the *focus*. This also must be set correctly to get a good picture. Your eye focuses automatically when you look at things that are different distances away from you. Do some research (read about it and/or ask someone) and find out how the focus is adjusted on the camera and what your eye does to focus on things you look at. Share your information with your group.

Why do some people wear glasses, and what do they do for the wearer? Write your hypothesis, then find the answer to this question while you are researching the focus of the eye and the camera.

Teacher Information

This activity should be carefully supervised. If you have to borrow a camera and are not acquainted with the operation of it, it will take only a few minutes for someone to brief you on it for this activity. This is also an excellent time for inviting a resource person into your classroom if you have a camera buff available. They could talk about the light and focusing adjustments of the camera and compare these to the adjustments made by the eye. Many cameras use light-sensitive cells to adjust the diaphragm automatically.

INTEGRATING: Reading, math

SKILLS: Observing, inferring, communicating, comparing and contrasting, using space-time relationships, formulating hypotheses, identifying and controlling variables, experimenting, researching

Activity 11.5
WHAT IS A BLIND SPOT?

Materials Needed

- Prepared 5″ × 7″ index card (see Figure below)

Procedure

1. Close and cover your left eye.
2. Hold the index card at arm's length.
3. Stare at the X.
4. Slowly bring the card closer to your right eye.
5. What happened to the dot? Repeat this activity several times.
6. Discuss this with your teacher and the class.

For Problem Solvers: Find a diagram of the eye. Locate the lens and the optic nerve. Study about how the lens focuses an image on the back of the eye and what happens at the spot where the optic nerve is attached. What does this have to do with the disappearing dot on the card?

Experiment, varying the size of the X and the dot and varying the distance between them.

Teacher Information

As the student slowly brings the card near while staring at the X, at some point the dot will momentarily disappear. This is because each eye has a blind spot where the optic nerve exits the eye. At this point there are no rods or cones to detect an image. The blind spot occurs only at a specific distance. We usually see beyond or within this distance, and we use two eyes, so we usually don't notice the blind spot.

INTEGRATING: Reading

SKILLS: Observing, inferring, communicating, researching

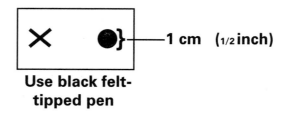

Use black felt-tipped pen

Index Card with X and Dot

Activity 11.6
HOW EFFECTIVE IS YOUR SIDE VISION?

 Take home and do with family and friends.

Materials Needed

- Pencil or ruler

Procedure

1. Do this activity with a partner.
2. Have your partner sit down and look straight ahead.
3. Hold the pencil vertically about one meter (or one yard) away from your partner's ear.
4. Move the pencil forward slowly and ask your partner to tell you when he or she can see it (eyes still straight ahead).
5. Move the pencil slowly forward and back as necessary to find the point at which your partner can first see it.
6. Test your partner's side vision of the other eye in the same way.
7. Trade places and have your partner help you test your side vision.
8. Compare results. Are they the same? Discuss situations where good side vision might be important.
9. Have you ever had an eye specialist perform this examination?

For Problem Solvers: Side vision is called *peripheral* vision. Test the peripheral vision of many people and see how they compare. Is it the same for everyone? Does it become stronger or weaker with age? Is it about the same for people who wear glasses as for people who do not? What about for people who wear contact lenses? Before you begin testing the peripheral vision of these people, write your prediction of how the different groups will compare.

Interview a professional driver (truck driver, taxi driver, etc.) or a pilot and find out how important side vision is for them.

Teacher Information

Peripheral vision (side vision) is the ability to see at the side while focusing straight ahead. It is used frequently by everyone, but for some it is narrower than for others. In some situations, good peripheral vision is critical, such as when driving an automobile or walking across a busy street. Students should easily recognize the importance of side vision to a football player or basketball player. Many other examples can be discussed.

INTEGRATING: Language arts, social studies

SKILLS: Observing, classifying, measuring, predicting, communicating, comparing and contrasting, formulating hypotheses, identifying and controlling variables

Activity 11.7
HOW CAN OUR EYES MAKE COLORS SEEM TO CHANGE?

 Take home and do with family and friends.

Materials Needed

- Prepared 5″ × 7″ index card

Procedure

1. Stare at the blue and red squares for 30 seconds.
2. Now stare at the flat white surface.
3. What happened? What can you say about this?

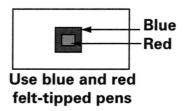

Blue
Red

**Use blue and red
felt-tipped pens**

Index Card with Red and Blue Squares

For Problem Solvers: Make another card, using the same pattern but with different colors, and try the activity again. Make different patterns and use different colors. Each time you use a new color or a new pattern, predict what colors will show up on the blank wall.

Can you make a picture of the U.S. flag that shows up in its true colors when you look at the blank wall?

Learn about complementary colors and find out how they relate to this activity.

Teacher Information

A simple explanation for elementary children might be: When we stare at bright colors for a length of time, the cones in our eyes that see the bright colors get tired. When we look at a white surface, the tired cones rest and the other cones near the same place in the eye take over. We will still see the image we have been staring at but it will be in different colors. (This may be a place to explore the idea of complementary colors in art.)

172

A related idea is the after-image effect. Darken the room and stare at a vivid object for several seconds (try a large black X on a white sheet of paper). After the object is removed you will still be able to see it faintly; however, the colors will be reversed (white X on a black square) just as in a negative of a black-and-white photograph.

INTEGRATING: Art

SKILLS: Observing, measuring, predicting, communicating, comparing and contrasting, using space-time relationships, formulating hypotheses, identifying and controlling variables, experimenting

Activity 11.8
HOW IS TASTE AFFECTED BY SMELL?

Materials Needed

- Variety of food samples
- Paper cups (one for each type of food)
- Box of toothpicks
- Blindfold
- Markers

Procedure

1. Find a partner to do this activity with you.
2. Blindfold your partner.
3. Have your partner hold his or her nose so the foods being tasted cannot be smelled.
4. Using a toothpick, place a small amount of one type of food in the center of your partner's tongue.
5. Have your partner close his or her mouth and move the tongue around for a thorough taste of the sample. Then describe the food as sweet, sour, salty, or bitter. Record the results on a chart something like this:

Name of taster: _____

FOOD   TASTE

_____   Sweet   Sour   Salty   Bitter

6. Follow the same procedure for each of the food samples, using a new toothpick for each food. The person tasting should rinse his or her mouth with water between food samples. Place the food in the center of the tongue each time.
7. After your partner has tasted all the food samples, trade places and have your partner put the food samples on your tongue. Put the food in the center of the tongue each time and use a new toothpick for each type of food. Your partner should record your judgment of each food type as sweet, sour, salty, or bitter.

Teacher Information

People are sometimes heard to say that food just doesn't taste the same when they have a cold. Taste is affected by smell, sometimes enough to alter the judgment of the type of taste if the salty, sweet, sour, or bitter tastes are not very strong. Have students share their findings and discuss them.

INTEGRATING: Language arts

SKILLS: Observing, inferring, classifying, communicating, comparing and contrasting, identifying and controlling variables

Activity 11.9
HOW CAN YOU TELL IF TASTE IS AFFECTED BY SMELL?

Materials Needed

- Small slices of potato, apple, and onion
- Three blindfolds
- Chart paper
- Markers

Procedure

1. Find three volunteers to help you do this activity.

2. Blindfold all three volunteers. Seat them about two meters (six feet) apart.

3. Hold a slice of one of the three foods under the nose of one volunteer as you put another of the foods in the same person's mouth. Ask him or her to identify the food in the mouth.

4. Use various combinations of the food slices with the same volunteer, placing a slice of apple in the mouth as you hold a slice of onion under the nose. Place a slice of potato in the mouth as you hold a slice of apple under the nose, and so forth.

5. Record the foods used and what the volunteer identifies them to be.

6. Follow steps 3 to 5 with the other two volunteers.

7. Analyze and discuss the results. Did the volunteers identify the foods accurately in all cases? Were the results consistent from one volunteer to the next? If identifications were inaccurate in some cases, which smells seem to fool the tongue?

For Problem Solvers: Do this activity with several more people. Keep accurate records and compare their ability to identify food types when distracting smells are introduced. Discuss the results with your group.

Teacher Information

The senses of taste and smell work together in helping us to identify what we are eating and to enjoy it. Either of these senses can be affected by strong signals from the other. Students might enjoy trying this same activity with other combinations of foods.

INTEGRATING: Language arts, math

SKILLS: Observing, inferring, classifying, communicating, comparing and contrasting, identifying and controlling variables, experimenting

Topic 12:   Health and Nutrition

TO THE TEACHER

Every person needs to develop wise eating habits and understand some basic concepts and principles for proper care of the body. Some children have access to little food and need to be especially careful that what they eat is nutritious. Many have excessive amounts of junk food available to them and considerable social pressure or desire to consume unhealthful amounts of it. The activities of this section will help to increase awareness of good eating habits, proper hygiene, and care of the teeth.

Someone said commitment comes partly through ownership of an idea. This is a good time to get students involved in researching, writing, and sharing reports on topics related to the activities herein, and in teaching one another. The process of teaching someone else good health habits will increase the level of commitment, on the part of the presenters, to develop those habits themselves.

Activity 12.1
HOW CAN WE TEST FOODS FOR PROTEIN?

(Teacher-supervised activity)

Materials Needed

- Lime powder
- Copper sulfate
- Water
- Two stirring sticks
- Two eyedroppers
- Small measuring cup
- Small amounts of common foods, such as meat, flour, butter, eggs, cheese, bread, salt, and sugar
- Paper towels
- Two cup-size containers

Procedure

1. Measure about two tablespoons of water into each of two containers.
2. Mix lime powder in one of the containers and copper sulfate in the other. Put in as much as you can get to dissolve.
3. Keep the two solutions separate. Put a clean dropper in each.
4. Put a small piece of meat on a paper towel.
5. Put two or three drops of lime water on one spot on the meat. Then put an equal amount of the copper sulfate solution on the same spot.
6. What happened?
7. Try putting equal amounts of the two solutions on some sugar.
8. Do the same with a piece of bread.
9. The different reactions you see are an indication of the amount of protein. Which of these substances has the most protein? Which does not have any?
10. Test the other foods you have and make a list, beginning with the foods having highest protein content and ending with those that have none.

Teacher Information

Proteins help to make up the protoplast, or living portion, of body cells. Our bodies cannot manufacture their own protein, so we depend on the plants and animals we eat for our protein supply. Proteins are a vital food element, so it is important that we know which foods are the best sources of protein.

If a food containing protein is mixed with lime and copper sulfate, the mixture will turn to a violet color. The higher the protein content of the food, the darker the violet color will be.

Your high school or junior high school chemistry teacher can help you obtain lime powder and copper sulfate.

SKILLS: Observing, inferring, classifying, comparing and contrasting, formulating hypotheses, identifying and controlling variables, experimenting

Activity 12.2
WHICH FOODS CONTAIN SUGAR?

Materials Needed

- Empty food containers with labels intact
- Pencils
- Paper
- Chart paper
- Markers

Procedure

1. Write a list of the foods your food containers represent. Put a check mark beside each food in your list that you think contains sugar.

2. Select one of the food containers. Write the name of the food on a chart.

3. Look at the list of contents on the container. Does the list include sugar? If so, write the type(s) of sugar used. Here are some types of sugar that might be included:

Sugar	Syrup
Corn syrup	Dextrose
Maltose	Glucose
Sucrose	Lactose
Fructose	Molasses
Corn sweetener	

4. The food contents are listed in order of quantity used. If one or more types of sugar are in the list, indicate on the chart whether they are listed first, second, third, and so forth.

5. Continue steps 2 to 4 for the food containers you have.

6. Now go back to the list you made in step 1 and put an X beside those foods you found that do contain sugar. Compare these with your predictions (check marks from step 1).

7. Are you surprised?

Teacher Information

The object of this activity is to make students aware that most foods we eat contain sugar and that sugar comes in many different forms. It is important that students complete step 1, including their predictions. Their findings will be more meaningful as they compare them with their own predictions if they complete step 1.

INTEGRATING: Reading

SKILLS: Predicting, communicating, formulating hypotheses, researching

Activity 12.3
WHICH FOODS CONTAIN STARCH?

Materials Needed

- Tincture of iodine
- Stirring sticks
- Eyedropper
- Paper cups
- Cornstarch
- Raw potato
- Bread
- Other foods, such as cooked egg white, cooked macaroni, meat, sugar, salt, crackers, and boiled rice
- Paper and pencils

Procedure

1. Fill a paper cup about half full of water and add a small amount of cornstarch.
2. Using the dropper, add a drop or two of iodine to the cornstarch solution and stir. The blue-black color indicates the presence of starch.
3. Using the dropper, place a drop of tincture of iodine on a slice of raw potato.
4. What happened? Does potato contain starch?
5. Use the iodine test on a variety of other foods. With each one, make your prediction before you do the iodine test.
6. Make a list of those foods that contain starch and a list of those that do not.

Teacher Information

Have one or more students look up starch in the encyclopedia or other reference books and prepare a short report on the nutritional value of starchy foods. They will learn that carbohydrates, including sugar and starch, provide heat and energy and are a necessary part of the diet. Excessive amounts, however, can be harmful.

SKILLS: Observing, inferring, classifying, predicting, communicating, comparing and contrasting, formulating hypotheses, experimenting

Activity 12.4
WHICH FOODS CONTAIN FAT?

Materials Needed

- Water
- Eyedropper
- Paper
- Pencils
- Brown paper bag
- Butter (melted)
- Variety of foods, such as salad dressing, boiled egg, leafy vegetable, meat, bread, nuts

Procedure

1. Tear the brown paper bag up into small pieces, about 5 cm (2 in.) in diameter.
2. Put a small amount of butter on one of the small pieces of paper. If the butter isn't melted, hold the paper in the sun for a few minutes.
3. Put a few drops of water on a second piece of paper.
4. Hold both pieces of paper up to the sunlight. Notice they are both translucent, letting some light through.
5. Leave both papers in the sun until the water dries.
6. Hold both pieces of paper up to the sunlight again. Are they both still translucent?
7. Fatty foods, like the butter, leave a permanent stain on the paper. Use the brown paper test on several other foods. With each one, predict whether they contain fat before you test them.
8. Make a list of foods you found to contain fat and those in which you did not detect fat.

For Problem Solvers: Do some research about fats in foods and find out if fats are always bad for you. Do we need any fat in our food at all? If so, why? If not, how can we avoid it? Is it healthful for us to be fanatical about avoiding fats in foods? Discuss your findings with your group.

Teacher Information

Have one or more students look up fatty foods in their health book or the encyclopedia and report to the class. They will learn that fats provide energy. If excessive amounts of carbohydrates are consumed, these are changed to fat and stored in the body. Fats have a much higher caloric content than do carbohydrates.

INTEGRATING: Reading, language arts, math

SKILLS: Observing, inferring, classifying, predicting, communicating, comparing and contrasting, experimenting, researching

Activity 12.5
HOW DO PEOPLE COUNT CALORIES?

Materials Needed

- Encyclopedia or cookbook
- Calorie chart for each student

Procedure

1. For one full day, record on a "Calories for a Day" chart everything you eat. Be sure to include the number of servings of each item.

2. Find a calorie chart in the encyclopedia or cookbook.

3. Determine as closely as you can the number of calories in each of the food items you consumed. Record these numbers with the foods on your list.

4. Compare the number of calories you consumed with the average indicated for your age and height.

5. Make a realistic judgment as to whether the number of calories you consumed is appropriate. Don't be concerned about your total calories being a little above or below average. You might want to ask your teacher or your parent for his or her opinion.

6. If you determine that you should change your calorie intake, make adjustments in your diet and keep track of what you eat for an additional day or more.

7. Compare the results from step 6 with those from the first day. How did you do?

Teacher Information

Caution students that to some people the number of calories eaten is considered personal information, so they shouldn't ask others for information from their lists. Before, during, or after this activity is an excellent time to invite a school nurse (or other available nurse, doctor, or nutrition expert) to talk to the group about nutrition and normal caloric intake.

INTEGRATING: Reading, math

SKILLS: Observing, inferring, classifying, measuring, communicating, formulating hypotheses, identifying and controlling variables, experimenting

Activity 12.6
HOW MANY CALORIES DO YOU USE?

Materials Needed

- Three copies of "My Daily Exercise Chart" for each student
- Calorie table
- Pencils

Procedure

1. Keep a record of the types of exercise you do for one full day and the number of minutes you spend with each one. Use "My Daily Exercise Chart."
2. From information in the calorie table, write on your chart the number of calories used per minute for each exercise you listed.
3. Compute the total number of calories you used in each exercise and record it on your chart.
4. Determine the total number of calories you used in exercising during the entire day.
5. Keep a record of your exercising for an additional two or three days and compare with the first day. What kinds of exercises are you doing most? How many calories do you seem to be using with exercise on an average day?

For Problem Solvers: Ask your teacher to gather all of the individual calorie charts, remove the names and assign a number to each one. Prepare a chart of the information without names, so that each member of the class can compare his or her calorie information with that of the class.

Try to get a nurse or other nutrition expert to visit the class and discuss the implications of the information on the chart. Ask everyone to respect the privacy of the information on the chart and to not try to guess which numbers belong to specific individuals.

Teacher Information

A calorie table can be found in a health book or encyclopedia. In addition to keeping track of their own calories used in exercising, students might enjoy comparing their charts with those of others. Make a class chart, without names, showing the types of exercises that seem to be the most popular and the number of calories used by each. Your problem solvers can do this. Total numbers of calories used daily in exercising can also be charted without names so each student can compare his or her results with those of the group. Students should understand that these figures represent only part of the total calories used. The body uses calories constantly, whether it is walking, running, resting, or even sleeping.

INTEGRATING: Reading, math

SKILLS: Observing, inferring, classifying, communicating, comparing and contrasting, formulating hypotheses, identifying and controlling variables

Name _____   Date _____

MY DAILY EXERCISE CHART

Type of Exercise	No. of Minutes Spent Doing It	No. of Calories Used per Minute	Total No. of Calories Used During This Exercise

Total No. of Calories
Used Exercising Today

Exercise Chart

186

Activity 12.7
HOW ARE TEETH SHAPED FOR THEIR TASK?

Materials Needed

- Model of a full set of teeth
- Encyclopedia and health books
- Pencil and paper
- Mirror

Procedure

1. Examine the model set of teeth and notice the different shapes.

2. Which teeth are sharpest? Which are most pointed? Which are flattest?

3. Use the mirror to look at your own teeth. Are yours shaped about the same as those in the model?

4. How are the front teeth shaped? What do you think they do best: cut, tear, or crush? How many of these are there? Write your answers on a sheet of paper.

5. How many teeth come to a single point? What do you think they do best? Write your answers on the paper.

6. Complete the paper by answering the same questions for teeth with two points and for those that are broad and flat.

7. When you are through, look up "Teeth" in the encyclopedia and find the names of the four types of teeth on your paper. Read about them and see if the information you wrote agrees with that in the encyclopedia.

For Problem Solvers: Now that you have examined human teeth and considered the specialized jobs they perform, compare these with the teeth of various animals. Study about them in the encyclopedia and other references you have available. What differences are there in the teeth of carnivores and herbivores? Compare the numbers and types of teeth of the various animals you find. Also compare the numbers and types of teeth with the numbers and types of human teeth.

Teacher Information

A full set of adult teeth includes the following types and numbers in the upper jaw (the same types and numbers are found in the lower jaw):

Four *incisors*, located in the center and front of the mouth. These are sharp and are used for cutting food.

Two *cuspids*, located at the corners of the mouth. These are pointed and are used to tear food.

Four *bicuspids*, located just behind the cuspids. These are used to tear and crush food.

Six *molars*, located at the back of the mouth. These are broad and flat and are used for grinding food.

In addition to examining human teeth and considering the specialized jobs they perform, your problem solvers might enjoy comparing these with the teeth of various animals. Note the differences in the teeth of carnivorous and herbivorous animals.

This is an excellent time to invite a dental technician into your classroom to talk about teeth and their proper care.

INTEGRATING: Reading, language arts, math

SKILLS: Observing, inferring, classifying, predicting, communicating, comparing and contrasting, researching

Activity 12.8
WHAT DOES TOOTH DECAY LOOK LIKE?

Materials Needed

- A healthy human tooth (or model)
- A decayed human tooth (or model)
- X-ray showing tooth decay
- Mirror
- Paper
- Pencil or crayons

Procedure

1. Examine the samples of healthy and decayed teeth. What differences can you see?

2. Use the mirror to look in your own mouth. Which of your teeth are most like the samples?

3. While you are examining your own teeth, look for places that are discolored or for possible signs of tooth decay.

4. Examine the X-ray. Can you tell where there is tooth decay? If not, ask your teacher to help you.

6. Draw a picture of a healthy tooth and a decayed tooth. Then draw a picture of what you think each of them would look like in an X-ray. You might need to look at the sample X-ray again and notice where the light and dark colorings are.

For Problem Solvers: Survey the class and find out how many have had teeth filled because of tooth decay. Find out how many go for a dental checkup at least once each year (every six months is better). Also find out how many brush their teeth regularly and floss regularly.

Prepare a chart with your information, with numbers only (no names), and discuss this information with the class. Decide what might be done by the class to take better care of their teeth and avoid tooth decay.

Teacher Information

If sample teeth or models cannot be obtained at your dentist's office, ask your school nurse to help you locate some samples. If they are not available, use pictures, but the real thing will leave a more lasting impression on students. You should be able to obtain one or more X-rays from your dentist. When you get the sample X-ray, have the dentist, a technician, the school nurse, or other qualified person brief you on reading the X-ray.

During discussions related to this activity, point out that the outer layer of the tooth is a hard enamel covering. When decay extends through this protective shell, the decay progresses more rapidly and becomes painful. This is one reason it is important for such problems to be detected and corrected early.

INTEGRATING: Language arts, math

SKILLS: Communicating, comparing and contrasting, using space-time relationships, formulating hypotheses, identifying and controlling variables, researching

Activity 12.9
WHY ARE HEALTHY TEETH IMPORTANT TO YOU?

(Teacher-directed small-group activity)

Materials Needed

- Pictures of smiling people of all ages and different nationalities with healthy teeth
- Dentist or dental hygienist as resource person
- Pictures of primitive people (eating if possible)
- Newsprint
- Pencils

Procedure

1. As you listen to the dentist or hygienist, use your pencil and paper to list as many reasons as you can that healthy teeth are important, and things you can do to keep your teeth healthy.

2. Look at the pictures of different people with healthy teeth. Some work very hard to keep them healthy and clean. Others do very little. Can you think of reasons why? Before you do step 3, write down any reasons you can think of.

3. Look at the pictures of the cave men and primitive people. Scientists have found evidence that these cave men and primitive people ate their food almost as they found it. They gnawed bones, chewed skins, and ate vegetables and fruit without boiling, softening, or tenderizing them. Because their teeth worked hard and were scraped, scratched, and brushed by tough foods, tooth and gum problems were rare. Broken teeth were common. Was this one of the reasons you listed on your paper?

4. Some highly developed and civilized people such as American Indians and Eskimos have very healthy teeth when they follow the customs and eating habits of their culture. Before white people came, most American Indians and Eskimos had very healthy teeth. Now many do not. Can you think of reasons why?

5. Good dental hygiene (brushing and flossing) is very important for everyone, but even if we try very hard, some people will have better teeth than others. This is also true of eyesight, hearing, and many other things. People adapt to different problems in different ways. Following is a list of some reasons for poor teeth and gums. Some you can change and some you cannot. Make a list of the things you can change and tell how.

   a. Tooth decay from eating and drinking foods with sugar.

   b. Tooth decay from improper care, such as not brushing and flossing.

   c. Tooth decay due to lack of fluoride in your drinking water.

   d. Crooked teeth

   e. Overbite

f. Sore gums

g. Color of teeth

h. Tooth problems of parents and grandparents

i. Eating foods that are hard to chew.

6. Discuss the list in step 5 with your teacher and your group.

Teacher Information

Although teeth have not changed significantly in the history of modern people, lifestyle and eating habits have. Good dental care, hygiene, and nutrition (sugar control) are ways of adapting teeth to constant change.

Different cultures and varying lifestyles influence the amount and type of care human teeth require. Heredity must also be considered when evaluating tooth development and care.

SKILLS: Observing, inferring, classifying, measuring, predicting, communicating, comparing and contrasting, using space-time relationships, formulating hypotheses, identifying and controlling variables, experimenting, researching

Activity 12.10
HOW CAN YOU CLEAN YOUR TEETH BEST?

Materials Needed

- Plaque-indicator pills (one for each student)
- Toothbrushes (one for each student)
- Toothpaste
- Toothpicks
- Dental floss
- Model set of teeth
- Sink and water
- Paper cups

Procedure

1. Chew up the pill.
2. Rinse your mouth with water and notice how much of the red coloring is left on your teeth.
3. Brush your teeth using a back-and-forth motion. Rinse your mouth and notice how much of the red coloring is left in your mouth.
4. Brush your teeth again, this time using an upward motion on your lower teeth and a downward motion on the upper teeth. Rinse your mouth and notice how much of the red coloring is left in your mouth.
5. Use dental floss between your teeth. Rinse your mouth and check for red coloring again.
6. Use a toothpick to clean places where the toothbrush and dental floss did not clean. Rinse your mouth and check for red coloring again.
7. Did each of these methods clean out some of the red coloring that was missed by the others? What can you say about that?

Teacher Information

If possible have the students bring their toothbrushes from home wrapped in plastic or foil. Each of the techniques used for cleaning teeth in this activity should clean out some of the red coloring that was missed by the other methods. Relative effectiveness in cleaning food out of the teeth is similar. Food that is between the teeth and missed by the toothbrush continues to provide feeding ground for bacteria. The waste product of the bacteria is called plaque. Plaque contains acid, which decays the teeth.

SKILLS: Observing, inferring, communicating, formulating hypotheses, identifying and controlling variables

PHYSICAL SCIENCE ACTIVITIES

Topics

- **Nature of Matter**
- **Energy**
- **Light**
- **Simple Machines**
- **Magnetism**
- **Static Electricity**
- **Current Electricity**

Topic 13:   Nature of Matter

TO THE TEACHER

Everything around us is matter of one form or another. The air we breathe, the food we eat, the books we read, our bodies—-all of these things are made of various types of chemicals and substances. The topic of this section is very broad and is related to many other science topics. No attempt has been made to be comprehensive in coverage, but only to expose students to a few of the basic properties and relationships of matter. Activities have been selected that involve materials and supplies common to the school or the home in preference to those requiring sophisticated equipment.

It is recommended that after a study of the nature of matter, you seek opportunities to apply the general concepts learned while studying other science topics. For example, in a study of weather, air, or water, the principles of evaporation and condensation are essential. The effect of temperature change on expansion and contraction is another idea common to weather, air, water, and the topic of this section. In a study of plants, animals, or the human body, the nature of matter has many applications.

Activity 13.1
HOW CAN THE DEPTH OF A BATHYSCAPH BE CONTROLLED?

Materials Needed

- Deep pan (or bucket) of water
- Small glass jar with tight-fitting lid
- Latex cement (such as Shoe Goo)
- Plastic tubing

Procedure

1. Make two holes in the lid. One should be just large enough to insert the tube through it and the other can be much smaller.

2. Insert one end of the tubing through the larger hole in the lid and put latex cement on the lid around the tubing to seal it from leakage of water or air. Allow the cement at least an hour to dry.

3. Fill the jar about half full of water and put the lid on tight.

4. Place the jar in the bucket of water.

5. Hold the lid-end of the jar under water. Put the end of the tube in your mouth and adjust the amount of water in the jar by blowing or drawing on the end of the tube until the jar floats just beneath the surface of the water.

6. Now draw on the tube very slightly to allow a little more water to enter the jar. What happened to the jar?

7. Blow and draw on the tube to change the amount of water in the jar. What happens to the jar?

8. How could this idea be used in a bathyscaph designed to study the ocean at different depths?

Teacher Information

A vessel in water can be caused to float at different depths by altering the density of the vessel. Density can be increased by displacing a chamber of air (or a portion of it) with water, or decreased by displacing the water with air. This is one way the depth of an underwater vessel can be adjusted.

SKILLS: Observing, inferring, predicting, communicating, identifying and controlling variables

Activity 13.2
HOW CAN CHEMICAL CHANGES HELP YOU WRITE A SECRET MESSAGE?

 Take home and do with family and friends.

Materials Needed

- Small jar
- Milk (only a few drops)
- Toothpick
- White paper
- Lamp with light bulb

Procedure

1. Dip the toothpick into the milk and use it as a pen to write a message on the paper. Let the milk dry.
2. What happens to your message as the milk dries?
3. Hold the paper close to a burning light bulb. What happens as the paper absorbs heat from the light bulb? What can you say about this?

Teacher Information

As the milk dries, the residue blends in with the white paper and becomes invisible. When heat is applied, a chemical reaction takes place in the milk residue, turning it dark and making it easily visible against the white paper.

Students could try the same activity using lemon juice instead of milk as their "ink."

SKILLS: Observing, inferring, predicting, comparing and contrasting

Activity 13.3
HOW DOES TEMPERATURE AFFECT THE SPEED OF MOLECULES?

Materials Needed

- Two tumblers
- Food coloring
- Paper and pencil
- Two eye droppers
- Hot and cold water

Procedure

1. Put very cold water in one tumbler and hot water in the other. Fill each about half full.

2. Draw four or five drops of food coloring into each of the two eye droppers. Put as near the same amount in each as possible.

3. Hold a dropper over each tumbler and squeeze to empty the contents of both at exactly the same time.

4. Compare the movement of the color in the two containers. In which tumbler did the color spread more rapidly?

5. If you have time, try different colors and different water temperatures. Record your observations.

For Problem Solvers: Try the same experiment, but using color as the variable. Put water of the same temperature in both containers. See if one color of food coloring diffuses through the water any faster than another color. Find a stopwatch and time them to find out exactly how long it takes to fully diffuse, so that the water is equal in color throughout.

Next, test water at different temperatures, timing the diffusion at each temperature. Does temperature make a big difference, a small difference, or none at all?

Compare diffusion time of various liquids. Do you think the food coloring will diffuse through milk at the same rate as water, if the two liquids are the same temperature? Try it. What other liquids could you compare?

Teacher Information

As temperatures increase, molecules move faster. The food coloring will diffuse noticeably more rapidly in the hot water than in the cold water. In this experiment, water temperature is the variable. Your "problem solvers" will try the same experiment with color as the variable.

For instance, use two tumblers of cold water and put red in one and green (or blue) in the other. They are also encouraged to use a stopwatch and a thermometer and record the actual time required for maximum diffusion (equal color throughout, as judged by the students).

INTEGRATING: Math

SKILLS: Observing, inferring, measuring, predicting, communicating, comparing and contrasting, using space-time relationships, formulating hypotheses, identifying and controlling variables, experimenting

Activity 13.4
HOW DOES TEMPERATURE AFFECT SOLUBILITY?

Materials Needed

- Two tumblers (equal size)
- Cold water
- Hot water (or a heat source)
- Two spoons (or other stirring instruments)
- Measuring spoons
- Sugar
- Marker

Procedure

1. Be sure the tumblers are equal size.
2. Make a mark on each tumbler about a fourth of the way down from the top. The mark should be at exactly the same point on each tumbler.
3. Using cold water for one tumbler and hot water (very hot) for the other, fill each exactly to the mark.
4. Using a measuring spoon (teaspoon is about right) put one level spoonful of sugar in each tumbler.
5. Stir the water in each tumbler until the sugar has completely dissolved in the water.
6. Add another level spoonful of sugar and again stir until completely dissolved.
7. Continue doing this, counting the spoonsful of sugar added to each tumbler. Stop adding sugar when you can no longer make it completely dissolve in the water.
8. Which dissolved more sugar, the cold water or the hot water? How much more? Why do you think this was so?

For Problem Solvers: Get some sugar cubes and see if they dissolve at the same rate as loose sugar. Compare them in hot and cold water. Time the dissolving rate with a stopwatch. Measure the temperature of the hot water and the cold water. Considering the dissolving rate for both of these, predict the dissolving rate if the water is halfway between these two temperatures. Try it.

Do you think stirring has an effect on dissolving rate? See what you can do to find out.

Do you think salt dissolves at the same rate as sugar? Do you think water temperature has the same effect on the dissolving rate of salt as it has on sugar? Devise an experiment to find out, and carry out your experiment.

Teacher Information

Hot water molecules move more rapidly than cold water molecules do. The dissolving sugar molecules are therefore dispersed more completely throughout the liquid and a greater amount of sugar is dissolved in the hot water.

Your "problem solvers" will compare the dissolving rate of sugar cubes with the dissolving rate of loose sugar. They will also investigate the effect of stirring on the dissolving rate of sugar. If their interest holds, they will find out if salt dissolves at the same rate as sugar. Your young scientists might think of other variables to test as well.

INTEGRATING: Math

SKILLS: Observing, inferring, measuring, predicting, communicating, comparing and contrasting, using space-time relationships, formulating hypotheses, identifying and controlling variables, experimenting

Activity 13.5
HOW CAN PERFUME GET INTO A SEALED BALLOON?

Materials Needed

- Two balloons
- Two small bowls
- Perfume
- Water
- String

Procedure

1. Put one-half cup of water in each of the two bowls.
2. Mix several drops of perfume into the water of one bowl.
3. Blow up both balloons and tie them. Use a string with a bow knot so they can be untied later.
4. Place one balloon in each bowl. Press them into the bowl to create an air-tight seal.
5. Leave the materials undisturbed for at least two hours.
6. After at least two hours, take the balloons to another room where the perfume in the bowl cannot be smelled.
7. Untie the balloon that was on the nonperfume bowl. Let the air out slowly and smell it.
8. Untie the balloon that was on the perfume bowl. Let the air out slowly and smell it.
9. What did you notice about the air in the balloons? What can you say about this?

For Problem Solvers: Do you think the perfume getting into the balloon would be affected by how tightly the balloon is blown up? Test this question by using three balloons. Be sure the balloons are identical, except that one will be blown up more and one less than before.

How about also testing the permeability of different plastic wraps? Put your perfume water in drinking cups or drinking glasses, and seal the plastic wrap over the tops of the containers; then see if you can smell the perfume through the plastic. Compare different brands of plastic wrap. Before you begin, make your predictions. Will they be the same? Do you think permeability of plastic wraps matters with foods that are stored in the refrigerator? Why?

Teacher Information

Molecules in the perfume are small enough to permeate the balloon. When the air is let out of the balloon after a two-hour period, the smell of perfume in the air of the balloon should be evident.

Foods sometimes take on odors from each other while wrapped and in the refrigerator. Your "problem solvers" will find out why.

INTEGRATING: Math

SKILLS: Observing, inferring, classifying, measuring, predicting, communicating, comparing and contrasting, using space-time relationships, formulating hypotheses, identifying and controlling variables, experimenting

Activity 13.6
HOW CAN YOU CAUSE MOLECULES TO MOVE THROUGH SOLIDS?

Materials Needed

- Balloon
- String
- Marker
- Paper and pencil

Procedure

1. Blow up a balloon and tie it.
2. Measure the size of the balloon by wrapping the string around it at the largest point and marking the string. Record the length of string required to go around the balloon.
3. Place the balloon where it will not be disturbed and where the temperature will remain quite constant.
4. For three days, measure the balloon twice a day with the same string and mark the string to indicate the length required to go around the balloon. Each time you measure, record the length of string required.
5. At the end of three days, describe your observations. Try to explain any changes you noted.

For Problem Solvers: Find some balloons of different brands and different quality and repeat this activity. Set up an experiment to compare the different types of balloons. Be sure to use balloons of the same size and shape, to blow them up to the same size, and to tie them in the same way.

Teacher Information

You might check to see that the balloon is tied tightly so air cannot leak through the opening. You can do this by submerging it in water to check for air bubbles. As the balloon sits, air molecules actually permeate the balloon walls and it will lose air slowly even though air is not escaping by any observable means. For the duration of this activity the air temperature should remain as constant as possible. If air temperature changes, the balloon will expand or contract (in warmer and cooler air, respectively), which will nullify the results.

INTEGRATING: Math

SKILLS: Observing, inferring, classifying, measuring, predicting, communicating, comparing and contrasting, using space-time relationships, formulating hypotheses, identifying and controlling variables, experimenting

Activity 13.7
WHAT IS VISCOSITY?

Materials Needed

- Four tall olive jars with lids (or other tall, skinny jars)
- Four marbles (different colors)
- Corn syrup
- Mineral oil
- Vegetable oil
- Water
- Paper and pencil

Procedure

1. Be sure all four jars are the same size.
2. Place a marble in each jar.
3. Fill each jar with one of the liquids and put the lid on it. There should be no air under the lid.
4. When all lids are tightly in place, get someone to help you turn all four jars upside down at once. Observe the marbles.
5. Record which marble sank to the bottom first, second, third, and fourth. Repeat and compare the results with your first trial.
6. Test other liquids and compare with these.
7. Discuss your findings with your friends or your teacher.

For Problem Solvers: Read about viscosity in a dictionary. Find an encyclopedia article that tells about the viscosity of oil and read the article. Talk to a mechanic and find out why oil is made at different viscosities for automobile engines. Why does it matter, and what are the advantages of light oil (low viscosity) and of heavy oil (high viscosity)? Some engine oils are even multiple-viscosity. What does that mean, and why do they make them that way?

Teacher Information

Other liquids can be substituted for those listed above, but they should vary in viscosity (thickness). The marbles will sink more slowly in liquids with greater viscosity. Viscosity is *resistance to flow.* If olive jars or other tall, thin jars are not available, baby-food jars can be used. Try to get the larger size, for height. Test tubes work very well, if they are available. They must have stoppers, of course.

The activity can even be done in open bowls. Put the liquids in separate bowls and a spoon in each bowl. Students should take a spoonful of the liquid and pour it back into the same bowl, observing how fast it pours out of the spoon. This doesn't have quite the interest or accuracy of the marble activity, but it will work.

As a practical application of this concept, your "problem solvers" will find out why automobile engines use oils of various viscosities. One factor is temperature. As is true of honey, oils become thinner (less viscous) as they become warmer. Heavier oil is generally preferred for hot weather and thinner oil for cold weather. Modern oils are also made in multiple viscosities; they have properties that cause them to behave as a heavier oil in hotter temperatures and as a lighter oil in colder temperatures.

INTEGRATING: Reading, math

SKILLS: Observing, inferring, classifying, measuring, predicting, communicating, comparing and contrasting, using space-time relationships, formulating hypotheses, identifying and controlling variables, experimenting, researching

Activity 13.8
HOW CAN A BLOWN-OUT CANDLE RELIGHT ITSELF?

(Teacher-supervised activity)

Materials Needed

- Two candles
- Metal pan
- Match

Procedure

1. For this activity, keep the candles over the pan and be sure you have a supervisor with you.
2. Light both candles.
3. Hold the two candles horizontally with one flame about an inch above the other.

Two Candles, One above the Other, Both Burning

4. Holding both candles steady, blow out the lower flame and observe for a few seconds.
5. What happened? Can you explain why?

For Problem Solvers: Observe the flame of a burning candle very carefully. Where is the flame resting? Does it seem to be sitting right on the wick, and burning the wick, or is it above the wick? What do you think is burning?

See what you can find out about flames. What part of a flame is the hottest? What causes the colors you see in the flame? Find answers to these questions and to other questions you think of.

Teacher Information

Wax, in solid form, does not burn. Heat changes wax to a vapor, which burns when combined with oxygen in the air. When a candle flame is blown out, hot gases continue to rise for a short time. These gases can ignite and act as a wick if another flame is close by and in their path. The flame will burn down the gases and relight the lower candle.

INTEGRATING: Reading, language arts, math

SKILLS: Observing, inferring, measuring, predicting, communicating, using space-time relationships, formulating hypotheses, identifying and controlling variables, experimenting, researching

Activity 13.9
HOW CAN YOU REMOVE THE FLAME FROM A CANDLE WITHOUT PUTTING IT OUT?

Materials Needed

- Glass jar with lid
- Birthday candle
- Tablespoon
- 30 cm (1 ft.) of pliable wire
- Baking soda
- Vinegar
- Match

Procedure

1. Put two tablespoons of vinegar and one tablespoon of baking soda in the bottom of the jar. Bubbles will form.
2. Set the lid upside down on the jar, to cover the jar without sealing it.
3. Let the jar sit until the bubbling has nearly stopped.
4. While you are waiting for the bubbles to stop, form a holder for the candle from the wire.
5. Place the candle in your wire holder and light the candle.
6. Remove the cover from the jar and slowly lower the candle into the jar until the top of the wick is about an inch below the rim of the jar, then bring the candle back up.
7. Try it again. Explain what happens.

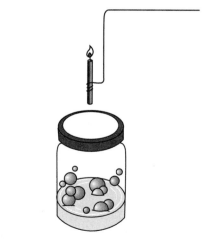

Candle Lowered by Wire into Jar

Teacher Information

CAUTION: Careful suprvision is required due to the involvement of fire. Combining vinegar and baking soda forms carbon dioxide, which is heavier than air and therefore drives the air out of the jar, leaving the jar filled with carbon dioxide. As the flame is lowered below the rim of the jar, it is starved for oxygen and the candle actually burns out. Gases continue to rise from the candle for a short time, however, and the flame sits on top of the layer of carbon dioxide, burning the rising gases in the presence of oxygen.

SKILLS: Observing, inferring, measuring, predicting, communicating

Activity 13.10
HOW CAN YOU MAKE A FIRE EXTINGUISHER?

(Teacher-supervised activity)

Materials Needed

- Large soda bottle (or quart jar)
- Vinegar
- Baking soda
- Candle
- Match
- Sink or pan
- Tablespoon
- Measuring cup

Procedure

1. Stand the candle in the sink or pan. Be sure there are no flammable materials nearby. Light the candle.

2. Put one tablespoon of baking soda into the bottle.

3. Measure about 3–4 ounces of vinegar with the measuring cup and pour it into the bottle.

4. As bubbles form, hold the bottle over the candle flame and tip it as though you were pouring water from the bottle onto the flame, but do not tip it far enough to pour out the vinegar.

5. What happened to the flame? Explain why you think this happened.

For Problem Solvers: Carbon dioxide is heavier than air. Why does that help it to be effective in putting out fires? See what you can learn about fire fighting, and what chemicals are commonly used for putting out fires.

Teacher Information

CAUTION: This activity must be carefully supervised due to the involvement of fire.

Baking soda is sodium bicarbonate. Vinegar contains acetic acid. When the two mix, carbon dioxide (CO_2) is formed. Carbon dioxide is heavier than air, so when the bottle is tipped, the CO_2 pours out. You don't see it pour because carbon dioxide is colorless. As it pours over the flame, the CO_2 deprives the flame of oxygen and the flame is extinguished. Carbon dioxide is commonly used in some fire extinguishers.

Carbon dioxide is one of the more common gases. Humans and other animals produce it and breathe it into the air. Plants absorb it and, in turn, make oxygen. Carbon dioxide is put into soft drinks to give them bubbles, or fizz. Dry ice is carbon dioxide, frozen to make it solid. If dry ice is available, have students repeat this activity, using a small piece of dry ice in the place of vinegar and baking soda. **CAUTION: Any use of dry ice must be carefully supervised, as it can burn the skin. It should never be put in the mouth. Also, dry ice must not be placed in a sealed bottle (or any other sealed container), because it can build up enough pressure to explode the bottle.**

INTEGRATING: Reading, math

SKILLS: Observing, inferring, measuring, predicting, communicating, identifying and controlling variables, experimenting, researching

Activity 13.11
HOW CAN YOU MAKE A BALL BOUNCE BY ITSELF?

(Teacher-supervised activity)

Materials Needed

- Old tennis ball
- Scissors

Procedure

1. With the scissors, cut the tennis ball in half to make two dish-shaped halves. You will need to start the cut by punching a hole with the point of the scissors or with a knife.
2. Trim around the edge of one of the halves until its diameter is about 5 cm (2 in.).
3. Turn the ball dish inside out and set it on the floor or on a table. Observe for several seconds.
4. What happened? Explain why you think it behaved this way. What might you do to make it happen faster or more slowly?

For Problem Solvers: Get your friends to help you ask around for and locate several tennis balls that are old and not needed any more. Experiment with the amount that you trim off for this activity. Try to create the ball that will bounce the highest. See if you can control the delay time (from the time you set it down until it flips up) by how much of the ball you trim off.

Teacher Information

After a brief observation, the "dish" should jump. Rubber molecules act like tiny springs, giving rubber the tendency to spring back to its original shape when distorted. This property gives rubber its bounce. With the inverted "dish," the restoring action of the rubber first has to overcome the resistance of the backward bend. When it reaches a certain point, though, the movement is very quick. The edges strike the surface with considerable force and the ball flips into the air.

As students ponder the last question in step 4, you might need to encourage them to try trimming a little more off the edges of the dish or taking the other half of the ball and trimming off less than they did with the first one. Trimming less will delay the action and trimming more will speed it up. Your "problem solvers" are encouraged to investigate with these factors.

INTEGRATING: Math

SKILLS: Observing, inferring, classifying, measuring, predicting, communicating, using space-time relationships, formulating hypotheses, identifying and controlling variables, experimenting, researching

Activity 13.12
WHAT IS POLYETHYLENE?

Materials Needed

- One polyethylene bag with tie
- One nonpolyethylene plastic bag with tie
- Sharpened pencil
- Water
- Sink or large pan

Procedure

1. Check to be sure one of the bags is polyethylene. It will be indicated on the container.
2. Fill both bags with water and put ties around the tops. Keep them over a sink or large pan.
3. Stab the pencil through the nonpolyethylene bag and observe what happens.
4. Stab the pencil through the polyethylene bag. Compare the results with what happened in step 3.
5. What can you say about this?

Teacher Information

Polyethylene has the strange property of shrinking together when it is torn. When the bag is punctured, the polyethylene shrinks and stops (or reduces) the flow of water. This property is a factor in puncture-resistant tires.

SKILLS: Observing, inferring, classifying, measuring, predicting, communicating, comparing and contrasting, using space-time relationships, formulating hypotheses, identifying and controlling variables, experimenting

Activity 13.13
WHAT DOES LITMUS PAPER TELL US ABOUT SUBSTANCES?

Materials Needed

- Red litmus paper
- Blue litmus paper
- Glass containing a small amount of vinegar water (about half vinegar and half water)
- Glass containing a small amount of baking soda mixed in water
- Glass containing a small amount of tap water
- Paper and pencil

Procedure

1. Write "Vinegar Water," "Baking Soda Water," and "Water" across the top of your paper.
2. Write "Blue Litmus Paper," Red Litmus Paper," and "Acid, Base, or Neutral" down the left side of your paper.
3. Dip one end of a strip of blue litmus paper into the vinegar water.
4. Did it change colors? If so, what color is it now?
5. Write the color in the space for vinegar water and blue litmus paper.
6. Dip one end of a strip of red litmus paper into the vinegar water.
7. What happened this time?
8. Write the color in the space for vinegar water and red litmus paper. If the litmus paper stayed the same color, write "no change."
9. Repeat steps 3 through 8 for the baking soda water.
10. Repeat steps 3 through 8 again for the water.
11. If a substance turns blue litmus paper red we say the substance is an acid. If the substance turns red litmus paper blue we say the substance is a base. If the substance does not change the color of either litmus paper we say the substance is neutral.
12. Fill in the bottom line of your chart, identifying each of the three substances as either acid, base, or neutral.
13. Compare your information with others. Did they get the same results?

	VINEGAR WATER	BAK. SODA WATER	WATER
BLUE LP	_____	_____	_____
RED LP	_____	_____	_____
A, B, or N	_____	_____	_____

For Problem Solvers: Stronger acids turn blue litmus paper darker red, and stronger bases turn red litmus paper darker blue. Find other substances to test with litmus paper. Some of the materials you could test are milk, tea, coffee, window cleaner, bathtub cleaner, and mouthwash. You will think of others as you go. Identify which of the materials you tested are strong acids, which are weak acids, which are strong bases, and which are weak bases.

Test a variety of brands of soft drinks. Before you test them, predict whether they will be acid, base, or neutral. If you think they will be acid or base, predict which drinks will be the strongest. After testing them, list them in the order of their strength, as shown by the litmus test.

Find as many sources of water as you can find in your area. These might include tap water, rain water, pond water, swamp water, river water, and others. Use the litmus paper test on each one, and list them in order according to your litmus test results.

Teacher Information

This activity will provide an introduction to the terms "acids" and "bases" and to the use of litmus paper as an indicator for determining which is which. It will also become a practical and useful experience for your problem solvers who decide to extend the activity into various drinks and into water from various sources. If acid rain is sometimes a problem in your area, you might also want to have your students collect samples of rain water during each storm and keep record of the acid levels from each. Do the same with snow; melt it down and test it.

As a long-term project, consider having your students determine whether the acidity of rainwater changes throughout the year in your area.

In the absence of litmus paper, or in addition to it, try red cabbage juice. You can either boil the cabbage, then strain the juice to remove the solids, or put red cabbage and water in a blender, again straining the juice. To use it as an acid-base indicator, take a small amount of juice, such as in a spoon, and add a drop or two of the liquid being tested. Compare the color changes to the changes in litmus paper.

INTEGRATING: Math, social studies

SKILLS: Observing, inferring, classifying, measuring, predicting, communicating, comparing and contrasting, experimenting

Topic 14:   Energy

TO THE TEACHER

We use many forms of energy every day, yet we never see it. The sun's energy literally powers the earth, but it is so common we take it for granted. It is just there. Energy comes in many forms, none of which looks like "energy." It is disguised as a match stick, a lump of coal, a gallon of gasoline, or a glass of orange juice; it is never just energy. In a broad sense, energy is so much a part of us and our surroundings that it would be impossible to deal with it as a topic separate from other topics treated in this book. The sun's energy keeps us warm and gives us light. Part of the sun's energy is converted by plants into food for animals. Cattle convert some of that energy from plant form to muscle, which we eat (beefsteak, hamburger, and so forth). Energy is consumed by people in both plant and animal form. We, in turn, convert it into human flesh and bones. The sun's energy is a vital ingredient of our own bodies and of a great deal of our surroundings.

In a narrower sense, energy is sometimes defined as the capacity for performing work (*Webster's New Collegiate Dictionary*). It exists in two forms, potential energy and kinetic energy. *Potential energy* is the ability to do work. Work is defined as force acting through a distance. Specifically, Work = Force × Distance. *Kinetic energy* is the energy of motion. A rubber band stretched out has potential energy. When it is released, its potential energy is converted to kinetic energy. A stick of dynamite has potential energy. When a small electrical charge or the right amount of heat is applied, the potential energy is converted to kinetic energy with great force.

The potential energy in dynamite is chemical energy. The potential energy in the rubber band, or in a set mousetrap, or in a raised hammer is mechanical energy.

The energy we consume in the form of meat, fruit, and vegetables isn't all used to build body cells. We use some of it to walk and talk. We even use some of this energy as we think.

Activity 14.1
HOW DO POTENTIAL ENERGY AND KINETIC ENERGY COMPARE?

(For older children or teacher demonstration)

Materials Needed

- Mousetrap
- Ball
- String
- Pencil eraser

Procedure

1. Set the mousetrap. What kind of energy does it have?

2. Drop the pencil eraser on the release lever. What kind of energy is present at the moment the trap springs shut?

3. Drop the ball and let it bounce a few times. Describe one full bounce, from the top of the bounce to the bottom and back to the top, in terms of the presence of kinetic and potential energy.

4. Tie the eraser to the string. Hold the end of the string and swing the eraser like a pendulum. Describe one full swing, back and forth, in terms of the presence of kinetic and potential energy.

For Problem Solvers: Think through the actions involved in a baseball game. List as many examples of potential energy as you can, and list as many examples of kinetic energy as you can. What about the pitcher standing in a relaxed position with ball in hand? The moment when the pitcher is wound up and ready to release the ball? The moment the ball connects with the bat? When the ball is zooming toward left field and the left-fielder is jumping to catch it? Add all of the actions you can think of, and list them as examples of either potential energy or kinetic energy.

Teacher Information

This activity requires the student to distinguish between kinetic and potential energy. When the mousetrap is set, the presence of the loaded spring gives it potential energy. At the moment the spring is released, the potential energy is converted to kinetic energy, or moving energy. Great care should be taken to assure that fingers are not injured by the mousetrap.

As the ball is held above the floor, it has potential energy. The ball is released and the potential energy is converted to kinetic energy as the ball falls toward the floor. When the ball strikes the floor, it is compressed and the kinetic energy is converted to potential energy. The potential energy in the compressed rubber propels the ball into the air, again converting the potential energy to kinetic energy. Some of the energy escapes in the form of heat as the ball meets resistance with the air and the floor. Thus, the height of the cycle decreases as the ball bounces.

The swinging pendulum passes through a cycle similar to that of the bouncing ball. All energy contained in the system is potential energy at the instant the pendulum is all the way to the top on either side of the cycle. At the moment the pendulum is at the bottom, moving neither upward nor downward, all of the energy is kinetic.

If the pendulum is at rest, it has neither potential nor kinetic energy. When in a position that gravity can cause movement when released, it has potential energy.

Your baseball stars and fans will enjoy dissecting a baseball game in terms of what they have learned about potential energy and kinetic energy and identifying the changes from one form of energy to the other.

INTEGRATING: Math

SKILLS: Observing, inferring, classifying, measuring, predicting, communicating, comparing and contrasting, using space-time relationships, formulating hypotheses, identifying and controlling variables, experimenting

Activity 14.2
HOW MUCH HORSEPOWER DO YOU HAVE?

(For upper grades)

Materials Needed

- Stairs
- Stopwatch
- Paper and pencil

  Note: The formula for computing horsepower was proposed by James Watt, who found that a horse could do 550 foot-pounds of work in one second. This formula is still used in determining the horsepower of automobile engines. The formula is

  $$Horsepower = \frac{Foot\text{-}pounds}{Seconds \times 550}$$

Procedure

1. Measure 10 feet (vertical distance) up the stairs or ladder.
2. Have someone time you as you climb that distance as fast as you can.
3. Compute your "horsepower" by using the above formula. For "foot-pounds," multiply your weight by 10 (number of vertical feet climbed).
4. A small motorbike has about 30–50 horsepower. A medium-sized car has about 100–300 horsepower. How many horsepower do you have?

Teacher Information

Using the formula should not be too difficult for students of the upper elementary grades. The following example assumes the student's weight to be 100 pounds and the time required to climb 10 vertical feet to be 3 seconds:

$$Horsepower = \frac{100 \times 10}{3 \times 550} = \frac{1000 \ foot\text{-}pounds}{1650} = 0.61$$

INTEGRATING: Math

SKILLS: Observing, inferring, measuring, predicting, communicating, using space-time relationships, formulating hypotheses, identifying and controlling variables, experimenting

Activity 14.3
HOW IS WORK MEASURED?

Materials Needed

- One-pound weight
- Foot ruler

Procedure

1. Stand the ruler on the table or the floor.

2. Raise the one-pound weight to the top of the ruler. The amount of work you did to raise one pound a distance of one foot is called one foot-pound.

3. Raise the one-pound weight six inches. How much work did you do? How much potential energy does the weight have at that point?

4. Raise the weight two feet. How much work did you do this time? How much potential energy does the weight have?

5. Set the weight on the table. How much potential energy does it have now?

6. Slide the weight to the edge of the table. How much potential energy does it have at that position?

7. Try to determine the amount of potential energy of various objects from different positions and the amount of work required to move those objects certain distances.

8. Climb a flight of stairs. How much work did you do to get to the top? What is your potential energy, assuming the possibility of falling or jumping to the bottom?

For Problem Solvers: Find a ten-pound weight. Lift the weight over your head. Measure the distance from the floor to the highest point you lifted the weight. Measure the height, in feet, and multiply that number by 10. That's the number of foot-pounds of work you did in lifting the weight one time. How much work can you do with the same weight in one minute? Do the same exercise every other day for two weeks. Make a graph showing the amount of work you do with the weight each time. It's okay to practice between your measured sessions if you want to. See how much you can improve in two weeks. Maybe your friends would like to join you and see how much they can improve, too.

Teacher Information

The foot-pound is a standard unit for measuring work or potential energy. Mechanics use a torque wrench to measure the degree of stress on a bolt as it is turned to hold the head or some other part of an engine. The torque wrench indicates the stress in foot-pounds, which is a measure of the work done to turn the bolt. (The metric system equivalent to foot-pounds is Newton-meters, or joules, not at all in common usage in the United States.)

A durable plastic or cloth bag filled with one pound of sand, beans, or other material would be an excellent weight for this activity. If a hard object is used, newspaper or other material could be placed on the table or floor to muffle the sound when the weight is dropped and to protect the surface from possible damage.

INTEGRATING: Math

SKILLS: Observing, inferring, measuring, predicting, communicating, using space-time relationships, identifying and controlling variables, experimenting

Activity 14.4
HOW MUCH ENERGY IS STORED IN A BOW?

(Teacher-supervised activity to be done outdoors)

Materials Needed

- Toy bow
- Toy arrow tipped with suction cup
- Spring scale
- Foot ruler
- Measuring tape

Procedure

1. Do this activity outdoors. Find an isolated area.
2. Put the arrow on the bow. Hold the bow and arrow at a comfortable height and point the arrow straight ahead in a direction away from people.
3. Draw the bowstring back six inches and let it go.
4. Measure the distance the arrow traveled.
5. Attach the spring scale to the bowstring and pull the string back six inches. How many ounces or pounds of force were required to pull the string back six inches?
6. Predict the amount of force required to pull the string back one foot. Measure it with the spring scale.
7. Predict the distance the arrow will travel with the string pulled back one foot.
8. Shoot the arrow with the string pulled back one foot. Be sure the bow is held at the same height as before and still aimed straight ahead.
9. Measure the distance and compare with your predictions.
10. Predict the force required to pull the string back 1.5 feet and the distance the arrow will travel. Try it and test your predictions.

For Problem Solvers: Try a similar test with your own throwing ability. Find a one-kilogram (2.5-pound) weight. With your arm fully outstretched, pull your arm back 10 cm (4 in.), and from that point see how far you can throw the weight. For this exercise, hold your body still and make your arm do the work. Have a friend measure the distance your arm moves. Try it again with a 20-cm (8-in.) throwing range, then 30 cm (12-in.), etc. Find your optimum throwing position (the position at which you can throw the farthest).

Where did the energy come from that shot the arrow? What about the energy that threw the weight? Trace the energy to its original source.

Teacher Information

Even though the arrow used in this activity is tipped with a suction cup for safety, close supervision is very important. Injury can still result if a child is hit in the face with the arrow. Young children can do the activity with less measuring and still predict the distances the arrow will travel. A ruler (or stick) could be marked at appropriate points to indicate the distance from the string to the bow. Children can indicate their predictions for distance the arrow will travel by placing a marker on the ground.

INTEGRATING: Math, physical education

SKILLS: Observing, inferring, classifying, measuring, predicting, communicating, comparing and contrasting, using space-time relationships, formulating hypotheses, identifying and controlling variables, experimenting

Activity 14.5
HOW CAN YOU POWER A RACER WITH A RUBBER BAND?

 Take home and do with family and friends.

Materials Needed

- Thread spool
- Cotton swab (or sandwich skewer)
- Washer
- Paper clip

Procedure

1. Thread the rubber band through the spool.
2. Put the paper clip through one end of the rubber band to prevent the rubber band from slipping back through the hole in the spool.
3. Thread the other end of the rubber band through the washer.
4. Insert the cotton swab through the rubber band, next to the washer.
5. Position the cotton swab so that one end is farther than the other from the rubber band.
6. Turn the cotton swab around and around to wind up the rubber band.
7. Set your racer on the floor and let it go!
8. Have races with others who made a similar racer.
9. What provides the energy for your racer? Is it really the rubber band? Think about it and discuss your ideas with others.

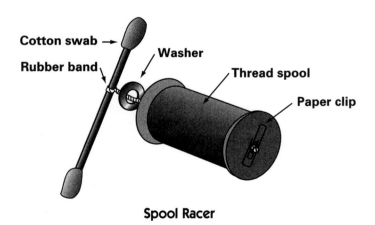

Spool Racer

228

For Problem Solvers: Find a shorter rubber band. Predict whether your racer will do better with the shorter rubber band, or not as well. Try a longer rubber band, but be sure to predict again before you test it. Find the best rubber band for the racer.

Could you make a similar racer with other cylinders? How about a small soup can? A larger can? A two-liter plastic bottle? Other things? Get creative—what else can you design that would be powered by a rubber band?

Teacher Information

This is a good opportunity for students to work with a familiar object as a source of energy and to trace energy sources. It's also a good opportunity for children to explore creatively and to share their ideas. As they work together they will learn of the benefits of cooperative efforts.

Students should recognize that the rubber band has no energy until energy is put into it by the winding action. The winding energy is fed into the rubber band by muscles of the human body. The muscles acquire their energy, directly or indirectly, from food made by plants—out of nutrients from the ground and the energy of the sun.

INTEGRATING: Math

SKILLS: Observing, inferring, measuring, predicting, communicating, comparing and contrasting, identifying and controlling variables, experimenting

Activity 14.6
WHAT HAPPENS TO SOLIDS AS THEY ARE HEATED AND COOLED?

(Teacher-supervised activity)

Materials Needed

- Wire, about 1 m (1 yd.) long
- Large nail or small bolt
- Candle
- Match

Procedure

1. Wrap one end of the wire around the nail and anchor the other end to a support. Adjust the wire so the nail swings freely but barely misses the table or floor.
2. Light the candle and heat the wire.
3. Observe the nail. What happened?
4. Remove the candle and allow the wire to cool.
5. Observe the nail. What happened?
6. What can you say about the effect of heat on solids?

For Problem Solvers: Did you ever notice how hard it is to remove the ring from a jar of fruit? Try running hot water over the lid, then remove it. What do you think makes the difference?

Why are sidewalks made with joints every few feet? See what you can learn about expansion joints. See if you can find expansion joints as you drive across overpasses or bridges on the highway. Why are these joints built into the bridge? Try to find expansion joints in large buildings.

If you know an automobile mechanic, ask him or her why wheel bearings are sometimes installed on axles when they are very hot.

Teacher Information

CAUTION: This activity uses open flame, necessitating close supervision.

As the wire is heated by the candle, it will expand and the nail, which was swinging freely above the surface, will drag. As it cools, the wire will contract and the nail will swing freely again. Other solids expand and contract similarly when heated and cooled.

SKILLS: Observing, inferring, predicting, communicating, comparing and contrasting, using space-time relationships, formulating hypotheses, identifying and controlling variables

Activity 14.7
WHAT HAPPENS TO LIQUIDS AS THEY ARE HEATED AND COOLED?

Materials Needed

- Narrow-necked jar with a one-hole rubber stopper
- Balloon stick (available from craft or party-supply stores)
- Marker, rubber band, or masking tape
- Water

Procedure

1. Fill the jar completely with cold water.
2. Insert the plastic tubing through the rubber stopper.
3. Place the stopper in the jar. As you press the stopper into place, there should be no air space beneath the stopper, and water should be forced part way (not more than halfway) up the tube above the stopper.
4. Mark the tube at the water level with a marker, or by putting a rubber band or tape around it.
5. Place the jar in a window in direct sunlight.
6. Check the water level in the tube every few minutes for at least two hours.
7. What happened to the water level as the water warmed in the sunlight?
8. Remove the jar from the sunlight and place it in a cool place.
9. Again check the water level in the tube every few minutes.
10. What happened to the water level as the water cooled?
11. What can you say about the effect of temperature change on liquids?

For Problem Solvers: If a motorist goes to the filling station on a hot day and fills the fuel tank clear to the brim, then parks the vehicle in the sun for two or three hours, sometimes the tank will overflow and spill fuel onto the ground. Think about the above activity and see if you can explain why the tank overflows. The manager at your local filling station would probably be glad to discuss it with you if you have any questions or if you'd just like to find out if your explanation is correct. Any experienced truck driver could also discuss it with you.

Teacher Information

The ideal tube for this activity is a balloon stick, available at party supply outlets.

As the jar of water warms in the sunlight, the water will expand and the water level will rise in the tube, demonstrating that as the temperature of a liquid increases the liquid expands. As the water cools it will contract, and the level of the water in the tube will drop.

If food coloring is available, have students add a few drops to the water. This makes the water level in the tube easier to see, and the change is more evident.

This device can become a thermometer if you have students attach a card to the tube and mark the card at different temperatures, by taking temperature readings from a commercial thermometer. Water evaporation in the tube will eventually destroy the accuracy of it as a thermometer and it will need to be recalibrated.

Filling stations store gasoline in large tanks beneath the ground. Thus, the fuel is cool. If a motorist fills the tank, then parks the vehicle in the sun for a time, the fuel will expand from the heat and will sometimes overflow onto the ground.

INTEGRATING: Math, social studies

SKILLS: Observing, inferring, classifying, measuring, predicting, communicating, comparing and contrasting, using space-time relationships, formulating hypotheses, identifying and controlling variables, researching

Activity 14.8
WHAT HAPPENS TO GASES AS THEY ARE HEATED AND COOLED?

Materials Needed

- Narrow-necked jar with one-hole stopper
- Balloon stick (available from craft or party-supply stores)
- Water

Procedure

1. Put a small amount of water in the bottom of the jar.
2. Insert the plastic tube through the stopper.
3. Place the stopper in the jar. The lower end of the tube must be in the water.
4. Notice the water level in the tube.
5. Place the jar in a window in direct sunlight.
6. Check the water level in the tube every three or four minutes for at least one-half hour.
7. What happened to the water level as the air warmed in the sunlight? Why?
8. Remove the jar from the sunlight and place it in a cool place.
9. Again check the water level in the tube every few minutes.
10. What happened to the water level as the air cooled? Why?
11. What can you say about the effect of temperature change on gases?

For Problem Solvers: Blow up a balloon and measure the distance around it with a string. Mark the string to show the length required to reach around the balloon. Place the balloon over a heat vent or in front of a heater for a few minutes. Use the same string to measure the distance around the balloon again. Is there a difference? Can you explain why?

Learn what you can about hot-air balloons. Why do they rise into the air? Why do they come down again? Do balloon pilots usually fly their ships in the cool air of morning or in the heat of the afternoon? Why?

Teacher Information

This activity is very similar to Activity 14.7, but this time the changes in water level in the tube are caused by expansion and contraction of air within the jar instead of expansion and contraction of liquid. As the air in the jar warms in the sunlight, it will expand, forcing water up the tube and very likely spilling it out the top of the tube, demonstrating that as the temperature of a gas increases, the gas expands. As the air cools, it will contract and the level of the water in the tube will drop.

If food coloring is available, add a few drops to the water to make the water level in the tube more visible. This is a type of thermometer.

INTEGRATING: Math

SKILLS: Observing, inferring, measuring, predicting, communicating, comparing and contrasting, using space-time relationships, formulating hypotheses, identifying and controlling variables, experimenting

Activity 14.9
HOW DOES A NAIL CHANGE AS IT IS DRIVEN INTO A BOARD?

(Teacher-supervised activity)

Materials Needed

- Hammer
- Nail, at least 5 cm (2 in.) long
- Board, at least 4 cm (1 1/2 in.) thick
- Pounding surface

Procedure

1. Place the board on a good pounding surface such as another board, a stack of newspapers, or concrete.
2. Pound the nail at least 2.5 cm (1 in.) into the board. Do not pound it all the way in.
3. As soon as you stop pounding, feel the nail. What difference do you notice in the nail?
4. Pull the nail out of the board with the hammer.
5. As soon as you get the nail out of the board, feel it again.
6. What difference do you notice in the nail by feeling it? What can you say about this?

For Problem Solvers: Rub your hands together, hard and fast. Do you feel a temperature change? How is this similar to what you experienced with the nail in the above activity?

Teacher Information

As the nail is pounded into the board, some of the energy from the hammer is changed to heat energy due to friction between the nail and the board. As the nail is removed from the board, friction again changes some of the energy to heat. If the nail is pulled out quickly, the heat might be even more noticeable than when it was pounded in.

SKILLS: Observing, inferring, comparing and contrasting

Activity 14.10
HOW CAN THE ENERGY OF SOUND CAUSE SOMETHING TO MOVE?

Materials Needed

- Two guitars

Procedure

1. Be sure the two guitars are tuned alike.
2. Stand the two guitars face to face, about 5–10 cm (2–4 in.) apart.
3. Strum the strings of one guitar. After two or three seconds, silence the strings of the guitar you strummed by putting your hand on them.
4. Listen carefully to the other guitar.
5. What do you hear? How did it happen?

Teacher Information

This activity shows that sound can actually do work. It can make something move. Energy is transferred from one guitar to the other by sound waves, and the strings of the second guitar vibrate. The two guitars should be tuned alike so the vibrating frequency is the same for the two sets of strings.

INTEGRATING: Music

SKILLS: Observing, inferring

Activity 14.11
HOW CAN MAGNETISM DO WORK?

Materials Needed

- Magnet
- Steel ball

Procedure

1. Place the magnet on the table.
2. Place the steel ball on the table about 2–3 cm (1 in.) from the end of the magnet.
3. Let go of the steel ball.
4. What happened?
5. What is work, and how was work done in step 3?

For Problem Solvers: Find a variety of magnets. Predict which ones are strongest and weakest, and lay them out in order from strongest to weakest, according to your predictions. Then continue with the above activity, comparing the strength of these magnets. Which one seems to attract the steel ball from the farthest distance?

Were your predictions accurate? Compare size with strength. Are larger magnets always stronger than smaller magnets?

Teacher Information

Work was defined in this section's "To the Teacher" as moving something (a force acting through a distance). The magnet should cause the steel ball to roll toward it. If this did not happen, try putting the steel ball a bit closer to the magnet or find a stronger magnet.

A paper clip can be used in the place of the steel ball if necessary.

INTEGRATING: Math

SKILLS: Observing, inferring, classifying, measuring, predicting, communicating, formulating hypotheses, experimenting

Activity 14.12
HOW DOES GRAVITY AFFECT HEAVY AND LIGHT OBJECTS?

 Take home and do with family and friends.

Materials Needed

- Large book
- Small book
- Wadded paper
- Pencil
- Eraser
- Paper clip
- Paper

Procedure

1. Take the large book in one hand and the small book in the other. Hold the two books at exactly the same height.

2. Drop both books at the same time, but before you drop them, predict which one will fall faster. Have someone watch to see which book hits the floor first.

3. Repeat the book drop three times to be sure of your results.

4. Which book falls faster, the large one or the small one?

5. Compare the pencil and the paper in the same way. First predict which you think will fall faster.

6. Compare the various objects, two at a time. In each case predict which will fall faster, then drop them together three times to test your prediction.

7. Of all the materials you tried, which falls fastest? Most slowly?

8. Explain how the force of gravity compares with objects that are large, small, heavy, and light, according to your findings. How do the falling speeds compare?

9. Compare the falling speed of the wadded paper with that of a flat sheet of paper dropped horizontally.

10. Compare the falling speeds of two flat sheets of paper, one dropped vertically and the other horizontally.

11. Compare the falling speed of the wad of paper with that of a flat sheet of paper dropped vertically.

12. Discuss your observations with your group.

For Problem Solvers: Go to encyclopedias and other resources and do some research about gravity. Can you find out what really causes gravity? How large does an object have to be in order for it to have a gravitational attraction for other things? How much do scientists know about gravity?

Teacher Information

The force of gravity pulls all objects to the earth at the same rate, regardless of the size or weight of the object. Air resistance can slow the rate of fall, so the flat paper held in horizontal position will fall more slowly. Except for the factor of air resistance, however, the rate of fall is equal. A rock and a feather will fall at the same speed if placed in a vacuum chamber.

Scientists are still trying to figure out exactly what gravity is. They have learned a great deal about it. They know that all objects have a gravitational attraction for all other objects, though the force is too weak to really notice unless the objects are huge, as with planets and stars.

INTEGRATING: Reading, math

SKILLS: Observing, inferring, predicting, communicating, comparing and contrasting, experimenting, researching

Activity 14.13
WHAT HAPPENS WHEN YOU BURN A CANDLE AT BOTH ENDS?

(Teacher demonstration)

Materials Needed

- Candle
- Match
- Toothpicks
- Water glasses

Procedure

1. Prepare a candle so the wick may be lighted at both ends.

2. Insert round toothpicks into the candle and balance it on the water glasses as shown in the illustration. It doesn't have to balance perfectly.

3. Predict what will happen if you light both ends of the candle.

4. Light both ends of the candle. Observe for several minutes. What happened?

5. Think about it, and explain what happened the best you can. Share your ideas with others in your group.

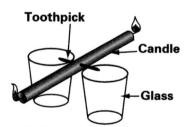

Candle Burning at Both Ends, Balanced Between Glasses

Teacher Information

CAUTION: Activities with fire or heat should be done only under close adult supervision or as a teacher demonstration.

When the candle is lighted at both ends, the end tilting downward will burn wax away more rapidly and become lighter. When it tilts up, the other end will be down, and it will burn wax away more rapidly. As this process continues to reverse, the candle will rock back and forth, often quite vigorously.

SKILLS: Observing, inferring, predicting, communicating, formulating hypotheses

Activity 14.14
WHAT IS CENTER OF GRAVITY?

 Take home and do with family and friends.

Materials Needed

- Meter stick (or yardstick)
- String
- Chair
- Various books

Procedure

1. Balance the meter stick on the back of the chair. It will balance at its "center of gravity," which should be at or very near the 50-cm (18-in.) mark. The part of the chair where the meter stick rests is the *fulcrum*.

2. Get two identical books and tie a string around each one.

3. Make a loop in the other end of each string and slide the loops over opposite ends of the meter stick. Leaving the books supported at the ends of the meter stick, where is the center of gravity (where the fulcrum has to be to balance the books)?

4. Replace one of the books with a smaller book. With the books still suspended at the ends of the meter stick, where is the center of gravity?

5. Replace the other book with a larger one. Where is the center of gravity now?

6. What can you say about the center of gravity when a large object is balanced with a small object? Consider the teeter-totter as you explain your answer.

For Problem Solvers: Do you know what a mobile is? Build one, then explain why it is important to know about center of gravity when constructing mobiles. If you do not know what a mobile is, ask your teacher, a parent, or a friend to help you get started.

Teacher Information

This activity is closely related to the activities on first-class levers in the section, "Simple Machines." Center of gravity is the balance point of an object. The center of gravity of spherical objects is at the center, assuming, of course, that the mass is equally distributed throughout the object.

Mobiles are fascinating to construct and provide excellent application of the concept of center of gravity. Encourage students to make a mobile, as suggested in the "For Problem Solvers" section.

INTEGRATING: Math

SKILLS: Observing, inferring, identifying and controlling variables

Activity 14.15
WHERE IS YOUR CENTER OF GRAVITY?

 Take home and do with family and friends.

Materials Needed

- Pencil or other small object

Procedure

1. Put your pencil on the floor.
2. Standing near the pencil, pick it up without bending your legs or moving your feet.
3. Stand against the wall, with your heels touching the wall.
4. Drop your pencil on the floor near your feet.
5. Bend over and pick up your pencil without moving your feet or bending your legs. You must also not lean against anything or hold onto anything for support.
6. What happened? Why?
7. Repeat steps 1 and 2. Notice your movements as you pick up the pencil. Explain what happened in step 5 in terms of the effect of the center of gravity.

For Problem Solvers: Try this activity with family members and friends. Try replacing the pencil with a coin or with a dollar bill. Can you find anyone who can pick up the object without breaking the rules?

Teacher Information

Any time we are on our feet, whether we are walking, running, standing, or bending over, we are constantly adjusting to the center of gravity in order to remain "balanced." The body makes these adjustments so automatically that we don't think about them.

The "For Problem Solvers" section invites students to try this activity with family members. Replacing the pencil with a dollar bill and offering it to the person who can pick it up without breaking the rules will increase interest and effort substantially. The money is as safe as if it were behind lock and key.

INTEGRATING: Physical education, dance

SKILLS: Observing, inferring, communicating

Activity 14.16
HOW CAN YOU BALANCE SEVERAL NAILS ON ONE NAIL?

 Take home and do with family and friends.

Materials Needed

- Wood base with nail hole in center
- Several flat-headed nails

Procedure

1. This is an activity you can use to trick your family and friends. After they give up, you can show them how smart you are.
2. Stand one nail (we'll call it #1) in the hole in the board.
3. Lay a second nail (#2) on the table.
4. Place the remaining nails on the table with their heads over nail #2, in alternating directions.
5. Lay the last nail on top of nail #2, where the nail-heads overlap.
6. Pick up nail #2 and the last carefully by the ends. If you have set it up correctly, the criss-crossed nails will come, too.
7. Carefully balance the whole system on nail #1.

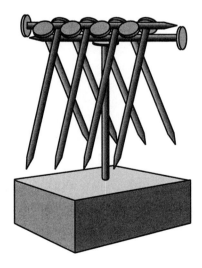

Balancing Nails

243

For Problem Solvers: In Activities 14.14 and 14.15 you learned about center of gravity. What is the role of center of gravity with the nail-balancer? Why don't the overhanging nails tip the system over?

Did you ever see a tightrope walker? They usually carry a low-bending pole. Can you see a similarity with the nail-balancer? Do some research about tightrope walkers and learn what you can about the way they use center of gravity to their advantage.

Teacher Information

First you might want to just give the materials to students with verbal instructions to stand one nail in the wood base and balance all of the other nails on the one that's standing. Let them struggle with it for a while. The instructions and illustration above will help students when you're ready for them to have it.

Although nails are stretching out in two directions, the fourteen nails will balance on the first nail, because the center of gravity is at the center of the system of nails. The overhanging nails actually hold the system in balance, instead of tipping it over as one might expect at first glance. Tightrope walkers use low-bending poles to help them balance for the same reason.

This is a great activity for students to do at home. Encourage them to let their victims struggle; don't be in a hurry to show them how to do it.

SKILLS: Observing, inferring, communicating, researching

Activity 14.17
WHAT IS INERTIA?

Materials Needed

- Two chairs
- Broom
- Four lengths of cotton thread about 45 cm (1.5 ft.) each
- Two rocks (or other weights) about 1 kg (2 lbs.) each

Procedure

1. Lay the broom across the backs of two chairs (or other supports).
2. Tie two pieces of thread to the broom handle, several inches apart.
3. Tie one of the rocks to each of the threads attached to the broom handle. The rocks should hang down several inches from the broom handle.
4. Tie one of the other two threads to each of the rocks. These threads should hang freely from the rocks.
5. Hold tightly to one of the lower threads and pull down slowly but firmly until a thread breaks.
6. Hold tightly to the other lower thread and jerk quickly, breaking a thread.
7. Which thread broke when you pulled slowly—the upper thread or the lower thread? Which one broke when you jerked? Explain.
8. Get some new thread and repeat the activity to verify your results.

For Problem Solvers: Pick a spot (target) on the floor or the sidewalk. Walk to the target and stop with your feet exactly on it. Now run to the target and stop with your feet exactly on it. Next, run as fast as you can, and try to stop with your feet exactly on it, without slowing down before you get there. What effect is inertia having on your effort to stop?

Think about seat belts. Why is it important to use them when riding in a motor vehicle? What does inertia have to do with the need for seat belts?

Why do Earth and the other planets remain in orbit around the sun, instead of being pulled into the sun by gravity? What do you think inertia has to do with this?

Teacher Information

As a lower thread is pulled slowly, the force of the pull is equal on both the upper and lower thread. In addition, the upper thread is supporting the weight of the rock (pull of gravity). Thus, the upper thread will usually break if the two threads are identical.

Newton's first law of motion states that an object at rest tends to remain at rest and an object in motion tends to remain in motion in the same direction and at the same speed unless it is acted upon by an outside force. This is sometimes referred to as the law of *inertia*. Inertia is the resistance to change in motion. The rock, in this case, is an object at rest. As the lower thread is given a quick jerk in step 6, the resistance, or inertia, of the rock protects the upper thread from receiving the full impact of the downward force. Thus, greater force is applied to the lower thread than to the upper thread, and the lower thread will break.

SKILLS: Observing, inferring, communicating, comparing and contrasting

Activity 14.18
WHAT IS CENTRIFUGAL FORCE?

Materials Needed

- Small tube, about 10 cm (4 in.) long
- String, about 1 m (1 yd.) long
- Two pencil erasers (or other small weights)

Procedure

1. Thread the string through the tube.
2. Tie one pencil eraser to each end of the string.
3. Hold the tube upright and move it around in a circular motion so the top weight swings around and around.

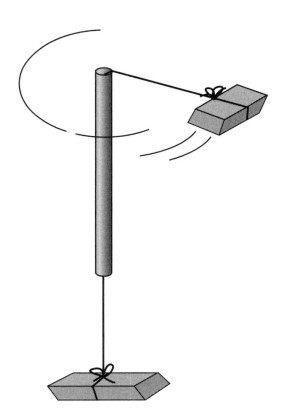

Tube, String, and Erasers—One Swinging

247

4. Swing the weight around faster. Do not swing it near anyone. The tendency of the upper weight to move outward when rotating is commonly called *centrifugal force*.

5. Change the speed of rotation, faster and slower, and observe the lower weight.

6. What happens to the lower weight as you increase and decrease the speed of rotation? What can you say about the speed of rotation and its effect on centrifugal force?

Teacher Information

The tube used in this activity could be a cardboard tube. It could even be the barrel of a ballpoint pen. If a small, sturdy tube is not available, use a wooden bead out of someone's toy box. The bead needs to be large enough to hold firmly in the hand without interfering with the movement of the string passing through it.

Centrifugal force is the force that tends to impel an object outward from a center of rotation. Newton's first law of motion states that an object at rest tends to remain at rest and an object in motion tends to remain in motion at the same speed and in the same direction unless it is acted upon by an outside force. The tendency of the object to continue moving in a straight line and at the same speed is called *inertia*. If the object is held back by another force, it cannot do that, thus the circular motion. The force that holds it back is called *centripetal force*, defined as the force that tends to pull an object toward the center of rotation. Thus, what we call centrifugal force is really an interaction between inertia and centripetal force.

SKILLS: Observing, inferring, comparing and contrasting

Topic 15: Light

TO THE TEACHER

Like many other scientific phenomena, light is so common that we take it for granted. Yet without it we could not live. Plants use light from the sun to produce oxygen, which is vital to all animal life, including humans. Without plants we would have no food. Light from the sun also heats the earth, and without heat there could be no life at all.

The question of what light really is has evaded scientists for centuries. Yet it is as fascinating as it is elusive, and continues to be the object of many studies. We know a great deal about light because of these studies. For instance, we know that light is a form of energy that travels freely through space. We also know that in addition to the sources of natural light (the sun and the stars), light can be created in various ways. When light comes from sources that people control, it is called artificial light. We use artificial light every day in the form of fluorescent lights and incandescent lights. The laser produces a form of light that has found widespread use in industry, medicine, and communications.

Activities included in this section encourage investigation into some of the ways in which light behaves. As students participate in these activities, the teacher should encourage them to ponder the relationship of this topic to the study of the eyes and to art.

The scope of the activities in this section is limited to a few very basic concepts about light. Students investigate shadows, color, reflection, and refraction, and they are introduced to prisms and lenses. Many of these concrete activities are easily adaptable for children in the early grades. For the student whose interests extend beyond these basic investigations, many resources are available—trade books, encyclopedias, science reference books, and suppliers of scientific equipment.

Activity 15.1
CAN YOU FIND THE COIN?

 Take home and do with family and friends.

Materials Needed

- Opaque bowl
- Water
- Coin (or button)

Procedure

1. Place the coin in the bowl.
2. Stand in such a position that the coin is just hidden from your view by the edge of the bowl.
3. Without shifting your position, have your partner slowly fill the bowl with water, being careful not to disturb the coin at the bottom of the bowl.
4. What happened to the coin as your partner poured water into the bowl?
5. What do you think could have caused this?

For Problem Solvers: Challenge your friends to a test of skills at spear fishing. Put some water in a dishpan or sink. Place a coin (that's the fish) at the bottom of the pan. Use a meter stick, a metal rod, or any other straight and narrow shaft as a spear. Place the tip of your spear on the edge of the pan, but not in the water. Aim at the fish, and quickly push the spear to the bottom of the pan, being sure to keep the spear at the same angle as when it was aimed.

Talk about eagles and bears, and their ability to strike at the right place when catching a fish. How do you think they learned to do that?

Teacher Information

Light travels in what appears to be a straight line in air, but when it passes from water to air, it is bent by refraction, because it travels more slowly through water than through air. As water is poured into the bowl, the light will bend and more of the bottom of the bowl will be exposed. The coin will appear.

Your students will enjoy the challenge of the "problem solver" activity. With trial and error they will improve their spearing accuracy. Perhaps eagles and bears also learn by trial and error.

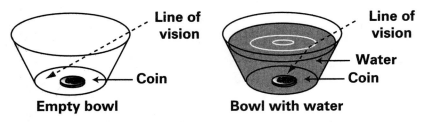

Bowl and Coin Showing How Water Bends Light

SKILLS: Observing, inferring, predicting, communicating, comparing and contrasting, identifying and controlling variables

Activity 15.2
HOW CAN A POSTAGE STAMP HIDE UNDER CLEAR GLASS?

 Take home and do with family and friends.

Materials Needed

- Empty short jar (such as peanut butter jar) with lid
- Water
- Postage stamp or sticker

Procedure

1. Put the stamp on the table.
2. Fill the jar with water and put the lid on.
3. Place the jar on the stamp.
4. Look at the stamp.
5. Explain your observations.

For Problem Solvers: Replace the jar with a plastic cup. Try this same activity with many different containers. They all need to be clear, of course, but try various shapes and sizes, using both glass and plastic. Do they all work the same? What are the differences? Can you tell why?

Teacher Information

As light passes from water to air the light bends (refracts) because it travels through these materials at different speeds. In this activity the refraction makes the stamp appear higher than it really is. When it is looked at from an angle, reflected light from the stamp doesn't reach the eyes, so the stamp seems to have disappeared. The lid on the jar prevents the observer from looking straight down on the stamp.

SKILLS: Observing, inferring, predicting, communicating

Activity 15.3
WHAT MAKES LIGHT BEND?

Materials Needed

- Aquarium three fourths full of water
- Flashlight or projector
- Milk
- Two chalkboard erasers that are chalky
- One sheet of paper
- Tape

Procedure

1. Pour milk into the aquarium, a little at a time, until the water has a *slightly* cloudy appearance. Easy does it—you might need only a spoonful.
2. Wrap and tape the paper around the flashlight like a tube, to concentrate the light into a narrow beam.
3. Turn the room lights off.
4. Aim the light at the water on an angle. Have someone clap the chalkboard erasers together over the aquarium to make the beam of light easier to see in the air.
5. Observe carefully the angle of the light beam as it extends from the flashlight to the water and as it continues through the water.
6. What happens to the light beam as it enters the water? What do you think causes the change?

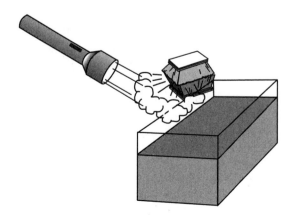

Aquarium, Flashlight, and Two Chalkboard Erasers

Teacher Information

This experiment makes the phenomenon of refraction easily visible. With the chalk dust the light can be seen in the air, and the milk makes it easily observable in the water.

SKILLS: Observing, inferring, comparing and contrasting

Activity 15.4
HOW DOES WATER AFFECT THE WAY LIGHT TRAVELS?

Materials Needed

- Glass jar with lid
- Paper
- Markers
- Water

Procedure

1. Draw a simple diagram on the paper and color it with dark or bright colors.
2. Hang the paper on the wall or lean it against something on a table.
3. Fill the jar with water and put the lid on.
4. Hold the jar between your eyes and your diagram.
5. What do you see?
6. Keeping your eyes on the diagram, hold the jar at different distances from your eyes and from the diagram.
7. Explain your observations.

For Problem Solvers: Try this activity with bottles of different sizes and shapes. What differences do you find? Do you see any patterns? Does the design look the same regardless of the size or shape of the bottle? Does the same thing happen at the same distance regardless of the size of the bottle?

Teacher Information

The jar filled with water acts as a convex lens and reverses the image.

SKILLS: Observing, inferring, comparing and contrasting

Activity 15.5
HOW CAN YOU MAKE A GLASS DISAPPEAR?

Materials Needed

- Two large glass jars
- Two small glass jars or drinking glasses
- Water
- Cooking oil

Procedure

1. Place the two small jars inside the large jars.
2. Fill one pair of jars with water.
3. Can you see the small jar?
4. Fill the other pair of jars with cooking oil.
5. Can you see the small jar?
6. Explain your observations.

For Problem Solvers: Think of some other ways to do this activity. Use containers with different shapes. Try plastic containers instead of glass containers. Does it work out differently in water if you put food coloring in the water? Think of other ways to test refraction of light.

Teacher Information

As light passes from one transparent material to another (such as air, water, and glass), the light is bent at the boundary between the two materials. This happens because of the differing speeds at which the materials transmit light. Light moves at about the same speed through petroleum products (including cooking oil) as it does through glass. Therefore, as light passes between glass and oil it doesn't bend at the boundaries, leaving the boundaries invisible.

SKILLS: Observing, inferring, communicating, comparing and contrasting, identifying and controlling variables

Activity 15.6
HOW DOES A CAMERA SEE THE WORLD?

(Teacher demonstration)

Materials Needed

- Pinhole camera
- Candle
- Match

Procedure

1. Darken the room.
2. Light the candle.
3. Point the pinhole in the box toward the candle.
4. Look at the image on the tissue paper at the back of the box. What do you observe about the image of the candle flame?
5. What can you say about this?

Teacher Information

As the light from the candle passes through the pinhole, the image is inverted because light travels in a straight line (Figures 15.6-1, 15.6-2, and 15.6-3).

The human eye also receives images upside down on the retina, but the brain somehow turns them right side up again as we "see" them. **CAUTION: Close supervision of candle flame is needed. This should be a teacher-demonstration activity.**

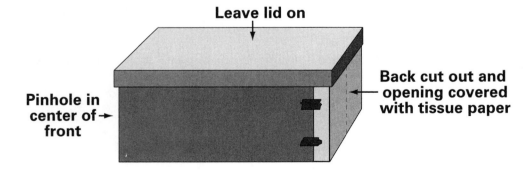

Figure 15.6-1

Shoe Box with Pinhole and Tissue Paper

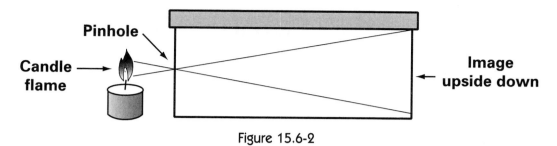

Figure 15.6-2

Diagram of Candlelight Going Through Pinhole Camera

Figure 15.6-3

End View of Box

SKILLS: Observing, inferring

Activity 15.7
HOW DOES A LENS AFFECT THE WAY LIGHT TRAVELS?

(Teacher-supervised activity)

Materials Needed

- Candle
- Match
- White cardboard
- Magnifying glass
- Pan

Procedure

1. Prop the cardboard on a table.
2. Stand the candle in a pan or other nonflammable container about 60–90 cm (2–3 ft.) away from the cardboard.
3. Light the candle.
4. Hold the magnifying glass near the cardboard. Move it slowly toward the flame until a clear image of the flame appears on the cardboard.
5. Do you see anything strange about the flame? What effect do you think the magnifying glass has on what you see?

Figure 15.7-1

Candle, Lens, and Cardboard

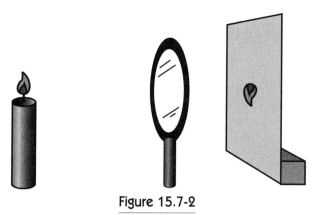

Figure 15.7-2

Candle, Lens, and Cardboard, with Inverted Image

For Problem Solvers: Try to find a variety of lenses—different types and sizes. Try the candle-flame activity with each lens. If you notice differences in what happens, describe those differences. If you have many lenses, put them in groups according to the way they worked for you.

Teacher Information

The bending of light through refraction (see also Activity 15.1) results in an inverse image of the flame as it is projected onto the cardboard. The same thing happens with the eye. Images are projected onto the back of the eye upside down, but they are reversed to their true perspective as they are interpreted by the mind.

SKILLS: Observing, inferring

261

Activity 15.8
HOW ARE CONVEX AND CONCAVE LENSES DIFFERENT?

Materials Needed

- Convex lens
- Concave lens
- Small sheet of clear glass
- Flashlight or projector
- Sheet of paper
- Tape
- White surface

Procedure

1. Roll the paper into a tube around the end of the flashlight and tape it in place.
2. Shine the light on a white surface.
3. Hold each lens and the sheet of glass, one at a time, in the path of the light. What happened each time?

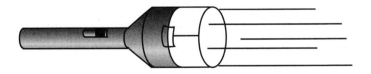

Figure 15.8-1

Flashlight with Paper Tube Around It

For Problem Solvers: Examine the surface of a book, a picture, your fingernail, and other objects using the two lenses. Explain the differences in the images you see. Examine the shapes of the lenses carefully. How are they alike? How are they different?

One of these lenses is called a concave lens and the other is called a convex lens. Do some research about lenses and see if you can find out why they have a different effect on images that are seen through them.

Teacher Information

When light passes between media of differing densities (such as air and glass or air and water) the light can be refracted, or bent. Convex lenses are thicker in the middle than on the edges and cause light rays to converge, or come together. Concave lenses are thicker on the edges than in the middle and cause light rays to diverge. A convex lens in the path of the light will concentrate the light on the white surface, causing it to appear brighter, while a concave lens will spread the beam of light over a larger surface. Convex lenses are used as magnifiers, while concave lenses are used to make things appear smaller.

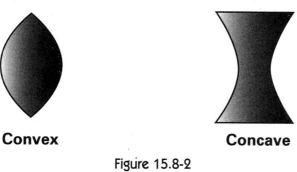

Convex   **Concave**

Figure 15.8-2

Convex and Concave Lenses

SKILLS: Observing, inferring, comparing and contrasting

263

Activity 15.9
HOW CAN YOU MEASURE THE MAGNIFYING POWER OF A LENS?

Materials Needed

- Hand lens
- Lined paper

Procedure

1. Lay the hand lens on the lined paper and count the number of lines from one edge of the lens to the other.
2. Pick up the lens and hold it in such a position that the lines on the paper come into focus.
3. How many lines do you see in the lens?
4. Compare the number of lines in step 1 with the number of lines in step 3.
5. From your information, what would you say is the magnifying power of your lens: Two power? Three power? Five power?

Teacher Information

If the lens itself spans six lines but only three lines can be seen through the lens when held in focus position, the lens is about two power. If only two of the six can be seen through the lens in focus position, the lens is about three power. It makes things look about three times as large as they are. This is not an accurate measurement of lens magnification, but it will provide a close estimate. If you are using a ten-power lens, you will need to use lines, or other equally spaced objects that are quite close together in order to get a workable count. The smaller and more powerful the lens, the closer the counted objects will need to be.

INTEGRATING: Math

SKILLS: Observing, measuring, predicting, communicating, comparing and contrasting

Activity 15.10
HOW DO DETECTIVES USE COLOR TO SOLVE CRIMES?

 Take home and do with family and friends.

Materials Needed

- Water-base markers
- Coffee filters (or other filter paper)
- Half-liter (pint) jars
- Paper clips
- Scissors
- Water

Procedure

1. Cut the filter paper into strips, about 2.5 cm (1 in.) wide.

2. Using one of the markers, place a dot about 2.5 cm (1 in.) from one end of one strip of filter paper.

3. Put a small amount of water in the jar.

4. Using an opened paper clip to hold the paper, and a pencil for support, suspend the strip of filter paper in the jar. Be sure the end of the filter paper is in the water and the colored dot is above the water.

5. Write your prediction of what will happen to the color as the water soaks up the filter paper.

6. Check the filter paper every few minutes for about 30 minutes.

7. Was your prediction accurate?

8. Discuss your observations. Try to explain what happened.

For Problem Solvers: Extend this activity to more than just water-base markers. Using water as the solvent, you can use a powdered drink mix (use only a small amount of water so it's highly concentrated), and food coloring. For permanent ink you can try rubbing alcohol or white vinegar as the solvent. Try various brands of markers—any you can find. Find out if all manufacturers use the same color combinations in making specific colors. Keep a record of your findings and share your information with others who are doing this activity, or who are interested in it.

If you had a friend who is allergic to a certain color of food dye, could you use this technique to find out if that color is in a particular package of powdered drink mix, or if it is used as a part of a combination of colors in another color of food dye?

How do you think police investigators might use this technique to help solve the mystery of a crime?

Teacher Information

This process is called "color chromatography." Many inks used in pens and markers have surprising combinations of coloring agents in them. (Among the markers you use, try to include the Bic Banana black.) This is also true of coloring agents used in powdered drink mixes and in food colorings. Colors that are soluble in water will dissolve into the water as the water soaks up the filter paper. How high the color will go up the paper will depend on how soluble that particular ingredient is and how well it binds, or sticks, to the filter paper.

Color chromatography is actually used by investigators in solving mysteries. For example, could the pen found on Joe Scribbler's body have been used in writing the suicide note?

INTEGRATING: Art, social studies

SKILLS: Observing, inferring, classifying, measuring, predicting, communicating, comparing and contrasting, using space-time relationships, formulating hypotheses, identifying and controlling variables, experimenting

Topic 16:   Simple Machines

TO THE TEACHER

Acquiring an understanding of simple machines can help open our eyes to the world around us. All machines, regardless of complexity, are composed of various combinations of the six simple machines. These are often applied in unique and creative ways, but they are nonetheless the same six. After some exposure to these activities, students will enjoy applying their newly acquired awareness in identifying the simple machines in common appliances and equipment—the shovel, the egg beater, the bicycle, the automobile, and so forth.

This section lends itself especially well to the discovery of scientific principles. Most of the activities suggested are safe for students to perform independently.

For most of the lever activities, a 1-in. board, which is approximately 1 m (1 yd.) long and 10 cm (4 in.) wide, is adequate. Others call for a lighter material, such as 1/2-in. plywood.

It is recommended that you prepare your levers by marking positions 1, 2, 3, 4, and 5, measured at equal intervals as indicated in Figure A.

Figure A

Lever with Points Marked and Eye Hooks

Eye hooks mounted at each point provide for attaching the spring balance.

Fulcrums ranging in height from 5 cm (2 in.) to 10 cm (4 in.) should be adequate and can be made by cutting a wedge shape from 4-in. × 4-in. post material (Figure B). Scraps that are adequate can usually be acquired at a lumber store for little or no cost.

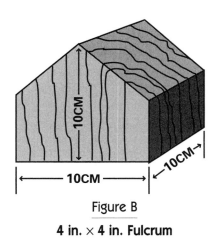

Figure B

4 in. × 4 in. Fulcrum

267

Activity 16.1
HOW CAN YOU PREDICT THE EFFORT REQUIRED TO LIFT A LOAD WITH A FIRST-CLASS LEVER?

Materials Needed

- Lever 1 m (1 yd.) long (preferably lightweight, such as 1/2-in. plywood)
- String
- Fulcrum 3–10 cm high (1–4 in.)
- Spring balance
- Two or three books
- "Record of Measurement I" chart
- Pencil

Procedure

1. Tie the books into a bundle. Place the fulcrum under position 3 as indicated in the figure below.

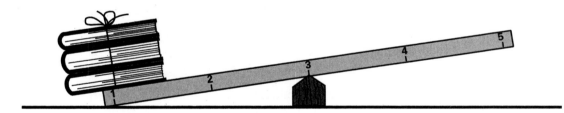

Lever with Fulcrum at Position 3

2. Place the books on the lever at position 1.
3. Use the "Record of Measurement I" chart for recording your measurements in this activity.
4. Attach the spring balance at position 5. Pull down and record the force required to lift the books.
5. Weigh the books and compare with the force required to lift them in step 4.
6. With the books on the lever at position 1 and the spring balance attached at position 5, move the fulcrum to position 4.

269

7. Pull down on the spring balance and record the force required to lift the books.

8. Repeat the above procedure with the fulcrum at position 2.

9. Compare your findings.

10. Estimate the force required to lift the books with the fulcrum halfway between positions 2 and 3. Record your estimate.

11. Try it. Record the actual force required. How close was your estimate?

12. Estimate the force necessary to lift the books with the fulcrum halfway between positions 3 and 4. Record your estimate.

13. Try it. Record your results. Was your estimate any closer this time?

Teacher Information

The effort required to lift an object with the first-class lever is proportionate to the relative lengths of the load arm and the effort arm. For example, with the fulcrum at position 3, the two arms are equal in length. If the load weighs 1 kg (or 1 lb.), the effort required to lift it should be 1 kg (or 1 lb.). (Note: 1 kg = 2.2 pounds, but load and effort are equal with fulcrum at position 3.)

With the fulcrum in position 4, the load arm is three times as long as the effort arm and the effort required to lift 1 kg (or 1 lb.) will be about 3 kg (or 3 lbs.).

With the fulcrum in position 2, the effort arm is three times as long as the load arm and the effort required to lift 1 kg (or 1 lb.) will be about 0.33 kg (or .33 lb.).

The degree of accuracy of the figures is affected by the degree of precision in positioning the load, fulcrum, and effort, and by the weight of the board itself. The results are therefore only approximate.

INTEGRATING: Math

SKILLS: Observing, inferring, measuring, predicting, communicating, comparing and contrasting, formulating hypotheses, identifying and controlling variables, experimenting

RECORD OF MEASUREMENT I

Actual weight of the load = _____ kg

Load Position	Effort Position	Fulcrum Position	Force
1	5	3	_____
1	5	4	_____
1	5	2	_____
1	5	between 2 and 3	Estimate: _____
			Actual: _____
1	5	between 3 and 4	Estimate: _____
			Actual: _____

Activity 16.2
WHAT DO WE LOSE AS WE GAIN FORCE WITH A LEVER?

Materials Needed

- Lever 1 m (1 yd.) long (preferably lightweight, such as 1/2 in. plywood)
- Pencil
- Spring balance
- Fulcrum at least 10 cm (4 in.) high
- Two or three books
- String
- "Record of Measurement II" chart
- Ruler

Procedure

1. Use the "Record of Measurement II" chart for recording your measurements in this activity.

2. Tie the books into a bundle. Place the fulcrum under position 3 as indicated in Figure 16.2-1.

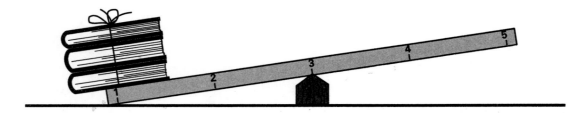

Figure 16.2-1

Lever with Fulcrum at Position 3

3. Review Activity 16.1 by doing the following. However, in addition to measuring the force required to lift the load for the various fulcrum positions, use the ruler to measure the distances traveled by the effort arm while the load arm travels the distances indicated on the chart.

   a. Place the books at position 1.

   b. Attach the spring balance at position 5, pull down, and record the force required to lift the books.

c. Weigh the books and compare with the force required above.

d. With the books on the lever at position 1 and the spring balance attached at position 5, move the fulcrum to position 4 (Figure 16.2-2).

e. Pull down on the spring balance and record the force required to lift the books.

f. Repeat the above procedure with the fulcrum at position 2.

g. Compare your findings.

4. With the last two fulcrum positions, estimate travel distances of the effort arm. Record your estimates.

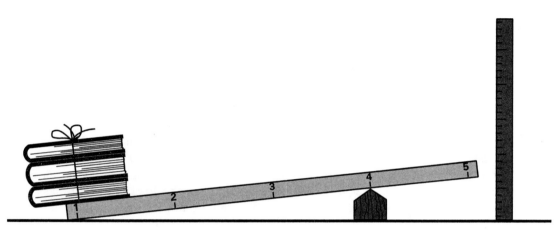

Figure 16.2-2

Lever with Fulcrum at Position 4

5. Try these and record the actual results.

6. As the force required at the effort arm decreases, does the distance the effort arm travels increase or decrease?

7. Write a statement about the force required to lift a load, the distance the load travels, and the distance the effort arm travels as the fulcrum is moved closer and closer to the load.

8. The lever you used here is called a first-class lever. Notice how it compares to the second-class lever and the third-class lever as you do other activities.

For Problem Solvers: Examine your list of levers and find all of them that are first-class levers. For each one, decide whether the advantage of using the lever in this application is to gain force or to gain distance and speed.

Continue to watch for more applications of the lever. Add them to your list as you find them.

Teacher Information

The total amount of work required to lift a load is neither increased nor decreased by the use of a lever. In using a first-class lever (as in this activity), we can decrease the amount of force required to lift a load by moving the fulcrum closer to the load. As the fulcrum moves closer to the load and the effort required to lift the load is decreased, the effort arm travels a greater distance and the load travels a lesser distance. We gain in terms of force required, but we sacrifice speed and distance.

The amount of force required to lift a given load using a first-class lever can be computed using the following formula:

$$load \times length\ of\ load\ arm = effort \times length\ of\ effort\ arm$$

For example, if we have a 200-kg load and we can apply only 50 kg of force to lift the load, the effort arm must be four times as long as the load arm. As the effort required to lift the load is divided by four, the speed and distance traveled by the load will also be divided by four.

In their list of first-class levers, your problem solvers should note that the advantage can go either way, depending on the position of the fulcrum. First-class levers can provide gain in force with a sacrifice of distance and speed, or a gain in distance and speed with a sacrifice of force. If the fulcrum is closer to the load, the gain is in force. If the fulcrum is closer to the effort position, the gain is in distance and speed. If the fulcrum is in the center of the lever, the only advantage is that it reverses the direction of the load. The first-class lever always reverses the direction of the load. For each example in their list, students should be able to easily determine the advantage by noting the position of the fulcrum.

INTEGRATING: Math

SKILLS: Observing, inferring, measuring, predicting, communicating, comparing and contrasting, formulating hypotheses, identifying and controlling variables, experimenting

NAME _____   DATE _____

RECORD OF MEASUREMENT II

Weight of the load = _____ kg

Load Position	Effort Position	Fulcrum Position	Force	TRAVEL DISTANCE Load Arm	Effort Arm
1	5	3	_____	10 cm	_____
1	5	4	_____	5 cm	_____
1	5	2	_____	5 cm	_____
1	5	Between 2 and 3	Estimate: _____ Actual: _____	5 cm	Estimate:_____ Actual: _____
1	5	Between 3 and 4	Estimate: _____ Actual: _____	10 cm	Estimate:_____ Actual: _____

275

Activity 16.3
HOW IS A SECOND-CLASS LEVER DIFFERENT FROM A FIRST-CLASS LEVER?

Materials Needed

- Lever
- Fulcrum
- Two or three books
- String

Procedure

1. Tie the books into a bundle.
2. Place the fulcrum at position 5 and hang the books, by their string, from position 4, as illustrated in the figure below.

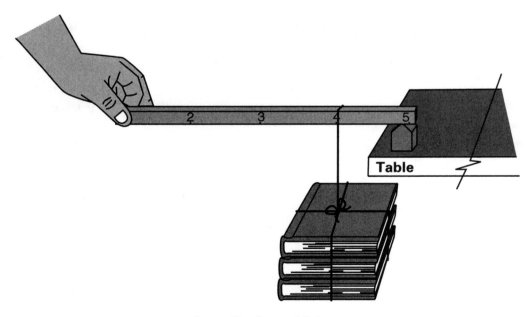

Lever, Books, and Fulcrum

276

3. Holding the lever at position 1, lift the books.

4. Move the books to position 3, then 2, then 1, each time lifting from position 1.

5. Is it easier to lift when the load is closer to the fulcrum or farther from the fulcrum?

6. With the books at position 4, the fulcrum still at position 5, and the effort still applied at position 1, what is the length of the load arm? The effort arm?

7. This is a second-class lever. Notice the relative positions of the fulcrum, the load, and the effort for this second-class lever. How do these compare with the first-class lever you used in the previous activities?

Teacher Information

With the load placed between the fulcrum and the effort, we now have a second-class lever. The length of both arms is measured from the fulcrum, so with the load at position 3, the effort arm is twice the length of the load arm.

As with the first-class lever, the shorter the load arm and the longer the effort arm, the less effort required to lift the load. The effort arm travels farther and faster, however, than the load.

A major difference between the first-class lever and the second-class lever is that the second-class lever does not reverse the direction of the load; both effort and load travel in the same direction.

Examples of second-class levers include the paper cutter, the nutcracker, and the wheelbarrow.

INTEGRATING: Math

SKILLS: Observing, inferring, measuring, predicting, communicating, comparing and contrasting, formulating hypotheses, identifying and controlling variables, experimenting

Activity 16.4
WHAT DO YOU GAIN AND WHAT DO YOU LOSE BY USING A SECOND-CLASS LEVER?

Materials Needed

- Lever
- Fulcrum
- Two or three books
- String
- Pencil
- Spring balance
- Meter stick
- "Record of Measurement III" chart

Procedure

1. Use the "Record of Measurement III" chart for recording your measurements in this activity.
2. Tie the books into a bundle.
3. Weigh the books and record the results.
4. Place the fulcrum at position 5 and suspend the books, by the string, from position 1.

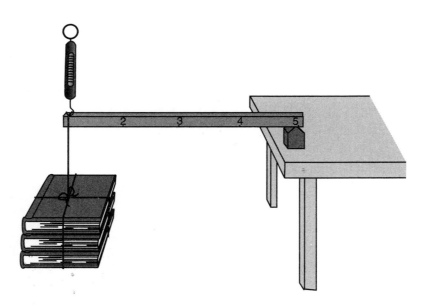

Lever with Books, Fulcrum, and Positions Noted

278

5. Record the amount of force required to lift the books, with the spring balance also at position 1, and compare this force to the weight of the books.

6. Measure the distance traveled by the spring balance (effort) as the books (load) travel 20 cm (8 in.).

7. Next, move the load to position 3 and record the force indicated on the spring balance. With the load between effort and fulcrum, you now have a second-class lever.

8. How does the amount of force required compare with the actual weight of the books?

9. Lift the load, measuring the distance traveled by the effort as the load is raised 10 cm (4 in.). Record the results.

10. How does the distance traveled by the load arm compare with the distance traveled by the effort arm?

11. If you were to move the load to position 4, how much force do you think would be required to lift the books? Record your estimate.

12. Try it and record the results. How close was your estimate?

13. With the load at position 2, how far do you think the load will travel as you lift the effort 20 cm (8 in.)? Record your estimate.

14. Try it and record the results. How close was your estimate?

For Problem Solvers: Examine your list of levers and find all of them that are second-class levers. For each one, decide whether the advantage of using the lever in this application is to gain force or to gain distance and speed.

Continue to watch for more applications of the lever. Add them to your list as you find them.

Teacher Information

The formula for computing effort and travel distance is the same for the second-class lever as for the first-class lever (see Activity 16.2). Remember to measure the length of each arm from the fulcrum.

All second-class levers provide gain in force with a sacrifice of distance and speed. In their list of second-class levers, your problem solvers should have included such things as the wheelbarrow, the nutcracker, and the paper cutter. The advantage of each one is in force.

INTEGRATING: Math

SKILLS: Observing, inferring, measuring, predicting, communicating, comparing and contrasting, formulating hypotheses, identifying and controlling variables, experimenting

RECORD OF MEASUREMENT III

Weight of the load = _____ kg

Load Position	Effort Position	Fulcrum Position	Force	TRAVEL DISTANCE Load Arm	Effort Arm
1	1	5	_____	20 cm	_____
3	1	5	_____	10 cm	_____
4	1	5	Estimate: _____ Actual: _____	Estimate: _____ Actual: _____	20 cm
2	1	5	Estimate: _____ Actual: _____	Estimate: _____ Actual: _____	20 cm

Activity 16.5
WHAT IS A THIRD-CLASS LEVER?

Materials Needed

- Lever
- Table
- Two or three books
- Strings

Procedure

1. Tie the books into a bundle and weigh them.
2. Use the edge of the table as a fulcrum. (You might need to have someone sit on the table to hold it down.)
3. Place the end of the lever under the edge of the table so your fulcrum (table's edge) is at position 5.
4. Suspend the books, by their string, at position 1.
5. Holding the lever at position 3, lift the books.
6. Is the effort required to lift the books greater or less than the actual weight of the books?
7. Move your hand to position 2 and lift the load.

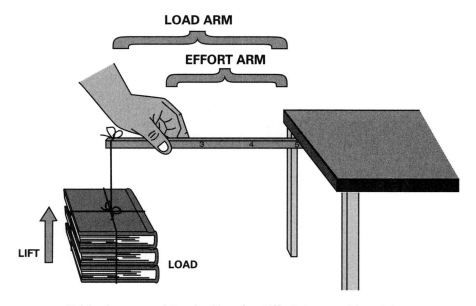

Table, Lever, and Books Showing Effort Arm and Load Arm

8. Lift the load from position 4.

9. Is it easier to lift the load as the effort (your hand) moves closer to the fulcrum (the table's edge)?

10. How is the third-class lever different from the first-class and second-class levers you have been using?

Teacher Information

As explained in earlier activities, second-class levers decrease the amount of effort required to lift a load, but in so doing they increase the distance the effort must travel to lift the load a given distance. The third-class lever reverses the advantage. With the effort now between the fulcrum and the load, the effort required to lift the load is greater than the actual weight of the load. The load, however, travels faster and farther than does the effort.

As with the other types of levers, the lengths of both the effort arm and the load arm are measured from the fulcrum. The load arm is always longer than the effort arm with a third-class lever.

The speed-and-distance advantage of the third-class lever is helpful in the use of such items as the fishing pole, ax, and broom. Our arms and legs are also third-class levers, with the joint as the fulcrum. The distance from joint to hand or foot is the load arm. The effort arm is from the joint to the point at which the tendons attach to anchor the muscle to the bone. These third-class levers offer advantages in speed and distance as a person swings a bat or a golf club, throws a baseball, or kicks a soccer ball.

INTEGRATING: Math

SKILLS: Observing, inferring, measuring, predicting, communicating, comparing and contrasting, formulating hypotheses, identifying and controlling variables, experimenting

Activity 16.6
WHAT IS GAINED AND WHAT IS LOST BY USING A THIRD-CLASS LEVER?

Materials Needed

- Lever
- Table
- Two or three books
- String
- Pencil
- Spring balance
- Meter stick
- "Record of Measurement IV" chart

Procedure

1. Use the "Record of Measurement IV" chart for recording your measurements in this activity.

2. Tie the books into a bundle.

3. Weigh the books and record the weight.

4. Use the edge of the table as a fulcrum. (You might need to have someone sit on the table to hold it down.)

5. Place the end of the lever under the edge of the table so your fulcrum (table's edge) is at position 5.

6. Suspend the books, by their string, at position 1.

7. Attach one end of the spring balance to the lever at position 3.

8. Holding the other end of the spring balance, lift with enough force to support the books. You are using a third-class lever.

9. Record the reading at the indicator and compare with the actual weight of the books.

10. Lift the load from position 3 and measure the travel distance of the load as the effort travels 10 cm.

11. Using your skills for predicting that you have learned in earlier activities, predict the force required to lift the load with the effort being shifted to position 2.

12. Try it, record the results, and compare with your prediction.

13. Leaving the effort at position 2, predict the travel distance of the load as the effort travels 10 cm.

14. Next, predict the outcomes with the effort being applied at position 4 and the effort traveling 5 cm, and record the results.

283

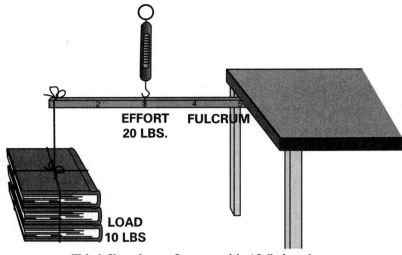

EFFORT 20 LBS.   **FULCRUM**

LOAD 10 LBS

Third-Class Lever System with 10-lb Load
and 20-lb Effort

15. Try it. Were your predictions close?

16. Select another point on the lever—somewhere between the numbers. Predict effort and distances and test your predictions.

For Problem Solvers: Examine your list of levers and find all of them that are third-class levers. For each one, decide whether the advantage of using the lever in this application is to gain force or to gain distance and speed.

Teacher Information

The formula for computing effort and travel distances for a third-class lever is the same as for first- and second-class levers. Remember to measure the lengths of the effort and load arms from the fulcrum.

With the system set up as indicated above, the effort required to lift a 10-lb. load would be 20 lbs., since the load arm is twice the length of the effort arm.

All third-class levers provide gain in distance and speed with a sacrifice of force. In their list of third-class levers, your problem solvers should have included such things as the fishing pole, the ball bat, ax, broom, golf club, and their own arms and legs. The advantage of each one is in distance and speed.

INTEGRATING: Math

SKILLS: Observing, inferring, measuring, predicting, communicating, comparing and contrasting, formulating hypotheses, identifying and controlling variables, experimenting

NAME _____   DATE _____

RECORD OF MEASUREMENT IV

Weight of the load = _____ kg

Load Position	Effort Position	Fulcrum Position	Force		TRAVEL DISTANCE	
					Load Arm	Effort Arm
1	3	5	_____		_____	10 cm
1	2	5	Estimate: _____ Actual: _____		Estimate: _____ Actual: _____	10 cm
1	4	5	Estimate: _____ Actual: _____		Estimate: _____ Actual: _____	5 cm
1	?	1	Estimate: _____ Actual: _____		Estimate: _____ Actual: _____	5 cm

Activity 16.7
WHAT IS THE WHEEL AND AXLE?

Materials Needed

- Compass
- Stiff paper at least 10 cm (4 in.) square
- Pencil
- Scissors
- Tape measure

Procedure

1. Use the compass to make a circle on the paper.
2. Cut out the circle.
3. Insert the pencil through the center of the circle. You have made a wheel and axle.

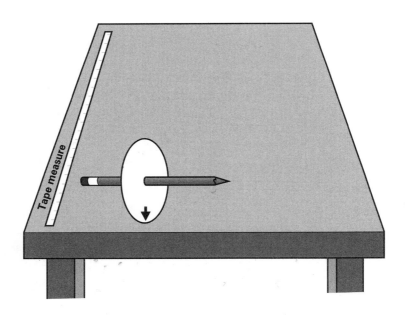

Figure 16.7-1

Pencil and Paper Wheel on Table

4. Roll your wheel and axle along the tabletop. How many times does the pencil rotate as the wheel rotates once?

5. Measure the distance the wheel traveled in one complete rotation.

6. Remove the pencil from the wheel, place the pencil on the table, and measure the distance it travels in one complete rotation.

7. How far would the pencil travel if rotated ten times?

8. Insert the pencil (axle) back into the wheel. How far does it travel now in ten rotations?

9. Name one advantage of the wheel and axle.

Teacher Information

The wheel and axle is a form of the lever. When the wheel or the axle turns, the other turns also. If the wheel turns around the axle, as on bearings, it is not a wheel and axle.

If the wheel is turning the axle, it is a form of second-class lever (Figure 16.7-2). The fulcrum is at the center of the axle. The radius of the wheel is the effort arm of the lever, and the radius of the axle is the load arm. There is increased force but less speed and distance.

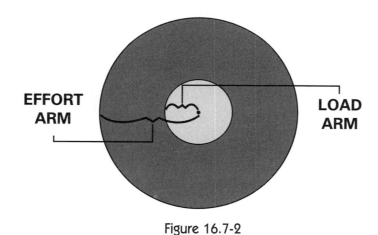

Figure 16.7-2

Wheel and Axle Showing Load and Effort as Second-Class Lever

Examples of the wheel and axle acting as a second-class lever include the doorknob, the screwdriver, and the steering wheel of an automobile.

If the axle is turning the wheel, it becomes a form of third-class lever, with a gain in speed and distance but a decrease in force (Figure 16.7-3). The fulcrum is at the center of the axle. The radius of the wheel is the load arm and the radius of the axle is the effort arm.

287

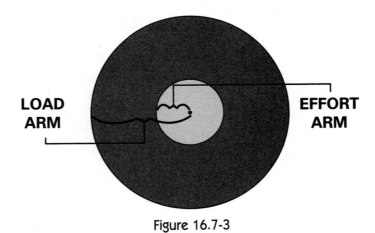

Figure 16.7-3

Wheel and Axle Showing Load and Effort as Third-Class Lever

Examples of the wheel and axle acting as a third-class lever include the drive wheels of an automobile and the rear wheel of a bicycle.

INTEGRATING: Math

SKILLS: Observing, inferring, measuring, predicting, communicating, comparing and contrasting, formulating hypotheses, identifying and controlling variables, experimenting

Activity 16.8
WHAT TYPE OF SIMPLE MACHINE IS THE PENCIL SHARPENER?

Materials Needed

- Pencil sharpener with suction mount
- String about 1 m long
- Book

Procedure

1. Clamp the pencil sharpener to the side of a file cabinet or other vertical surface and remove the cover.

2. Turn the handle of the pencil sharpener around, noting that it goes all the way around, just like a wheel.

3. Tie the book in such a way that a long string is left from which the book can be suspended.

4. Notice the amount of effort required to lift the book. Tie the end of the string firmly around the end of the pencil sharpener shaft. Use tape to keep it from slipping.

5. Allow the book to hang freely and support the pencil sharpener with your hands to keep it from pulling loose.

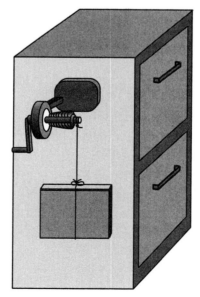

Pencil Sharpener on Vertical Surface, with Book Tied to It

289

6. Turn the pencil sharpener handle around several times, making sure the string is winding around the shaft.

7. Is more or less force required to lift the book with this wheel and axle than to lift the books directly?

8. See if you can locate a picture of an old well with a windlass for raising a bucket full of water. What similarities do you see between the windlass and your pencil sharpener?

9. What type of machine is the pencil sharpener? The windlass?

Teacher Information

A wheel does not have to be a complete wheel in order to be considered a wheel and axle. It can be just a crank, as with the pencil sharpener used above or the water-well windlass referred to. The crank makes a complete circle when used, just as though it were a complete wheel. A type of windlass called a winch is often found on boat trailers and four-wheel-drive vehicles.

INTEGRATING: Math

SKILLS: Observing, inferring, measuring, predicting, communicating, comparing and contrasting, formulating hypotheses, identifying and controlling variables, experimenting

Activity 16.9
WHAT IS A FIXED PULLEY?

Materials Needed

- Single-wheel pulley
- Crossbar
- Spring balance
- Meter stick
- Cord or heavy string
- Pencil
- "Measuring with a Fixed Pulley" chart
- Bundle of books (or other heavy object)

Procedure

1. Use the "Measuring with a Fixed Pulley" chart for recording your measurements in this activity.

2. Weigh the books with the spring balance and record the results.

3. Arrange your pulley, crossbar, spring balance, cord, and bundle of books as shown in Figure 16.9-1, with the pulley attached to the crossbar.

4. Pull down on the spring balance to lift the books. Be sure to pull straight down and not to the side.

5. Pull down steadily on the spring far enough to lift the load 20 cm. Record the following information on your chart:

   a. Direction the load (books) moved as the effort (spring balance) moved downward.

   b. Distance moved by the effort as the load moved 20 cm.

   c. Amount of force required to lift the books.

6. Examine the information in your chart. Was lifting the books using the pulley different in any way from lifting the books without the pulley? Consider these questions:

   a. Did the pulley decrease the amount of force needed to lift the books?

   b. Did the pulley cause the books to move a greater or lesser distance than the effort moved?

   c. Did the pulley cause the books to move in the opposite direction from that of the effort?

7. With the pulley fastened to the crossbar, as it has been for this activity, it is called a fixed pulley. This simply means that the pulley does not move up or down, but remains in a fixed position as the load is moved.

8. What is accomplished by using a fixed pulley?

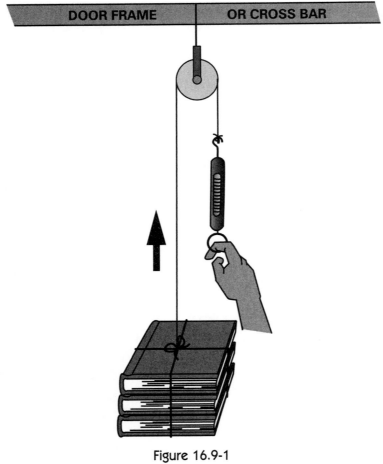

Figure 16.9-1

Pulley System with Books

Teacher Information

When you use a fixed pulley, the load moves up or down but the pulley itself is fastened to a stationary object and therefore remains in a fixed position.

A fixed pulley does not alter the amount of force required to lift an object, but it reverses the direction of the force; that is, as the force is applied in a downward direction the load is lifted in an upward direction.

The fixed pulley is a form of turning first-class lever (see Figure 16.9-2). Think of the fulcrum as being at the center of the axle, the effort at one edge of the pulley wheel, and the load at the other edge. As with other first-class levers, the fulcrum is between the effort and the load. Curtains, drapes, and louvered blinds use fixed pulleys.

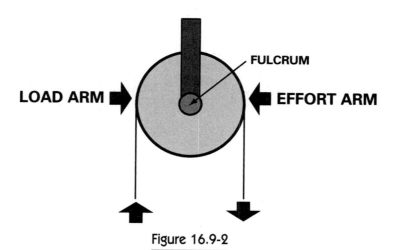

LOAD ARM FULCRUM **EFFORT ARM**

Figure 16.9-2

Fixed Pulley System Showing It As a First-Class Lever

INTEGRATING: Math

SKILLS: Observing, inferring, measuring, predicting, communicating, comparing and contrasting, formulating hypotheses, identifying and controlling variables, experimenting

MEASURING WITH A FIXED PULLEY

Weight = _____ kg

a. TRAVEL DIRECTION

What direction does the load (books) move as the effort (spring balance) moves downward?

b. TRAVEL DISTANCE

How far does the effort move as the load moves 20 cm?

c. FORCE

How much force is required to lift the load?

Activity 16.10
WHAT IS A MOVABLE PULLEY?

Materials Needed

- Pulley
- Crossbar
- Spring balance
- Meter stick
- Cord or string
- Pencil
- "Measuring with a Movable Pulley" chart
- Bundle of books (or other heavy object)

Procedure

1. Use the "Measuring with a Movable Pulley" chart for recording your measurements in this activity.

2. Weigh the books with the spring balance and record the results.

3. Arrange your pulley, crossbar, spring balance, cord, and bundle of books as shown in the figure, with one end of the cord attached to the crossbar.

4. Lift the books by pulling up on the spring balance. Note the force indicated on the spring balance as you lift in a steady motion. Record this amount as the force required to lift the books using a movable pulley.

5. Compare the weight of the books with the amount of force required to lift the books using the movable pulley.

6. Measure and record the distance traveled by the effort (spring balance) as the load (books) travels 20 cm.

7. Estimate the distance the load will travel as the effort travels 30 cm.

8. Try it. Record the results and compare with your estimate.

9. Notice and record the direction traveled by load and effort as you lift the load.

10. Examine the information in your chart and consider these questions:

    a. Did the pulley decrease the amount of force needed to lift the books?

    b. Did the pulley cause the load to move a greater or lesser distance than the effort moved?

    c. Did the pulley cause the load to move in the opposite direction from that of the effort?

11. With the pulley fastened to the load, as it has been for this activity, and one end of the cord fastened to the crossbar, the pulley is called a movable pulley. The pulley itself moves up or down with the load.

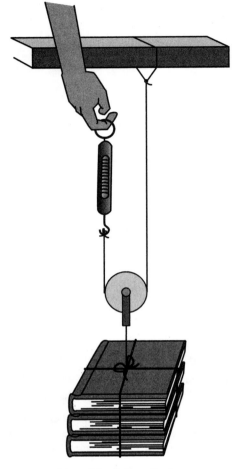

Movable Pulley System

12. What effect does a movable pulley have on the force required to lift a load?

13. What effect does a movable pulley have on the distance a load travels compared with the distance traveled by the effort?

14. What effect does a movable pulley have on the direction of the load compared with the direction of the effort?

Teacher Information

A movable pulley is attached to the load and therefore moves up and down with the load.

When you use a movable pulley, the direction of travel does not change; the load travels in the same direction as the effort. However, the amount of force required to lift a load is less than the actual weight of the object. The travel distance of the load is less than that of the effort. Thus, the movable pulley offers an advantage as to force required, but it does so at the expense of travel distance and speed.

In computing the gain or loss from using a movable pulley, use the following as a guide:

a. The load will travel half the distance of the effort.

b. The force required to lift the load is half the actual weight of the object.

Note: The force required will be increased by whatever friction is involved as the pulley turns on the axle, the cord rubs against the sides of the groove in the pulley, and so forth.

INTEGRATING: Math

SKILLS: Observing, inferring, measuring, predicting, communicating, comparing and contrasting, formulating hypotheses, identifying and controlling variables, experimenting

MEASURING WITH A MOVABLE PULLEY

Weight of books = _____ kg

Force required to lift books = _____ kg

Travel Distance

What is the distance traveled by the effort (spring balance) as the load (books) moves 20 cm?

_____

What is the estimated distance the load would travel as the effort moves 30 cm?

_____

What is the actual distance the load travels as the effort moves 30 cm?

_____

Travel Direction

What is the direction traveled by the load and effort as you lift the load?

Load _____

Effort _____

Activity 16.11
WHAT HAPPENS WHEN A SMALL PERSON TUGS ON A LARGE PERSON?

Materials Needed

- Pulley
- Rope
- Two chairs with sturdy legs

Procedure

1. Anchor the pulley to Chair A (see Figure below).
2. Thread one end of the rope through the pulley and tie the end of the rope to Chair B.
3. Have a large person sit on Chair A and a small person on Chair B.
4. When you pull on the other end of the rope, which chair will move?
5. After you make your prediction, pull on the rope.
6. What happened? Why?
7. Discuss your ideas with your group.

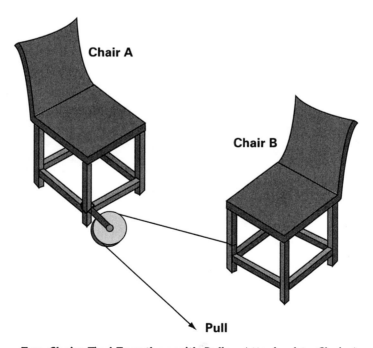

Chair A

Chair B

Pull

Two Chairs Tied Together, with Pulley Attached to Chair A

For Problem Solvers: Try to figure out a way to measure the force that is being exerted on each of the chairs. If you have more pulleys, figure out a way to make it still easier to pull the larger person sitting on a chair.

Teacher Information

Two ropes are pulling on Chair A, while only one rope is pulling on Chair B. The two ropes pulling on Chair A have equal tension. Twice as much force is exerted on Chair A as on Chair B.

INTEGRATING: Math, language arts

SKILLS: Observing, inferring, measuring, predicting, communicating, using space-time relationships, formulating hypotheses, identifying and controlling variables, experimenting

Activity 16.12
WHAT CAN BE GAINED BY COMBINING FIXED AND MOVABLE PULLEYS?

Materials Needed

- Two pulleys
- Crossbar
- Spring balance
- Meter stick
- Cord or heavy string
- Pencil
- "Measuring with a Combined Fixed and Movable Pulley" chart
- Bundle of books (or other heavy object)

Procedure

1. Use the "Measuring with a Combined Fixed and Movable Pulley" chart for recording your measurements in this activity.
2. Weigh the books and record the weight in Part One.
3. Arrange the pulleys, crossbar, spring balance, cord, and bundle of books as illustrated in the Figure on page 302. Notice that one pulley and one end of the cord are attached to the crossbar.
4. You now have a pulley system that includes a fixed pulley and a movable pulley.
5. From your previous experience, see if you can predict the answers to the following questions. Record your predictions in Part One of the chart.
   a. Which direction will the load (books) move as you pull down at the effort position (spring balance)?
   b. Considering the actual weight of the books, how much force will be required to lift the load?
   c. How far will the load travel as the effort travels 40 cm?
6. After recording your predictions, test them by actual measurement. Record your measurements and compare them with your predictions.
7. Now record the following in Part Two:
   a. Change the number of books in your bundle, record the weight of your new load, and predict the amount of force necessary to lift it with the pulley system.
   b. Predict the travel distance of the effort as you lift the load 5 cm.
8. After recording your predictions, test them and record your actual measurements.
9. Were your predictions closer this time?
10. Can you think of any situation where it would be helpful to combine a fixed pulley with a movable pulley?

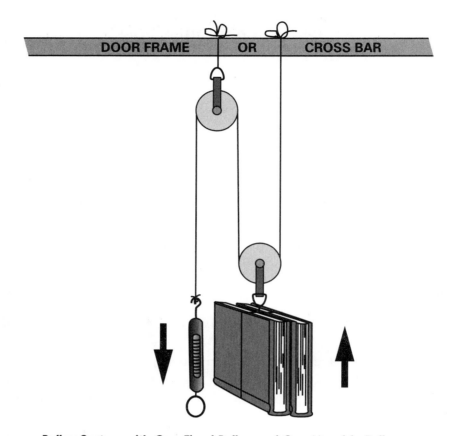

Pulley System with One Fixed Pulley and One Movable Pulley

For Problem Solvers: Try to find an opportunity to visit a crane while it is working at a construction site. Find as many simple machines as you can, including all three types of levers, fixed pulleys, movable pulleys, and combined pulleys.

Teacher Information

A combination of a fixed pulley and a movable pulley offers the advantages of both. A load can be lifted with half as much force as would be expected by considering the actual weight of the objects (because of the movable pulley) and the load can be moved upward by pulling downward (because of the fixed pulley).

This system, including a fixed pulley combined with a movable pulley, is called a block and tackle. It is used for lifting automobile motors, for raising and lowering scaffolds for painters, and for many other purposes.

Enrichment

Allow students to experiment with various combinations of pulleys and test the mechanical advantage of their creations.

Combinations of more than one fixed pulley and an equal number of movable pulleys multiply the mechanical advantage of the movable pulley and decrease efficiency in terms of travel distance. For instance, in a system involving a double fixed pulley and a double movable pulley, a load of 4 lbs. would be lifted with approximately 1 lb. of force at the effort position, but the effort must travel 4 cm (or inches) for each cm (or inch) the load is to be lifted.

If a strong overhead beam (such as a tree branch) is available, students would enjoy experimenting with their pulleys in lifting heavier objects, such as each other, the teacher, or several students at a time. Such an activity should be closely supervised to assure safety. Beware of possible broken ropes and falls. Vertical distance lifted should be limited to minimize risk of injury.

INTEGRATING: Math, social studies

SKILLS: Observing, inferring, measuring, predicting, communicating, comparing and contrasting, formulating hypotheses, identifying and controlling variables, experimenting

Topic 17:   Magnetism

TO THE TEACHER

A study of magnetism is often a very helpful beginning point for introducing structured inquiry/discovery activities. Be certain to warn the children that magnets can break or lose their magnetism if dropped or hit together. In the case of U-shaped magnets, a piece of soft iron called a keeper should be placed across the ends.

This material is nongraded. However, some activities may seem more appropriate to certain age levels. Each teacher should feel free to reorganize and eliminate materials according to the needs of students, keeping in mind the level of psychological development that may influence the understanding of certain concepts. Inquiry and the use of concrete materials is a major purpose of this unit.

Many of the activities in this section seem to be most effective when presented to individuals, small groups, or teams. If your classroom organization permits, consider placing the materials in a science learning center, with time provided for children to move through the sequence at their own rate. Classroom discussions to reinforce the concepts should follow. If classroom demonstrations are used initially, children should perform the activities, and then the materials should be left on the science table for children to explore individually.

Many children are fascinated by magnets. They seem almost like magic. There is a natural desire on the part of many children to explore and share their discoveries with friends and others outside the classroom. Most magnets are fairly expensive, but many school supply outlets sell small magnets (for notices on bulletin boards, refrigerator doors, and so on) at a reasonable cost. If possible, try to get a number of these small magnets for out-of-school activities. Ideally, each child should have a pair of these small alnico (aluminum, nickel, cobalt) magnets.

One excellent source of magnets is audio speakers. Every speaker contains a magnet. They come in many different sizes and strengths and they are generally fairly easy to remove with a hammer and screwdriver. They are usually riveted in place; some are held with bolts and nuts. Check with a local shop that installs car stereos; they usually throw the old speakers away. Occasionally a speaker system in a school, or other large building, will be replaced and you might be able to get some dandies.

Bar magnets can be given new life by stroking them lengthwise several times across one pole of a powerful magnet. Stroke in one direction only. If poles are reversed, stroke in the opposite direction *or* use the other pole of the large magnet.

CAUTION: Audio tapes, video tapes, and computer disks are magnetic. If they come near a strong magnet, they may be erased. Spring-operated watch mechanisms may also become magnetized in a strong magnetic field.

Activity 17.1
HOW DO MAGNETS GET THEIR NAMES?

Materials Needed

- A large collection of magnets of different sizes, shapes, materials, and colors

Procedure

1. Magnets often get their names from their shapes or from what they do. See if you can find magnets that might have the following names:

   bar magnet

   cylindrical magnet

   disk (or disc) magnet

   U-shaped magnet

   horseshoe magnet

   cow magnet

2. Can you name any others?

Teacher Information

This activity may have some value in helping children learn new names for certain shapes. It will also provide a basic vocabulary for further study of magnets. Since magnets are so much a part of our everyday life, your children may bring in many new and unusual magnets to add to the collection.

INTEGRATING: Language arts

SKILLS: Observing, inferring, classifying, comparing and contrasting

Activity 17.2
WHAT IS A SPECIAL PROPERTY OF MAGNETISM?

 Take home and do with family and friends.

Materials Needed

- Two bar magnets
- Thread

Procedure

1. Tie the thread to the center of one bar magnet.
2. Hold the bar magnet in the air by the thread so it can turn freely.
3. Bring each end of another bar magnet near the one that is suspended from the thread.
4. What happened?
5. What can you say about this?

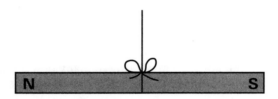

Bar Magnet Suspended from Thread

Teacher Information

Be sure the bars are correctly magnetized and that each has an "N" and an "S" marked on opposite ends. Like poles will push away. Unlike poles will attract one another. The poles of the bar magnet can be reversed by drawing the bar magnet several times across one of the poles of a powerful magnet. The direction in which the bar magnet is drawn across the pole of the larger magnet will determine the polarity of the bar magnet.

The ability to attract and repel each other is a special characteristic by which magnets can be identified.

SKILLS: Observing, inferring, predicting, communicating, experimenting

Activity 17.3
WHAT HAPPENS WHEN A MAGNET CAN TURN FREELY?

 Take home and do with family and friends.

Materials Needed

- Bar magnet
- Thread

Procedure

1. Hold the bar magnet by the thread.
2. If it spins, give it time to completely stop turning.
3. Observe the position in which it stops.
4. Do this several times.
5. What happened?
6. What can you say about this?

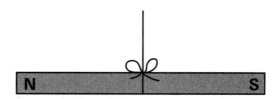

Bar Magnet Suspended from a Thread

Teacher Information

If the bar magnet is correctly magnetized, it should stop each time with the N end pointing toward magnetic north. Calling the N end of the magnet *north* has come about through common usage, as people knew about magnets and their behavior long before they understood them scientifically. Actually, since opposite poles attract, to be correct it should be called the *north-seeking* end.

INTEGRATING: Social studies

SKILLS: Observing, inferring, predicting, communicating

Activity 17.4
WHAT IS A COMPASS?

Materials Needed

- Sensitive compass
- Paper clip

Procedure

1. Bring the clip near the compass.
2. What happens to the compass needle?
3. What can you say about this?

Teacher Information

A compass is a freely suspended bar magnet. If a bar magnet is brought near, it will behave just as the suspended bar magnet did in Activity 17.2, showing that it has poles.

The children may also bring other known magnetic materials near the compass to further reinforce this idea. Understanding that a compass is a magnet is important for further investigations in this unit.

CAUTION: Very strong magnets may damage a compass by pulling the needle off its delicate support.

SKILLS: Observing, inferring, predicting, communicating

Activity 17.5
HOW CAN YOU MAKE A COMPASS?

Materials Needed

- Plastic, aluminum, or glass bowl
- Nonmagnetized needle
- Small piece of plastic foam
- Compass
- Water
- Bar magnet

Procedure

1. Is the needle a magnet? Don't guess. Devise a way to find out.
2. Rub the needle 30 times in the same direction with the bar magnet. Is the needle a magnet now?
3. Fill the bowl partly full of water.
4. Stick the needle through the plastic foam and float it in the pan of water.
5. Point the needle in different directions, then allow it to settle.

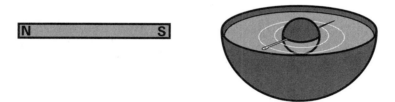

Needle in Floating Plastic Foam

6. What happened?
7. Can you see a relationship to the compass?
8. What can you say about this?

For Problem Solvers: If you were lost in the woods and you didn't have a compass, but you had a small bar magnet or a magnetized needle, what would you do to find your directions? Would you like to create a story about that? Try it—it will be fun.

Teacher Information

The floating needle will behave like a compass, with one end always pointing to magnetic north. A story is told that this is the same type of compass used by Christopher Columbus. Since the metal needles of the time were poor, Columbus had a lodestone to remagnetize his floating needle. A bar magnet will affect the floating needle in the same way it did the compass. By moving the bar magnet under the dish, the children can discover that magnetism goes through water.

INTEGRATING: Social studies

SKILLS: Observing, inferring, predicting, communicating

Activity 17.6
WHAT ARE THE EARTH'S MAGNETIC POLES?

(Classroom demonstration and total group discussion)

Materials Needed

- 13-cm (6-in.) plastic foam ball cut in half
- Bar magnet
- Compasses
- Toothpicks
- Index card
- Iron filings

For Problem Solvers: Find one or more reference books and learn all you can about the earth's magnetic field. When did people first know about the earth's magnetic field? Was it useful information to them? In what ways? Do the earth's magnetic poles always stay at the same place, or do they wander around? Are true north and south and magnetic north and south the same? Do other planets have magnetic fields? Does the moon? What about the sun?

Teacher Information

This activity does not provide procedural steps for students. The concept of the earth's behaving as a large magnet with magnetic north and south poles is difficult to teach with simple inquiry/discovery activities alone. You might want to begin with a classroom discussion using one half of a plastic foam ball (or a grapefruit or large orange) with a bar magnet running through it and a tip sticking out of each end to represent the magnetic north and south poles. Toothpicks nearby could represent *true north* and *true south*, the axis (an imaginary line from true north to true south) on which the earth turns.

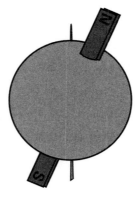

Ball, Bar Magnet, and Toothpicks

313

To further reinforce the idea, place an index card over the bar magnet with iron filings sprinkled on it. Scientists believe this pattern represents approximately the lines of force of the earth's magnetic field, with the strongest pull at the poles. With this basic idea in mind, a compass can be brought near the ball to show that it will point to the north and the south ends or poles.

See your encyclopedia for a discussion of northern and southern lights (aurora borealis and aurora australis). Scientists believe the stronger pull at the earth's poles attracts electrons given off from the sun. As they enter the earth's atmosphere they produce these unusual lights.

The earth's magnetic poles are offset somewhat from the true north and south poles. The difference between true north and magnetic north is called the *angle of declination*, and it varies according to your geographic location on Earth.

INTEGRATING: Reading, language arts, social studies

SKILLS: Observing, inferring, predicting, communicating, researching

Activity 17.7
HOW DO MATERIALS BECOME MAGNETIZED?

Materials Needed

- Plastic tube (toothbrush container or test tube) two thirds full of iron filings
- Strong magnet
- Compass

Procedure

1. Place the tube with the iron filings flat on a table.
2. Move the compass along the side of the tube. Observe the needle.
3. Rub the tube containing iron filings 30 times in the same direction across one pole of the strong magnet. Now move the compass along the side of the tube again. Observe the needle.
4. What happened?
5. Shake the tube several times. Move the compass along the side of the tube.
6. What do you think is happening?

For Problem Solvers: Find a screwdriver and try to pick up paper clips with it. If it will pick up one or more paper clips, the screwdriver is already a magnet. If it won't, stroke it the length of the shaft several times in the same direction with a good magnet. Then try to pick up some paper clips with the screwdriver.

What other tools or items do you think you can make into magnets? Wrenches? Scissors? Get permission before you try any of these things, unless they belong to you.

Teacher Information

This activity illustrates in concrete form one of the theories scientists use to explain what happens when an object becomes magnetized. In materials that can be magnetized are groups or *domains* of atoms that have north and south poles but are arranged randomly (Figure 17.7-1).

Figure 17.7-1

Domains Shown in Random Order

315

The iron filings in the plastic tube represent these domains. The compass will show that the tube does not have poles. When the *domains of atoms* come into the presence of a strong magnetic field, they line up, following the lines of force of the magnetic field (Figure 17.7-2).

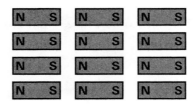

Figure 17.7-2

Domains Shown in Uniform Arrangement

When the plastic tube is rubbed with a strong magnet, the iron filings line up inside and the compass test will show the tube has poles. Shaking the tube several times mixes the filings up and the compass test will show the tube no longer has poles.

The mixing up of the domains is one way of explaining how magnets may lose their magnetism. When an object is heated, the molecules move more rapidly and bounce against one another. Dropping or striking a magnet may jar the domains out of alignment. Magnets stored with *like* poles together seem to gradually shift the domains out of position.

As the domain theory is presented to children with the plastic tube model, it is important to remember that it is a simplified version. More complex concepts consistent with this model are studied in later years.

SKILLS: Observing, inferring, predicting, communicating

Activity 17.8
HOW CAN YOU FIND THE POLES OF A LODESTONE?

Materials Needed

- Lodestone
- Compass

Procedure

1. Bring the compass near different parts of the lodestone.
2. Observe the needle.
3. What happened?
4. What can you say about this?

For Problem Solvers: Try to identify all the poles that you can on your lodestone. Draw two outlines of the lodestone on paper and label one outline "Front" and the other "Back." Every place that one of the ends of the compass needle is attracted to is a pole. Label each one as S or N. Do the poles seem to be always at the points of the rock, or in the hollows, or both? Do they seem to be always in pairs? How many pairs of poles did you find?

Teacher Information

The compass will indicate that lodestones do have poles. Some lodestones may have several poles, but they should have equal numbers of north and south poles. Some scientists believe that lodestones are magnetized and aligned to the earth's magnetic poles as the iron ore from which they are formed cools.

Since ancient deposits of lodestone have poles pointing in directions different from the present north and south it is suggested that our present north and south poles may have switched several times over the years.

The different directions in which the poles of ancient deposits point are also studied as indicators of earth movement and the theory of *continental drift*.

SKILLS: Observing, inferring, predicting, communicating

317

Activity 17.9
HOW CAN YOU SEE A MAGNETIC FIELD?

Materials Needed

- Two thin books
- Shaker of iron filings
- Bar magnet
- Card

Procedure

1. Place the bar magnet between the two books.
2. Cover the magnet with the card.
3. Sprinkle iron filings on the card.
4. Tap the card gently several times.
5. What happened?
6. What can you say about this?

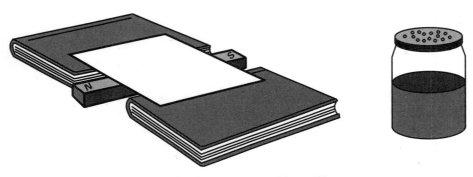

Books, Card, Magnet, and Iron Filings

For Problem Solvers: Let's explore with magnetic fields. Put a second bar magnet end to end with the first one, with unlike poles together, and center them under the card. Sprinkle iron filings on the card and see what the magnetic field looks like now. Next, turn one of the bar magnets around, so the like poles are together, and again sprinkle the card with iron filings. Find other sizes and shapes of magnets and make pictures of their magnetic poles with the iron filings.

Teacher Information

You can demonstrate to the entire class at once by putting the magnets on an overhead projector, using a sheet of glass instead of a card, and shining the image on the screen.

The iron filings will be aligned with the magnetic field of the bar magnet, making it visible. Note that the filings in the middle will point to the poles, while the greater number of filings will cluster at the poles. Iron filings may be purchased from science supply houses. They also occur naturally in many types of sand and may be collected by running a strong magnet through a sand pile. Put the magnet in a baggy before dragging it through the sand, for easy cleanup.

Your problem solvers will experiment with magnets of different types and will compare the pattern of filings created by their magnetic fields.

SKILLS: Observing, inferring, predicting, communicating

Activity 17.10
HOW CAN YOU PRESERVE A MAGNETIC FIELD?

Materials Needed

- Two thin books
- Shaker of iron filings
- Bar magnet
- Card
- Spray paint
- Newsprint or other protective cover

Procedure

1. Do this activity outdoors. You need plenty of ventilation.
2. Place the bar magnet between the two books.
3. Cover the books and magnet with newspaper.
4. Cover the magnet with the card (see Figure below).
5. What do you think the pattern of the magnetic field will be like for the magnet(s) you are using? Make your prediction before you sprinkle any iron filings.
6. Sprinkle iron filings on the card.
7. Tap the card gently several times.
8. When the magnetic field is formed, spray the card lightly with paint.
9. Allow the paint time to dry, then brush off the iron filings into a wastebasket.
10. Display your picture on a wall, along with those that are made by other students.

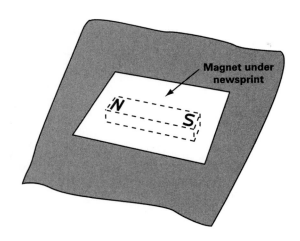

Newsprint, Card, and Magnet

320

For Problem Solvers: Experiment with different magnets and combinations of magnets to create interesting patterns of magnetic lines of force, and paint them so the patterns can be preserved and displayed.

If you can get some spray adhesive, ask your teacher to help you repeat the same activity but using adhesive instead of paint. This time, don't brush off the iron filings when the design has dried. Don't move the card or the magnet until the adhesive is completely dry, which will likely take about 30 minutes. Be sure to do this activity outdoors.

You could also use light-sensitive paper in place of the card to make a permanent record. Even purple construction paper will fade if left by a window in the sunlight and will make a permanent print of the pattern of filings.

Teacher Information

This is a great way to permanently preserve patterns of magnetic fields for viewing and discussion. Some very interesting patterns will evolve as students get involved. You will get face patterns and many other creative designs.

If spray adhesive is available, help your problem solvers to try at least one of the patterns using adhesive instead of paint. They will be excited to see the iron filings preserved as a part of the pattern. Be sure to let the adhesive dry completely before moving the card or the magnets, and the iron filings that are near the poles will retain their standing position. These patterns will need gentle handling to avoid knocking the iron filings off.

INTEGRATING: Art

SKILLS: Observing, inferring, classifying, predicting, communicating, identifying and controlling variables

Topic 18:   Static Electricity

TO THE TEACHER

The topic of static electricity has at least two things in common with magnetism: (1) the attraction and repulsion of one object for another, and (2) the attraction of all age groups to the topic. There is something, perhaps the element of mystery, that intrigues both young and old. Although our information about static electricity is still based largely on theory (another common thread with magnetism), much is known about its behavior. Through observation and experimentation, logical explanations of the phenomenon have developed.

Static electricity works best on a cool, clear day (moisture in the air tends to drain off the charge), but success with these activities is very high almost any time except, perhaps, on a hot, muggy day.

Static electricity is the object of curiosity, annoyance, and humor. During a severe electrical storm the emotion associated with it can be fear, in recognition of the all-too-real danger to life and property. The lightning bolt itself is current electricity because it is moving, but it results from the buildup of an electrostatic charge.

Several activities in this section involve objects receiving an electrostatic charge by induction. When two materials rub together, such as wool cloth and a balloon, electrons are transferred from one material to the other—from cloth to balloon, for instance. However, a neutral object can receive an *induced* charge simply by being near a charged object. If a neutral object is approached by a negatively charged object, the neutral object becomes positively charged. If the neutral object is approached by a positively charged object, the neutral object becomes negatively charged. The induced charge is always opposite that of the charged object. Thus, charged objects are attracted to neutral objects. A charged balloon will cling to a wall, a person, and so forth.

As you select materials to use with static electricity activities, avoid those that have been treated with antistatic chemicals. Such chemicals are often used in dishwashers (antispot substances), in clothes dryers (anticling products or fabric softeners), or on carpets and furniture (fabric protector). Sometimes these treatments can be washed out, and the materials can then be used for static electricity activities.

Although wool cloth is often suggested for use in static electricity activities because it gives up electrons readily to other materials rubbed by it, cotton cloth, flannel, and many other fabrics work well. Be sure the fabric is clean and is *not treated* by a fabric softener.

Activity 18.1
HOW CAN YOU FILL A STOCKING WITHOUT PUTTING A LEG INTO IT?

 Take home and do with family and friends.

Materials Needed

- Cool, dry day
- Sheer nylon stocking
- Clean lightweight plastic (such as a fresh vegetable bag from grocery store)
- Smooth wall, chalkboard, or cork board

Procedure

1. Holding it by the top, place the nylon stocking against the wall.
2. Use the plastic to rub and smooth the stocking against the wall. It is best to rub with long strokes in one direction from top to toe. Do this about 20 times.
3. Release your hold on the top of the stocking. What happened?
4. Keeping an arm's length away from the stocking, grasp at the top and slowly pull it away from the wall. Be sure nothing comes near it.
5. Still holding it at arm's length, do you observe any difference in the stocking?
6. Slowly bring the stocking toward you. What happened? Can you explain why this happened?

Teacher Information

This activity demonstrates induction and the attraction and repulsion of like and unlike static charges. Be sure the nylon you use has been washed thoroughly in clear water so any anticling treatment has been removed.

At first the nylon will hang limply against the wall. As the plastic is rubbed on the nylon it will remove electrons from the stocking, giving the stocking a positive charge. By the time the stocking has been stroked 20 times it should smooth out and cling to the wall without support. This is caused by a form of induction explained earlier in the section on static electricity.

When the stocking is pulled away from the wall and held at arm's length it will fill out in all directions as if an invisible leg were inside. This is because the entire stocking has a positive charge and like charges repel or push away from each other.

SKILLS: Observing, inferring, classifying, predicting, communicating, formulating hypotheses, identifying and controlling variables, experimenting

Activity 18.2
HOW CAN YOU BEND WATER?

 Take home and do with family and friends.

Materials Needed

- Sink
- Comb
- Wool cloth (or cotton)

Procedure

1. Turn on the water in the sink, just enough to get a very thin but steady stream.
2. Rub the comb vigorously with the cloth.
3. Bring the comb near the stream of water, being sure the comb does not touch the water.
4. What happened?
5. What do you think might have caused this? Discuss your ideas with your group.

Teacher Information

As has been the case with other activities, rubbing the comb with the cloth results in the comb taking on extra electrons and assuming a negative charge. Water molecules are polar, due to the way the two hydrogen atoms combine with an oxygen atom. This means the water molecule has a positive charge on one end and a negative charge on the other end. The negatively charged comb attracts the positive end of the water molecule, and the thin stream of water bends noticeably toward the comb.

SKILLS: Observing, inferring, communicating, formulating hypotheses

Activity 18.3
HOW CAN YOU MAKE AN ELECTROSCOPE?

(Upper grades)

Materials Needed

- Bottle with cork stopper
- Copper wire about 20 cm (8 in.) long
- Lightweight aluminum foil
- Nail
- Rubber comb
- Wool cloth
- Scissors
- Ruler

Procedure

1. Force the nail through the cork stopper to make a hole for the wire.
2. Remove the insulation from both ends of the wire.
3. Insert the copper wire through the cork stopper.
4. Bend the lower end of the wire (the end that will go inside the bottle) as illustrated in the following figure.

Assembled Electroscope

5. Cut a strip of aluminum foil approximately 1/2 cm (1/4 in.) wide and 3 cm (1.25 in.) long.

6. Fold the aluminum foil in half and let it hang over the end of the wire, as illustrated. *Be sure all insulation is removed from the wire where the foil rests.*

7. Put the stopper on the bottle, being careful not to jar the strip of aluminum foil off the end of the wire.

8. Rub the comb with the wool cloth and bring the comb near the top end of the wire. As you do this, observe the foil strip carefully.

9. What happened? Can you explain why?

10. Try the same thing with other charged objects.

For Problem Solvers: Examine the electroscope and explain why it works the way it does. Share your explanation with at least one of your classmates. When you and your classmates can agree on the way the electroscope works, explain it to your teacher.

Try to make a new design of the electroscope. What are the critical parts? What purpose does the bottle serve? The stopper? The wire? The foil? Can you make something else work in place of any of these? Maybe some of these parts are not even needed at all. Test out your ideas.

Teacher Information

The electroscope is an easy-to-make device and should not be difficult to assemble for students who are motivated. They can use it to demonstrate the presence of an electrostatic charge in a comb, a balloon, or other charged object. As the charged object is brought near the upper end of the copper wire, the wire, being a conductor, becomes charged by induction and transfers the charge to the foil. The entire foil strip receives the same charge, and the two ends repel each other.

The very thin foil stripped from a gum wrapper works better for this activity than does heavier aluminum foil used in wrapping food.

SKILLS: Observing, inferring, classifying, predicting, communicating, comparing and contrasting, formulating hypotheses, identifying and controlling variables, experimenting

Topic 19:   Current Electricity

TO THE TEACHER

The study of this topic should follow the studies of magnetism and static electricity, as it requires background information from both. The activities are nongraded, but teachers of young children will need to adapt language and instruction.

The amount of electric current used in these activities (1.5 to 6 volts) is perfectly safe if you follow directions to avoid overheating of circuits. If your flashlight has two batteries it uses three volts of electricity. **Caution: Never use household current directly for these activities.** In many activities, a high-quality transformer could substitute for batteries. Before using a transformer, be sure you know exactly how much voltage it produces and that it is safe to use. Flashlight cells may be wrapped together securely with electrical tape, end to end, just as they fit in a flashlight.

The majority of these activities suggest using a lantern battery, while a few of them suggest flashlight batteries. The flashlight battery has the advantage of cost, while the advantages of the lantern battery are (1) it will last much longer, and (2) it has connectors, making it much easier to connect wires to the batteries. Battery holders with easy connectors can be purchased or made for flashlight batteries, eliminating that problem.

Be sure that your bulbs are compatible with the voltage of the batteries being used. A bulb designed for 1.5 volts will burn out if you attach it to a 6-volt lantern battery.

Technically a *battery* consists of two or more cells connected together, and the flashlight battery is not a battery at all, but is more properly called a *dry cell*. However, single dry cells are so commonly called batteries that to insist on technically proper use of the terms is futile. The popular square 6-volt lantern battery is a true battery, containing four cells of 1.5 volts each (voltage of the four cells is added because they are connected in series within the battery). The rectangular 9-volt lantern battery contains six cells of 1.5 volts each.

Materials such as light sockets, bulbs, and insulated copper wire can be purchased at a hardware or electronics store. An inexpensive wire cutter and stripper (to remove insulation) is a necessary item.

Most activities are designed for individuals or small groups. Costs can be reduced by setting up a learning center and rotating groups through it.

Before you begin this section it would be helpful to read all activities. Some of the same materials are used several times in different ways.

Many schools have magnets that have become weak. You can rejuvenate magnets by wrapping a coil of wire around them and sending an electric current through the wire (see activities on electromagnets in the Current Electricity section). If you recharge bar magnets, be sure the current flows through the wire in the proper direction to produce the correct poles as marked (use a compass to check). A simple device for making bar magnets stronger can be made from a toilet tissue tube with a coil of wire wrapped in one direction around it. Simply insert a bar magnet in the tube and turn on the current for a few seconds. If the poles are reversed, repeat the process but turn the bar magnet around or switch the wires on the battery terminals to send the current in the opposite direction through the coil. Bar magnets can also be given new life by stroking them lengthwise several times across one pole of a powerful magnet. Stroke in one direction only. If poles are reversed, stroke in the opposite direction *or* use the other pole of the large magnet.

Enrichment activities for this unit could focus on new ways to produce electric current. Evaluation should use concrete materials, not just pencil and paper.

Activity 19.1
WHAT MATERIALS WILL CONDUCT ELECTRICITY?

Materials Needed

- Circuit as shown in the Figure on page 332, consisting of a lantern battery, lengths of insulated copper wire of 20 or 22 gauge, and a small light socket with miniature bulb
- Small objects made of different materials, such as paper clips, nails, wire, wood, rubber bands, glass, plastic, coins, rocks

Procedure

1. Test your circuit by touching the bare wires together. The light should go on.
2. Choose objects from the pile on the table. Touch both bare wires to each object about 2 cm (1 in.) apart and observe the light. If the item conducts electricity, the light will turn on.
3. Explain what is happening the best you can.

For Problem Solvers: Now that you have tested several small items to find out if they conduct electricity, take your circuit and test a lot of other things. Each time you think of a new material to check, first make a prediction of whether the material will conduct electricity, then check it out.

Classify the materials you used by making separate lists of materials that conduct electricity, materials that do not conduct electricity, and materials that surprised you. If you found some items that conduct electricity but not very well (the light came on, but it was dim), put them in a separate list.

Teacher Information

This activity introduces the idea of conductors and nonconductors. Nonconductors are sometimes called insulators. Most metals are conductors to some degree, since electricity will move through them. Some materials, such as glass, rubber, and plastic, are insulators, and electricity does not flow through them.

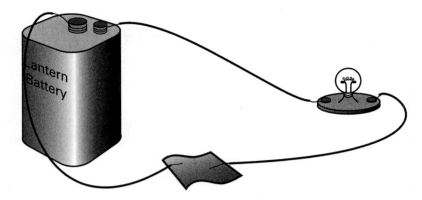

Battery, Bulb, and Wires

SKILLS: Observing, inferring, classifying, predicting, communicating, comparing and contrasting, formulating hypotheses, identifying and controlling variables, experimenting

Activity 19.2
WHAT IS A CIRCUIT?

 Take home and do with family and friends.

Materials Needed

- One 1.5-volt flashlight battery
- Two 25-cm (10 in.) lengths of single-strand insulated copper wire of 20 or 22 gauge
- Small light socket with flashlight bulb
- Small screwdriver

Procedure

1. In front of you are all the materials needed to make the light turn on. Can you connect them together so the bulb lights up? If you have trouble, read the following hints:

    a. Electricity will flow from the battery (power source) only if it has a complete path from one battery terminal (end) to the other.

    b. Electric current will go through the copper wire but not through the plastic or rubber insulation (covering).

    c. The bulb must be tight in its socket.

    d. The wires must be tightly connected.

2. What happens if the path from one battery terminal to the other is broken? Can you explain why?

3. When the light is on, this is called a complete circuit because it forms a complete path from the battery to the light and back to the battery.

For Problem Solvers: Remove the bulb from the socket and try to make the bulb light up without the socket. Use only the bulb, two wires, and the flashlight battery.

Make the bulb light by using only one wire.

Now that you know how to make a complete circuit, so the light comes on, try the activity with other people. You only need two wires, a flashlight battery, and a flashlight bulb. Give the materials to your dad, mom, brother, sister, a friend, or Great Uncle Newberry. See if they can make the light come on. Help them only if you have to, and don't be in too big a hurry to help—let them struggle for a while. Try it with several different people.

Teacher Information

One and one-half volts of electric current from a flashlight battery is perfectly safe for classroom use. This activity may be varied according to the age of the children. For younger children you may want to attach the wires to the socket and let them discover how to make it work by screwing the bulb in and touching the bare ends to the battery. Older children should be able to hook up the circuit by following the hints. You may need to help them clean off (strip) insulation from about 2 cm (1 in.) from each end of each wire. An inexpensive wire cutter and stripper obtainable from any hardware store is most helpful.

When completed, the circuit should look like the one shown in the figure below.

Numbers indicating the gauge (thickness) of wire are in the reverse order of their thickness. For example, 20-gauge wire is heavier than 22-gauge. An ideal gauge for most of these activities is often called bell wire.

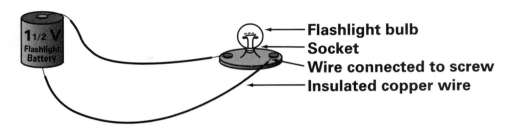

Battery and Bulb Connected in a Circuit

Your problem solvers will have an exciting time testing others on their newly learned skill. Your students will probably be surprised to learn that few adults can make the bulb light without a lot of struggle. They might even need help, which will do wonders for the self-confidence of the child. The real value will be that the child will learn how to make a complete circuit so well that he or she will probably never forget.

INTEGRATING: Language arts, social studies

SKILLS: Observing, inferring, classifying, predicting, communicating, comparing and contrasting, formulating hypotheses, identifying and controlling variables, experimenting, researching

Activity 19.3
HOW CAN WE MODEL A COMPLETE CIRCUIT?

(Group activity)

Materials Needed

- Group of students
- Labels "Battery" and "Light"
- Labels "Negative" and "Positive"

Procedure

1. Assign one person to be the battery and one person to be the light.
2. Put the labels on these two people.
3. Put the "Negative" label on the left arm of the "Battery" and the "Positive" label on the right arm of the "Battery." The arms now represent the negative and positive terminals of the battery.
4. Form a circle, with everyone holding hands.
5. Have the "Battery" squeeze the hand of the person on his or her left. That person should, in turn, squeeze with the left hand, and so goes the signal around the circle and back to the positive terminal of the "Battery."
6. This shows a complete circuit, with electricity flowing from the battery, all the way through the circuit, and back to the battery. The "Light" could smile brightly to show that the light turns on when the signal is received. This is called a *complete circuit*.
7. Have two people—any two—break the hand grip.
8. The "Battery" squeezes with the left hand again, but this time the signal stops where the break is, so it does not get back to the battery.
9. This time the "Light" does not smile, because electricity flows *only* if it has a complete circuit from the negative terminal of the battery all the way back to the positive terminal of the battery. This time it was an *incomplete circuit*.
10. Discuss this activity, sharing ideas about what happened and the difference between a complete circuit and an incomplete circuit.
11. Draw a complete circuit and an incomplete circuit, showing the battery, the bulb, and wire.

Teacher Information

It is hoped that this activity will help students begin to understand the difference between a complete circuit and an incomplete circuit and that electricity flows only if the circuit is complete.

In a good battery, chemicals react together in such a way that an abundance of electrons builds up at the negative terminal, with a shortage of electrons resulting at the positive terminal. That's why the terminals are called negative and positive. The natural tendency is toward neutrality, so when a conductor connects the negative terminal to the positive terminal, electrons flow through the conductor, from negative to positive, until the materials inside the battery are electrically neutral. Whether there is a light or other appliance in the circuit is immaterial to whether or not electrons will flow. We simply place an appliance in the circuit to take advantage of the fact that the battery will send electrons from the negative terminal to the positive terminal if the two terminals are connected.

If we remember that the reason electrons flow is to reduce the excess at the negative terminal and make up the shortage at the positive terminal, it's easy to understand why the circuit must be complete in order for electricity to flow. And incidentally, if the battery is still in good condition, the chemical reaction that caused the imbalance of electrons at the two terminals will continue and the battery will be ready to use again. It might take a few days for the battery to recharge itself, but if it isn't too old it will happen. This is not true of rechargeable batteries; these batteries use different chemicals and must be placed in a charger.

SKILLS: Observing, inferring, communicating, comparing and contrasting, using space-time relationships, formulating hypotheses

Activity 19.4
WHAT IS A SHORT CIRCUIT?

Materials Needed

- Complete circuit constructed in Activity 19.2
- One 25-cm (10-in.) length of copper wire, similar to that used in Activity 19.2, stripped on both ends

Procedure

1. Connect your circuit so there is a complete path and the light turns on.
2. Strip (clean off) the insulation from 1 cm (1/2 in.) in the center of each wire. Does the light still go on?
3. Put the bare ends of the extra piece of wire across the bare sections of your circuit wires. Does the light go on?
4. What do you think has happened? Why?
5. Feel the ends where the bare ends are touching. Do you notice anything?
6. You have made a short circuit. Discuss with your teacher and the other class members what that means.

Battery and Bulb, Short-circuited

Teacher Information

When the additional wire is placed across the circuit, the light goes out. A general rule in electrical circuits is that electricity will follow the path of least resistance. This means it will follow the shortest, easiest path back to its source (battery). In this example you have made the path shorter and avoided a resistor (the light bulb). If you permit current to flow through the short circuit for more than a few seconds, the wire will begin to heat up. This is caused by providing an easy path for electricity to flow. The amount of electricity going through the wire increases beyond its normal capacity.

Caution: Do not leave the circuit connected this way for more than a few seconds. If the battery is strong the wire might become hot enough to burn fingers, though it will still not cause an electrical shock. It will also run the battery down very rapidly.

SKILLS: Observing, inferring, predicting, communicating, comparing and contrasting, formulating hypotheses, identifying and controlling variables, experimenting

Activity 19.5
HOW CAN YOU MAKE A SWITCH?

(Teacher-supervised activity)

Materials Needed

- Complete circuit used in Activity 19.2
- Metal strip 10 cm (4 in.) long by 2 cm (1 in.) wide
- Strip of wood (lath) 15 cm (6 in.) long
- Two small wood screws
- Hammer and nail
- Screwdriver

Procedure

1. Use the hammer and nail to punch a hole near one end of the metal strip.
2. Use a screw to attach the metal strip near one end of the piece of wood (if you punch a small nail hole in the wood, the screw will go in more easily).
3. Install the other screw in the wood so that the loose end of the metal strip touches but is not attached to it. Bend the metal strip up about 2 cm (1 in.).
4. Cut one of your circuit wires in the middle of the bare place you made when you were constructing a short circuit.
5. Attach one end of the bare wire to each screw.
6. When you finish, your circuit should look like the figure below.
7. Can you use the switch to make the light turn on and off?
8. Discuss what the switch does.

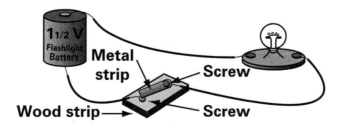

Battery and Bulb with Switch in Circuit

For Problem Solvers: In this activity you made a switch. An electrical switch is a device that allows you to easily turn electricity on and off. There are many ways you can make a switch. What other ways can you think of to make a switch? Can you make a switch out of a paper clip? Make several different kinds and test them in your circuit.

Teacher Information

If available, sheet copper should be used because it is easier to cut than sheet metal, and there is less chance of injury from sharp edges and corners. For best results, the wires should be under the screws when they are tightened down.

This circuit has the following parts:

a. A power source (battery).

b. A path through which the current can flow (wire).

c. An appliance (light) to use current.

d. A switch to turn it on and off.

SKILLS: Observing, inferring, measuring, predicting, communicating, identifying and controlling variables, experimenting

Activity 19.6
HOW CAN YOU MAKE A SERIES CIRCUIT?

Materials Needed

- Lantern battery
- Circuit from previous activity, including switch
- Two additional small light sockets with flashlight bulbs
- Two pieces of insulated single-strand copper wire 10 cm (4 in.) long
- Small screwdriver

Procedure

1. For this and some of the following activities, we will use a lantern battery instead of a flashlight battery. It is easier to use and will last longer.
2. In this activity, we will add two lights to our circuit.
3. Test to be certain your circuit will light the bulb.
4. Disconnect one wire from your light socket and connect it to one terminal of another socket with one 10-cm length of wire. Use another 10-cm length of wire to connect the other terminal of your second socket to the third socket. Connect the long wire from the battery to the third socket. When you finish, your circuit should look like the figure shown below.
5. Now close the switch. Do the lights come on? Unscrew one bulb. What happened? Can you explain why?

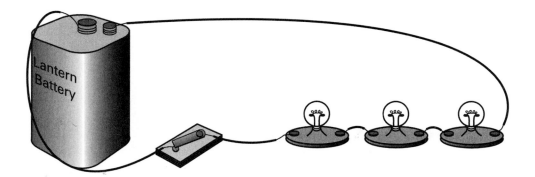

Battery, Switch, and Three Bulbs Wired in Series

Teacher Information

Before letting the children use the lantern batteries, you may want to remove the screw caps on the terminals to remind the children not to leave the wires connected when they are not in use. Lantern batteries have the advantage over flashlight batteries of being easier to handle and simpler to hook up. There is no danger of electrical shock from these batteries.

Be certain the two 10-cm lengths of wire are stripped on both ends. The circuit the students have constructed is called a series circuit because the electric current travels through the wire in one path and the resistors (lights) and switch are all part of that single path. If one portion of a series circuit is missing, the current will not flow, because it must have a complete path *from* the power source *to* the power source. If a light bulb is removed, the path is broken and all the lights go out.

INTEGRATING: Math

SKILLS: Observing, inferring, measuring, predicting, communicating, comparing and contrasting, formulating hypotheses, identifying and controlling variables, experimenting

Activity 19.7
HOW CAN YOU MAKE A PARALLEL CIRCUIT?

Materials Needed

- Series circuit from Activity 19.6
- Screwdriver
- Wire stripper
- Two additional pieces of insulated single-strand copper wire 10 cm (4 in.) long

Procedure

1. Use the additional pieces of wire to change your circuit so it looks like the one in the figure shown below.

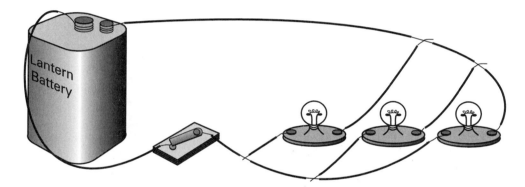

Battery, Switch, and Three Bulbs in Parallel

2. Close the switch so all bulbs are lit. Unscrew one bulb. What happened? Unscrew two bulbs.

3. Can you explain how this circuit is different from the one in Activity 19.6?

For Problem Solvers: In this activity and in Activity 19.6 you have learned about series and parallel circuits. You learned that an important difference is that if lights are wired in series, they all go out if one goes out. If they are wired in parallel, one light can go out and the rest of them stay on. Most sets of Christmas lights are wired in series. When one bulb burns out it's very difficult to tell which one is bad. Why do you think manufacturers make them that way? Talk to your family about it. Discuss it with your class. When Christmas season comes along, see how many light sets you can find that are wired in series and how many you can find that are wired in parallel. Which will you buy?

Teacher Information

A parallel circuit provides an independent path for the electric current to travel to each light and back to the power source. The lights will burn brighter because the current does not have to travel through a series of resistors (the other lights). And guess what—when one light goes out, the rest of the lights stay on.

The best living example of series versus parallel wiring comes to us each year at Christmas time. Thousands of perfectly good sets of Christmas lights are replaced each year because they are wired in series. One light goes out on the set and the entire set turns off. It simply isn't worth it to us to replace all of the bulbs one at a time in an effort to determine which bulb really is burned out. We trash the entire set and buy a new set. Manufacturers know that's what we'll do, so they keep making light sets in series. A very simple twist in the manufacturing process would wire the lights in parallel and we could easily replace one burned-out bulb, but we would then use the same set of lights for years and years. That would not sell lights! Search for the box that says something like "When one light goes out, the rest remain lighted." That set is worth much more than the one that invites you to replace the lights one at a time until the set comes on again. Think about that before you buy your next set of Christmas lights.

INTEGRATING: Reading, language arts, math, social studies

SKILLS: Observing, inferring, classifying, predicting, communicating, comparing and contrasting, formulating hypotheses, identifying and controlling variables, experimenting, researching

Activity 19.8
WHAT IS RESISTANCE?

Materials Needed

- Circuit used in Activity 19.1
- Large writing pencil with about 8 cm (3 in.) of wood removed on one half to expose the graphite core

Procedure

1. Touch the ends of the bare wire to the graphite ("lead") core of the pencil, as far apart as possible.
2. Slowly slide the bare wires closer together along the graphite and observe the light.
3. Can you use the information you have learned about conductors to explain this?
4. Have you seen anything like this principle used in a home or an automobile?

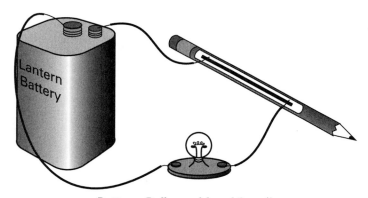

Battery, Bulb, and Lead Pencil

For Problem Solvers: If you have a switch at home that dims the lights, it works in about the same way as the pencil lead you used for this activity. A resistor switch is called a rheostat. This device makes it possible to change the amount of current going to an appliance (light, heater, etc.). Make a list of all the things you can think of that use resistor switches. Think about the kitchen. Think about the car. Share your list with others who are doing this activity and with your teacher.

Teacher Information

This is a demonstration of variable resistance. The core of a lead pencil isn't lead at all, but graphite. Graphite will conduct electric current, but not nearly as well as copper. Because it resists the flow of current, it is an example of one kind of resistor. As the bare copper wires are moved closer together, the resistance is gradually reduced and the light gradually becomes brighter. This is the principle of the rheostat used to dim automobile dash lights and some lights in homes, theaters, and public buildings.

INTEGRATING: Language arts, social studies

SKILLS: Observing, inferring, classifying, predicting, communicating, comparing and contrasting, formulating hypotheses, identifying and controlling variables, experimenting, researching

Activity 19.9
HOW DOES ELECTRIC CURRENT AFFECT A COMPASS?

Materials Needed

- Insulated 22-gauge copper wire, 50 cm (20 in.) long, stripped on each end
- Lantern battery
- Compass

Procedure

1. From your study of magnetism, do you remember that a compass is a magnet suspended so it can turn freely? The magnetic field of the earth causes it to point north unless another magnet or magnetic material comes near it.

2. Put your compass flat on the table and notice in which direction it is pointing.

3. Connect one end of the wire to a terminal of the battery and place the wire across the top of the compass.

4. Touch the other end of the wire to the second terminal of the battery (don't connect it).

5. Move the wire to different positions on top of the compass and observe the needle as you send current through the wire.

6. What is happening? Discuss this with the class.

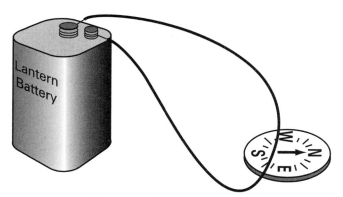

Battery, Wire, and Compass

Teacher Information

When an electric current flows through a wire, a magnetic field is formed around the wire. Through this activity, students may decide that electricity is in some way related to magnetism. The next activity will help them visualize what is really happening.

CAUTION: When the copper wire is connected, it creates a short circuit. The wire should be connected only momentarily; otherwise, it will get very hot and the electricity will drain rapidly. Many fires are started by short circuits.

SKILLS: Observing, inferring, predicting, communicating, formulating hypotheses, identifying and controlling variables, experimenting

Activity 19.10
WHAT HAPPENS WHEN ELECTRIC CURRENT FLOWS THROUGH A WIRE?

Materials Needed

- Circuit used in Activity 19.9
- Iron filings
- 5 × 7 inch card

Procedure

1. Connect one end of the wire to a terminal of the battery.
2. Place the card flat and level over the middle part of the wire.
3. Connect the other end of the wire to the battery and quickly sprinkle iron filings on the card.
4. Disconnect the wire and observe the card. *Do not* leave the wire connected to the battery for more than a few seconds at a time.
5. Have you seen something like this before? Look carefully at the filings.
6. What conclusions can you make? Discuss this with the class.

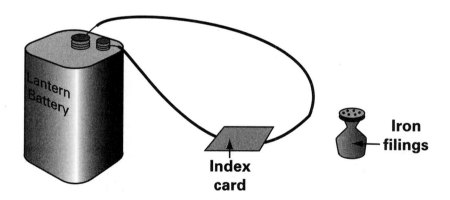

Battery, Wire, Card, and Iron Filings

Teacher Information

When current flows through the wire, the iron filings will line up along the path of the wire because of the magnetic field created around it. Note that iron filings do not line up with the wire, but perpendicular to it instead. This indicates that the lines of force of the magnetic field are perpendicular to the direction of the flow of current.

SKILLS: Observing, inferring, predicting, communicating, formulating hypotheses, identifying and controlling variables, experimenting

Activity 19.11
WHAT IS AN ELECTROMAGNET?

Materials Needed

- 1 m (1 yd.) of 22-gauge insulated copper wire stripped on both ends
- Lantern battery
- Large iron nail no longer than 10 cm (4 in.)
- Paper clips

Procedure

1. In Activities 19.9 and 19.10, we learned that when an electric current flows through a wire, a magnetic field is formed around the wire.

2. Coil the wire ten times around the nail. Bring the nail near some paper clips. What happened?

3. Attach one end of the wire to a terminal of the battery. Bring the nail near some paper clips. Touch the other end of the wire to the other terminal of the battery. What happened?

4. Hold the nail above the table and disconnect the wire from one terminal of the battery.

5. What happened?

6. Explain why you think this happened.

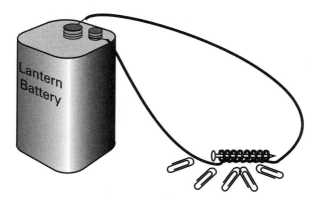

Electromagnet with Paper Clips

Teacher Information

The nail will not pick up paper clips until current flows through the coil of wire. When current flows through the coil of wire, a magnetic field is created around the coil and causes the soft iron nail to become a temporary magnet and attract the paper clips. When the electric current is cut off, the nail will lose its magnetism and the clips will fall off.

The nail you use should be no longer than about 10 cm (4 in.). Very large, thick nails will sometimes retain their magnetic properties for a longer period of time and will not release the paper clips readily when the current is turned off.

INTEGRATING: Math

SKILLS: Observing, inferring, comparing and contrasting, identifying and controlling variables, experimenting

Activity 19.12
WHAT IS A WAY TO CHANGE THE STRENGTH OF AN ELECTROMAGNET?

Materials Needed

- Same as for Activity 19.11

Procedure

1. As you perform the activities with electromagnets, remember not to leave the electromagnets connected to the battery for more than a few seconds at a time.

2. Use your electromagnet with 10 coils to pick up as many paper clips as you can at one time. Record the number of clips it picked up.

3. Wrap 10 more coils of wire around the nail, connect it to the battery, and see how many clips you can pick up at one time. Record the number.

4. What do you think would happen if you wrapped 10 more coils around your electromagnet? Try it.

5. What can you say about this?

Teacher Information

Increasing the number of coils of wire will increase the strength of the magnetic field. This is one way to make an electromagnet stronger. Using a stronger electric current will also increase the force of an electromagnet.

INTEGRATING: Math

SKILLS: Observing, inferring, measuring, predicting, communicating, comparing and contrasting, formulating hypotheses, identifying and controlling variables, experimenting

Activity 19.13
WHAT IS ANOTHER WAY TO CHANGE THE STRENGTH OF AN ELECTROMAGNET?

Materials Needed

- Two lantern batteries
- 1 m of insulated copper wire
- One 10-cm (4-in.) length of insulated copper wire stripped at both ends
- One large nail
- Box of paper clips
- Paper and pencil

Procedure

1. Make an electromagnet with ten coils of wire wrapped around the nail.

2. Use one battery with your electromagnet and see how many clips you can pick up at one time. Record the results.

3. Observe your lantern battery. Notice it has a terminal (connector) in the center and one near the outside edge. Unless otherwise marked, the center terminal is called positive (+) and the outer terminal is called negative (–).

4. Use the 10-cm wire to connect a second battery in series (connect the wire from the negative terminal of one battery to the positive terminal of the other battery). This increases the voltage to the sum total of the voltage of both batteries.

5. Connect your electromagnet as shown in the figure below and pick up as many clips as you can. Record the number of clips.

6. What do you think would happen if you used two batteries and 20 coils of wire? Try it.

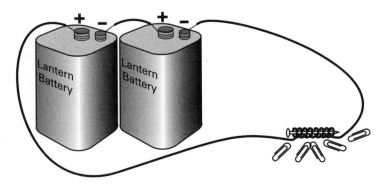

Electromagnet with Two Batteries and Paper Clips

For Problem Solvers: In this activity and Activity 19.12, you learned two ways to change the strength of an electromagnet. Earlier you learned how to make a switch. Build an electromagnet with a switch in the circuit, so it's easy to turn the magnet on and off. Try different sizes and types of nails and bolts as the core. See if you can find a brass bolt to try as the core. Find a steel bolt to use instead of iron. Find out what works best and what doesn't work so well.

Use the shaft of a screwdriver as the core of an electromagnet. How does it work differently from the nail or bolt? Does it release all the paper clips when you turn off the power? Oops.

Do some research about electromagnets. Make a list of some ways they are used.

Teacher Information

Series wiring is commonly used to increase the voltage of dry-cell batteries. Six- and nine-volt batteries contain four and six cells. Each cell produces 1.5 volts, and when they are connected in series the voltage is added. More about batteries and how they work is developed later in this section.

INTEGRATING: Math

SKILLS: Observing, inferring, measuring, predicting, communicating, comparing and contrasting, formulating hypotheses, identifying and controlling variables, experimenting

Activity 19.14
WHAT HAPPENS WHEN CURRENT FLOWING THROUGH A WIRE CHANGES DIRECTION?

Materials Needed

- 50-cm (20 in.) length of insulated single-strand copper wire stripped at both ends
- Lantern battery
- Compass

Procedure

1. Place the center of the wire over the compass as you did in Activity 19.9. Touch the ends of the wire to the terminals of the battery and watch the needle.

2. Now touch the ends of the wire to the opposite terminals of the battery. Since electricity flows *from* the negative (–) terminal *to* the positive (+), you have reversed the flow of current through the wire.

3. Switch the ends of the wires several times. What happens to the compass needle?

4. Discuss your observations with your group.

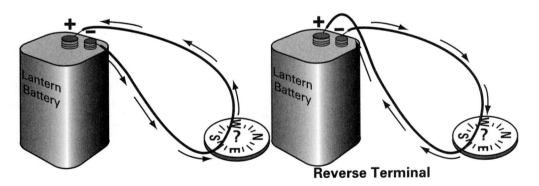

Reverse Terminal

**Compasses Near Wires
with Current Flowing in Opposite Directions**

Teacher Information

The direction of flow of electric current has not been a factor until now. At this point you should emphasize that electricity that is produced by a battery flows in one direction through the wire. It flows from the negative terminal of the battery to the positive terminal when a path is provided. We will discover later that some current moves back and forth, or *alternates*, within a wire.

Each time the direction of the flow of current changes in this activity, the compass needle will reverse, indicating that the poles of the electromagnetic field reverse when the direction of the flow of current is reversed.

SKILLS: Observing, inferring, communicating, comparing and contrasting, formulating hypotheses, identifying and controlling variables, experimenting

Activity 19.15
HOW DOES THE DIRECTION OF THE FLOW OF CURRENT AFFECT AN ELECTROMAGNET?

Materials Needed

- Electromagnet used in Activity 19.13
- Lantern battery
- Compass
- Two bar magnets
- String 20 cm (8 in.) long

Procedure

1. **Important: Throughout this activity, disconnect one wire from the battery except for the moment that you are using the electromagnet.**

2. Place the compass flat on the table. Connect your electromagnet to the battery and bring one point of it near the compass. Observe which end of the needle points to the electromagnet.

3. Switch the ends of the wires leading to the battery terminals. What happens to the compass needle?

4. Suspend one bar magnet from the piece of string. Bring each end of the other bar magnet near the N end of the suspended magnet. What happened? This should help you remember a characteristic of magnets that you learned when you were studying magnetism.

5. Bring your nail and coil of wire near both ends of the suspended bar magnet (don't connect it to the battery yet). What happened?

6. Connect the wires to the battery and bring the pointed end of the nail near the N end of the suspended bar magnet.

7. Now turn your electromagnet around so the flat end of the nail comes near the N end of the suspended bar magnet. What happened?

8. Keep the flat end near the suspended bar magnet and reverse the flow of current through your electromagnet by switching the wires on the battery terminals. Do this several times and observe the behavior of the bar magnet (don't move the electromagnet).

9. Describe your observations. What can you say about this characteristic of an electromagnet?

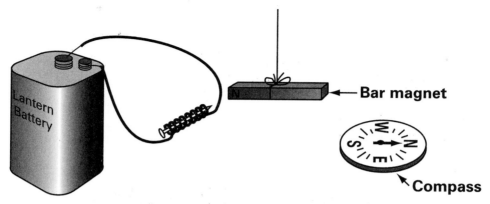

Electromagnet, Compass, and Suspended Magnet

For Problem Solvers: You have discovered a very important relationship between magnetism and electricity. All electric motors work on two principles that you have learned—first, that a flow of electricity through a wire creates a magnetic field around the wire, and second, changing the direction of the current reverses the poles of an electromagnet.

Now do some research and see how much you can learn about electric motors and how they work on these principles of magnetism and electricity. You might want to even try building a simple electric motor that actually runs.

Teacher Information

Like permanent magnets, electromagnets have poles. When the direction of the flow of current is reversed (in this case by switching wires on the terminals), the poles of the electromagnet reverse. This characteristic of electromagnets gives them an advantage over permanent magnets in some applications. Because of this phenomenon, electric motors are possible. To demonstrate this try the following:

Have one student hold the electromagnet near the suspended bar magnet. Have another student touch the wires to the battery. As soon as the poles of the two magnets come close to each other, switch the wires on the terminals of the battery. The pole of the electromagnet, which was attracting a pole of the bar magnet, will reverse and repel the same pole of the bar magnet (remember opposites attract, likes repel). With practice, the students can make the bar magnet spin around by reversing the poles of the electromagnet. Now all that is needed is a device to switch the direction of current automatically and you have a simple electric motor.

SKILLS: Observing, inferring, communicating, comparing and contrasting, formulating hypotheses, identifying and controlling variables, experimenting

Activity 19.16
HOW CAN YOU TELL IF ELECTRIC CURRENT IS FLOWING THROUGH A WIRE?

Materials Needed

- 10 m (11 yds.) of 24-gauge insulated copper wire stripped at both ends
- Three 10-cm (4-in.) lengths of wire
- One 30-cm (12-in.) length of wire
- Sewing needle
- One 20-cm (8-in.) strip of wood lath
- Lantern battery
- Thread
- Paper clip
- Bar magnet

Procedure

1. Make a coil with your long piece of wire by winding it around a lantern battery or small fruit jar. Leave about 50 cm (20 in.) of wire at each end.

2. Remove the coil from the battery and use the 10-cm (4-in.) pieces of wire to hold the coil together in three places.

3. Use the 30-cm (12-in.) wire to secure the coil in an upright position on the lath.

4. Magnetize the needle by rubbing it 30 times in the same direction with a bar magnet. It should now pick up a paper clip.

5. Use thread to hang the needle balanced in the middle of the coil. Compare your finished product with the following figure.

6. We have learned that electric current flowing through a wire creates a magnetic field around the wire. We found that when the wire is coiled, the magnetic field is stronger. The needle is a magnet. If an electric current flows through the coil of wire, what do you predict will happen to the needle?

7. Touch the bare ends of your coil of wire to the dry cell. Was your prediction correct?

8. This is a simple galvanometer used to detect the direction and flow of electric current. Touch the wires to a battery and notice the direction the needle points. Now, switch the wires on the terminals of the battery and notice the direction the needle points. This device can be used to detect the flow of even small amounts of electric current.

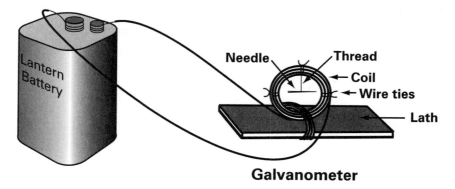

Coil of Wire with Suspended Needle

For Problem Solvers: In this activity you made a galvanometer. Design your own galvanometer. Try more windings in the coil. Try fewer windings in the coil. Try placing a directional compass within the coil instead of a suspended needle on a thread. What other variables can you think of to change it and perhaps make it better or easier to use?

Teacher Information

Ideally, each child should construct a galvanometer. Groups of three or four students working on one galvanometer should be maximum. If a student is able to construct, explain, and predict the behavior of a galvanometer, it will indicate that he or she understands some of the important ideas about magnetism and electricity.

Your problem solvers will substitute a directional compass for the suspended needle.

Very thin insulated wire is best for this activity in order to provide many windings without excessive bulk. The more windings the galvanometer has, the more sensitive it will be to small amounts of current electricity.

SKILLS: Observing, inferring, communicating, comparing and contrasting, formulating hypotheses, identifying and controlling variables, experimenting

Activity 19.17
HOW IS ELECTRICITY PRODUCED BY CHEMICALS?

Materials Needed

- Wide-mouthed glass cup or jar
- 8-cm (3-in.) zinc strip
- 8-cm (3-in.) copper strip
- Salt
- Lemon juice
- Water
- Galvanometer

Procedure

1. Pour water into the jar or cup until it is three-fourths full.
2. Dissolve two teaspoons of salt in the water.
3. Tightly connect one end of your galvanometer to the copper strip and put it in the glass. Bend the zinc strip into a hook on one end and hang it inside the glass.
4. Wait a few seconds. Then observe the needle of your galvanometer as you firmly touch the other wire to the zinc strip.
5. What happened? Wait a few seconds, then touch the wire to the zinc again.
6. Discuss your observations with your group.

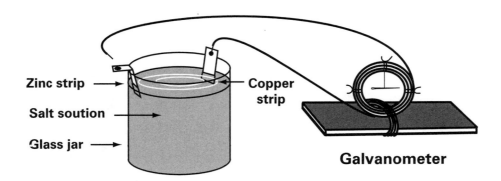

Homemade Cell and Galvanometer

For Problem Solvers: Try vinegar as the electrolyte instead of saltwater, and do the activity again. (Be sure to rinse the jar thoroughly whenever you change the electrolyte.) Try lemon juice. Replace the copper strip with the carbon rod. Try a penny in the place of the copper strip, and a silver dime instead of the zinc (you'll have to find a dime that's several years old in order to get silver).

Teacher Information

When placed in an acid or base (alkaline) solution, some materials give up or take on electrons readily through a chemical process called ionization. Zinc metal builds up electrons and becomes the negative terminal. When a negative material (zinc) is connected to a positive material (copper or carbon) in the solution, electrons flow along the path from the zinc to the copper or carbon. In this circuit the galvanometer is in the path and detects the flow of current. You can explain this using the diagram in the figure by adding plus (+) along the side of the copper or carbon rod and minus (–) along the zinc strip.

The reason the children are asked to wait a few seconds before touching the wire to the zinc is to allow time to build opposite charges on the copper and zinc strips.

Carbon rods and zinc strips may be obtained by dismantling old-style flashlight batteries. A carbon core runs through the center and the case is made of zinc. The newer long-life batteries are constructed differently, though the same basic principles apply as they develop an electrical charge. Six-volt lantern batteries contain four 1.5-volt cells.

SKILLS: Observing, inferring, communicating, comparing and contrasting, formulating hypotheses, identifying and controlling variables, experimenting

Activity 19.18
HOW DOES A LANTERN BATTERY OR FLASHLIGHT BATTERY WORK?

(Teacher-supervised activity or teacher demonstration)

Materials Needed

- Flashlight battery (old style–lead-acid) cut in half
- Paper and pencil
- Figure in Activity 19.17 (for comparison)

Procedure

1. Compare the half battery with the materials you used in Activity 19.17.
2. Except for the galvanometer, all the types of materials used in Activity 19.17 can be identified in the battery. Can you find them?
3. Draw a picture of a battery cut in half. Label the parts. Compare your picture with those made by other members of the group. Explain how you think it works.
4. Have you ever seen a battery leak and damage a flashlight? Batteries contain a weak acid or alkaline solution, usually in a tightly packed absorbent material. Since your battery is old, this solution has probably dried up.

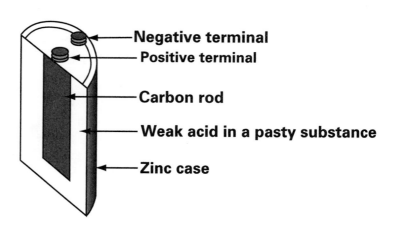

- Negative terminal
- Positive terminal
- Carbon rod
- Weak acid in a pasty substance
- Zinc case

Cross Section of Lantern Battery

For Problem Solvers: With close supervision, dismantle a flashlight battery that is a newer, long-life variety. How is it different? Do some research and find out what materials are in this particular battery and how they react together to cause electrons to flow.

Teacher Information

By the end of this experience, students should be able to explain in general terms how electricity is produced by chemical means. Elementary-age students should simply understand that certain materials will develop a positive or negative charge in the presence of an acid or a base (salt), and that when these materials are connected by a conductor (wire), electricity flows through the conductor from negative to positive.

The battery shown in this activity is the lead-acid battery, which has been used for many years. Newer long-life batteries operate on the same principles, but they use different materials. You might choose to open both for comparison.

The old-style tall 1.5 volt lantern battery and the old-style lead-acid flashlight battery are constructed similar to the one shown. The six-volt lantern battery has four such cells connected in series. The nine-volt lantern battery has six such cells, again connected in series. Each cell produces one and one-half volts.

Technically the word battery implies a collection, so the four-cell and six-cell units are true batteries, while the single units are more properly called "cells." However, the single-cell unit is so commonly called a battery that to carefully distinguish between them is probably more confusing than helpful. Flashlight cells are even labeled as *batteries*.

Note: Batteries can be cut with a hacksaw.

CAUTION: This activity involves the use of cut-open flashlight cells, exposing acid substances. Close supervision is very important to keep the acid from getting in eyes or on skin, or on clothing or other materials that might be damaged by the acid. Wash hands thoroughly after handling the cells.

SKILLS: Observing, inferring, comparing and contrasting, formulating hypotheses

Activity 19.19
HOW CAN ELECTRICITY BE PRODUCED BY A LEMON?

(Close supervision is required)

Materials Needed

- Large, fresh lemon
- Zinc and copper strips
- Galvanometer
- Knife

Procedure

1. Just for fun, let's try to make a battery from a lemon.

2. Make two small slits in the lemon, close together, with the knife.

3. Attach the copper strip to one wire of the galvanometer and insert it into one of the slits in the lemon.

4. Push the zinc strip into the other slit. The zinc strip must not touch the copper strip.

5. Wait a few seconds, then observe the needle on the galvanometer as you firmly touch the wire to the zinc strip. What happened? Wait a few seconds more and try again.

6. Using information you learned in Activities 19.17 and 19.18, explain what is happening.

7. Could you use another fruit such as a grapefruit or a tomato? Try it.

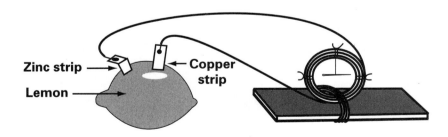

Zinc strip →

Lemon →

← Copper strip

Lemon Cell with Galvanometer

For Problem Solvers: There are many chemicals that can be used to create a flow of electrons. Try this activity with other citrus fruits. Try it with the juice in a cup instead of using the fruit itself. Try a penny in the place of the copper strip, and a silver dime (you'll have to find one that's several years old to get silver) instead of the zinc. Take it from there and continue your exploration. Be sure to write everything you use and what happened, so you will remember and be able to share your information.

Teacher Information

The lemon contains citric acid, which will cause the same reaction as other weak acids. Tomatoes and citrus fruits usually contain enough acid to affect the galvanometer.

SKILLS: Observing, inferring, communicating, comparing and contrasting, formulating hypotheses, identifying and controlling variables, experimenting

Activity 19.20
HOW CAN MECHANICAL ENERGY PRODUCE ELECTRICITY?

Materials Needed

- Galvanometer
- Galvanometer coil without needle
- Strong magnet

Procedure

1. Securely attach the wires from one coil to the other.
2. Hold the coil without the needle in one hand and with the other hand move the strong magnet back and forth through the center of the coil or around the coil.
3. Observe the needle on the galvanometer. Can you see a relationship in what is happening?
4. Think of some words to describe the behavior of the needle. Discuss this with your teacher and other students.

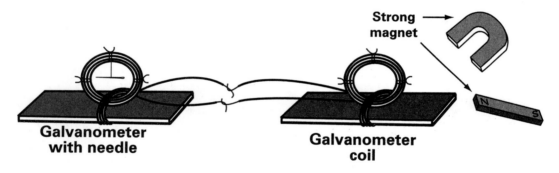

Figure 19.20-1

Coil of Wire, Galvanometer, and Two Magnets

For Problem Solvers: Can you use the idea from this activity to design a generator? Figure out a way that you can spin a magnet within a coil of wire, or spin a coil of wire within a magnetic field. Try to design your generator with more than one coil or more than one magnet.

Teacher Information

When electric current flows through a coil of wire, a magnetic field is created around the wire. You will remember that from your experience in making electromagnets; that's why electromagnets work. In this activity the opposite is happening. Instead of producing a magnetic field around a coil of wire by sending an electric current through the wire, we are causing electrons to flow by moving a coil of wire within a magnetic field. Because of this phenomenon, the generator, which turns coils of wire through a magnetic field, has made electricity relatively inexpensive and plentiful.

Observe the needle closely as the magnet goes through the coil and you will notice that it reverses the direction in which it is pointing each time the magnet moves back and forth. This shows that as the magnetic field moves back and forth, the electrons move back and forth or *alternate* their direction within the wire. Electricity produced in this manner is called *alternating current*.

If you examine a small hand generator (crank type) you will notice it is nothing more than a coil of wire turned mechanically in a magnetic field. Commercial electricity is usually produced by water or steam. A turbine, which is an enclosed wheel with curved blades, spins rapidly when water or steam is directed into it under great pressure. This provides the mechanical energy to turn huge generators. Atomic energy is sometimes used to heat water and create steam to turn the turbines.

Many people think that hydroelectric plants somehow *extract* electricity from water as the water rushes through the dam. The dam is engineered to direct falling water through turbines, providing the power to spin coils of wire within magnetic fields, stimulating the flow of electrons through the wire. See your encyclopedia for further information.

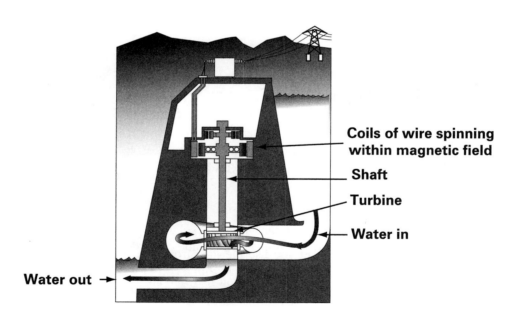

Figure 19.20-2
Generator

SKILLS: Observing, inferring, communicating, formulating hypotheses, identifying and controlling variables, experimenting

369

Activity 19.21
HOW CAN SUNLIGHT PRODUCE ELECTRICITY?

Materials Needed

- Solar cells
- Galvanometer
- Light source

Procedure

1. In recent years scientists have been trying to find new sources of electricity to replace our rapidly diminishing fossil fuel resources (coal and oil). A most promising source is solar (sun) energy. Look at your solar cell. When light strikes this cell, a very small amount of electrical energy is produced.

2. Connect your cell to the galvanometer and shine a bright light on it. As you turn the light on and off, observe the needle on the galvanometer. What happens to the needle?

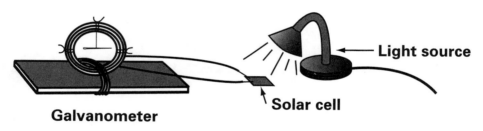

Solar Cell in Galvanometer Circuit, with Light Source

For Problem Solvers: If you can get some solar cells, learn how to connect them to operate a small light bulb. Perhaps you can find some discarded calculators and use the solar cells from them.

Do some research and see what you can learn about solar energy as a source of electricity. Make a list of all of the things you can find that are powered by solar energy. Will it likely ever be a major source of electricity for our homes and factories?

Can solar energy be used as a power source for electric cars? Write to General Motors (ask about their Sun Racer) and to Ford Motor Company and ask for information about their research on solar batteries and solar-powered cars.

Teacher Information

Solar energy is becoming increasingly important and common in our lives. Most children have seen solar cells used in calculators, cameras, and other devices that require small amounts of electricity.

The space program has rapidly expanded the development of this energy source. Satellites use electricity produced in this manner to recharge the batteries that provide electrical power.

A major obstacle to wide use of solar power is the limited amount of electric current each cell can produce. Huge areas of solar cells are required to produce significant amounts of electrical energy. The current produced flows in one direction, just as in flashlight batteries. Also, on the earth, solar cells as primary producers of electrical energy are limited to daylight hours and further inhibited by cloudy days.

Solar cells (often in clusters connected in series) can be obtained from many electronic supply stores.

INTEGRATING: Social studies

SKILLS: Observing, inferring, classifying, communicating, comparing and contrasting, formulating hypotheses, researching

Activity 19.22
HOW CAN ELECTRICITY HELP US COMMUNICATE?

Materials Needed

- Two small light sockets with bulbs
- Two switches
- Lantern battery
- Six 1-m (1-yd.) lengths of insulated copper wire

Procedure

1. Use your materials to construct a circuit like the one in the figure shown below.
2. Press one switch. What happened?
3. Release the first switch and press the second one. What happened?
4. Press both switches at once.
5. Can you think of some use for a device like this?
6. If it is available, you could splice more wire into the circuit and take one switch and light into another room.

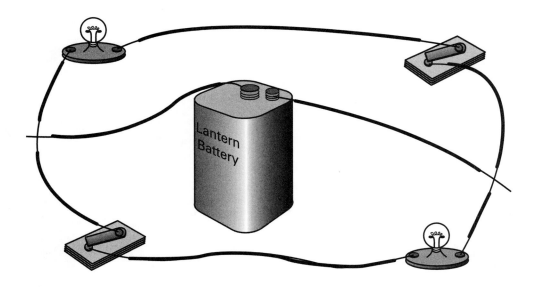

Two Telegraphs Wired to One Battery

For Problem Solvers: Look up the Morse Code in an encyclopedia. If you and a friend would care to learn the Morse Code, you could have a lot of fun sending messages to each other. Or you might prefer to create your own code. Set up your telegraph sets so that you can be in separate rooms, or in separate parts of the room, and make each other's light blink with your switch.

Teacher Information

This is a variation of the telegraph. There are several ways to wire the circuit. This one is parallel. The original telegraph sets were wired in series so all keys but one had to be closed and all messages went through all the *sounders* in the circuit. Telegraph offices often followed the railroads and needed only one wire on the poles. The iron rails were used as the second or *ground* wire. The original telegraph, patented by Morse, used an electromagnet to attract a magnetic material (soft iron) and make a loud clicking sound. Telegraphers were trained to hear combinations of long and short "dots and dashes" to represent letters of the alphabet. This is called the Morse Code.

The completion of the transcontinental telegraph near the end of the Civil War was extremely significant. For the first time, a message could travel across the nation in seconds rather than in weeks. The circuit above uses the electric light, which was not invented until much later.

In addition to the activity suggested in the "For Problem Solvers" section, your motivated students might enjoy designing and constructing a telegraph using electromagnets.

INTEGRATING: Social studies

SKILLS: Communicating, comparing and contrasting, identifying and controlling variables

BIBLIOGRAPHY

Selected Professional Texts

Carin, Arthur A., *Teaching Science Through Discovery* (7th ed.). New York: Macmillan Publishing Co., 1993.

Esler, William K., and Mary K. Esler, *Teaching Elementary Science* (6th ed.). Belmont, CA: Wadsworth Publishing Co., 1993.

Gega, Peter C., *Science in Elementary Education* (7th ed.). New York: Macmillan Publishing Co., 1994.

Tolman, Marvin N., and Garry R. Hardy, *Discovering Elementary Science: Method, Content, and Problem-Solving Activities*. Needham Heights, MA: Allyn & Bacon, 1995.

Victor, Edward, and Richard D. Kellough, *Science for the Elementary School* (7th ed.). New York: Macmillan Publishing Company, 1993.

Periodicals for Teachers and Children

Astronomy. Astro Media Corp., 625 E. St. Paul Ave., Milwaukee, WI 53202.

Audubon. National Audubon Society, 950 Third Ave., New York, NY 10022.

Cricket. Open Court Publishing Co., Box 100, LaSalle, IL 61301. Published monthly.

The Curious Naturalist. Massachusetts Audubon Society, South Lincoln, MA 01773. Nine issues per year.

Discover. Time Inc., 3435 Wilshire Blvd., Los Angeles, CA 90010.

Ladybug. Carus Publishing Co., 315 Fifth St., Peru, IL 61354. Published monthly.

National Geographic. National Geographic Society, 17th and M Sts. NW, Washington, DC 20036.

National Geographic School Bulletin. National Geographic Society, 17th and M Sts. NW, Washington, DC 20036. Published weekly during the regular school year.

National Geographic World. National Geographic Society, 17th and M Sts. NW, Washington, DC 20036.

Natural History. American Museum of Natural History, Central Park West at 79th St., New York, NY 10024.

Odyssey. AstroMedia, 625 E. St. Paul Ave., Milwaukee, WI 53202. Published monthly.

Ranger Rick. 1412 16th St. NW, Washington, DC 20036. Eight issues per year.

Science. American Association for the Advancement of Science, 1515 Massachusetts Ave. N.W., Washington, DC 20005.

Science and Children. National Science Teachers Association, 1840 Wilson Blvd., Arlington, VA 22201. Published monthly during the regular school year.

Science Digest. 3 Park Avenue, New York, NY 10016. Published monthly.

Science Scope. National Science Teachers Association, 1840 Wilson Blvd., Arlington, VA 22201. Published monthly during the regular school year.

Smithsonian. Smithsonian Associates, 900 Jefferson Dr., Washington, DC 20560.

Super Science. Scholastic, Inc., 730 Broadway, New York, NY 10003-9538.

3–2–1 Contact. Children's Television Workshop, P.O. Box 2933, Boulder, CO 80322. Published monthly during the regular school year.

SELECTED SOURCES OF FREE AND INEXPENSIVE MATERIALS FOR ELEMENTARY SCIENCE

Note: Requests for free materials should be made in writing and on school or district letterhead. Only one letter per class should be sent to a given organization. It is a courtesy, when requesting free materials, to provide postage and a return envelope. It is most important to send a thank-you letter when free materials have been received.

The following list includes only those organizations and agencies who specifically approved their being included in the list.

American Gas Association
Education Programs
1515 Wilson Blvd.
Arlington, VA 22209

American Museum of Natural History
Education Dept.
Central Park W. at 79th St.
New York, NY 10024-5192

American Petroleum Institute
Public Relations Dept.
1220 L St. NW
Washington, DC 20005

American Water Works Association
Student Programs Manager
6666 W. Quincy Ave.
Denver, CO 80235

Animal Welfare Institute
P.O. Box 3650
Washington, DC 20007

Freebies: The Magazine with Something
    for Nothing
1145 Eugenia Place
Carpinteria, CA 93013

National Aeronautics & Space
    Administration
Education Services Branch FEE
Washington, DC 20546

National Cotton Council of America
Communications Services
P.O. Box 12285
Memphis, TN 38182-0285

National Geographic Society
1145 17th St. NW
Washington, DC 20036

National Institute of Dental Research
P.O. Box 547-93
Washington, DC 20032

Procter & Gamble
Educational Services
P.O. Box 599
Cincinnati, OH 45201-0599

For more comprehensive listings of sources of free and inexpensive materials, see the following sources. Annual editions are available for purchase from: Educators Progress Service, 214 Center St., Randolph, WI 53956.

Educators Guide to Free Audio and Visual Materials

Educators Guide to Free Films

Educators Guide to Free Filmstrips and Slides

Educators Guide to Free Science Materials

SELECTED SCIENCE SUPPLY HOUSES

American Science & Surplus/Jerryco
601 Linden Place
Evanston, IL 60202

Arbor Scientific
P.O. Box 2750
Ann Arbor, MI 48106-2750

Astronomical Society of the Pacific
390 Ashton Ave.
San Francisco, CA 94112

Baxter Diagnostics, Inc.
Scientific Products Division
1430 Waukegan Rd.
McGaw Park, IL 60085-6787

Brock Optical
P.O. Box 940831
Maitland, FL 32794

Carolina Biological Supply Co.
2700 York Rd.
Burlington, NC 27215

Celestial Products, Inc.
P.O. Box 801
Middleburg, VA 22117

Central Scientific Co. (CENCO)
11222 Melrose Ave.
Franklin Park, IL 60131

Chem Shop
1151 S. Redwood Rd.
Salt Lake City, UT 84104

Creative Teaching Associates
P.O. Box 7766
Fresno, CA 93747

Cuisenaire Co. of America, Inc.
P.O. Box 5026
White Plains, NY 10602-5026

Dale Seymour Publications
P.O. Box 10888
Palo Alto, CA 94303-0879

Delta Education
P.O. Box 915
Hudson, NH 03051-0915

Denoyer-Geppert Science Co.
5225 Ravenswood Ave.
Chicago, IL 60640-2028

Didax Educational Resources
One Centennial Dr.
Peabody, MA 01960

Discovery Corner
Lawrence Hall of Science
University of California
Berkeley, CA 94720

Edmund Scientific
101 E. Gloucester Pike
Barrington, NJ 08007-1380

Educational Rocks & Minerals
P.O. Box 574
Florence, MA 01060

Energy Sciences
16728 Oakmont Ave.
Gaithersburg, MD 20877

Estes Industries
1295 H St.
Penrose, CO 81240

Fisher Scientific
4901 W. LeMoyne St.
Chicago, IL 60651

Flinn Scientific, Inc.
131 Flinn St.
P.O. Box 219
Batavia, IL 60510

Forestry Suppliers, Inc.
P.O. Box 8397
Jackson, MS 39284-8397

Frey Scientific
905 Hickory Lane
P.O. Box 8101
Mansfield, OH 44901-8101

General Supply Corp.
303 Commerce Park Dr.
P.O. Box 9347
Jackson, MS 39286-9347

Grau-Hall Scientific
6501 Elvas Ave.
Sacramento, CA 95819

Hawks, Owls & Wildlife
R.D. 1, Box 293
Buskirk, NY 12028

Hubbard Scientific
3101 Iris Ave., Suite 215
Boulder, CO 80301

Idea Factory, Inc.
10710 Dixon Dr.
Riverview, FL 33569

Ideal School Supply Co.
11000 S. Lavergne Ave.
Oak Lawn, IL 60453

Insights Visual Productions
P.O. Box 230644
Encinitas, CA 92023-0644

Let's Get Growing
1900-B Commercial Way
Santa Cruz, CA 95065

Nasco
901 Janesville Ave.
Fort Atkinson, WI 53538-0901

National Geographic Society
1145 17th St. NW
Washington, DC 20036

National Wildlife Federation
1400 Sixteenth St. NW
Washington, DC 20036-2266

Radio Shack
Tandy Corp.
Fort Worth, TX 76102

Sargent-Welch Scientific Co.
911 Commerce Ct.
Buffalo Grove, IL 60089

Science Kit
777 E. Park Dr.
Tonawanda, NY 14150

The Science Man
P.O. Box 56036
Harwood Hts., IL 60656

Scott Resources
P.O. Box 2121F
Ft. Collins, CO 80522

Southwest Mineral Supply
P.O. Box 323
Santa Fe, NM 87504

Summit Learning
P.O. Box 493F
Ft. Collins, CO 80522

Tap Plastics
6475 Sierra Lane
Dublin, CA 94568

Teachers' Laboratory, Inc.
P.O. Box 6480
Brattleboro, VT 05302-6480

Tops Learning Systems
10970 S. Mulino Rd.
Canby, OR 97013

Uptown Sales, Inc.
33 N. Main St.
Chambersburg, PA 17201

SELECTED SUPPLIERS OF VIDEO TAPES, VIDEODISCS, AND CD-ROM FOR ELEMENTARY SCIENCE

Beacon Films
1560 Sherman Ave., Suite 100
Evanston, IL 60201

Carolina Biological Supply Co.
2700 York Road
Burlington, NC 27215

Churchill Media
12210 Nebraska Ave.
Los Angeles, CA 90025-3600

Elementary Specialties
917 Hickory Lane
Mansfield, OH 44901-8105

Emerging Technology Consultants, Inc.
P.O. Box 120444
St. Paul, MN 55112

Encyclopaedia Britannica Educational
     Corp.
310 S. Michigan Ave.
Chicago, IL 60604

Everyday Weather Project
State University of New York College at
     Brockport
Brockport, NY 14420

Hubbard Scientific, Inc.
1120 Halbleib Rd.
P.O. Box 760
Chippewa Falls, WI 54729

Insights Visual Productions, Inc.
P.O. Box 230644
Encinitas, CA 92023

Instructional Video
P.O. Box 21
Maumee, OH 43537

Kons Scientific Co., Inc.
P.O. Box 3
Germantown, WI 53022-0003

Miramar Productions
200 Second Ave., W.
Seattle, WA 98119-4204

Modern Talking Picture Service, Inc.
5000 Park St. N.
St. Petersburg, FL 33709

National Geographic Society
Educational Services
1145 17th St. NW
Washington, D.C. 20036-4688

Optical Data Corporation
30 Technology Drive
Warren, New Jersey 07059

Phoenix/BFA Films and Video, Inc.
2349 Chaffee Dr.
St. Louis, MO 63146

The Planetary Society, Education Div.
65 N. Catalina
Pasadena, CA 91106

Sargent-Welch Scientific Co.
911 Commerce Ct.
Buffalo Grove, IL 60089

Scholastic Software
730 Broadway
New York, NY 10003

Scott Resources
P.O. Box 2121F
Ft. Collins, CO 80522

Society for Visual Education
1345 Diversey Parkway
Chicago, IL 60614-1299

Tom Snyder Productions
80 Coolidge Hill Rd.
Watertown, MA 02172

Videodiscovery, Inc.
1700 Westlake Ave. N.
Suite 600
Seattle, WA 98109-3012

SELECTED SUPPLIERS OF COMPUTER SOFTWARE FOR ELEMENTARY SCIENCE

Apple Computer Co.
20525 Mariana Ave.
Cupertino, CA 95014

Carolina Biological Supply Co.
2700 York Rd.
Burlington, NC 27215

Denoyer-Geppert Science Co.
5225 Ravenswood Ave.
Chicago, IL 60640-2028

Emerging Technology Consultants, Inc.
P.O. Box 120444
St. Paul, MN 55112

Eureka!
Lawrence Hall of Science
University of California
Berkeley, CA 94720

MECC
6160 Summit Dr. North
Minneapolis, MN 55430-4003

Milliken Pub. Co.
P.O. Box 21579
St. Louis, MO 63132-0579

Optical Data Corp.
30 Technology Dr.
Warren, NJ 07059

Scholastic Software
730 Broadway
New York, NY 10003

Society for Visual Education
1345 Diversey Parkway
Chicago, IL 60614-1299

Special Times, Special Education Software
Cambridge Development Laboratory, Inc.
214 Third Ave.
Waltham, MA 02154

Wings for Learning/Sunburst
1600 Green Hills Rd.
P.O. Box 660002
Scotts Valley, CA 95067-9908

Videodiscovery, Inc.
1700 Westlake Ave. N., Suite 600
Seattle, WA 98109-3012